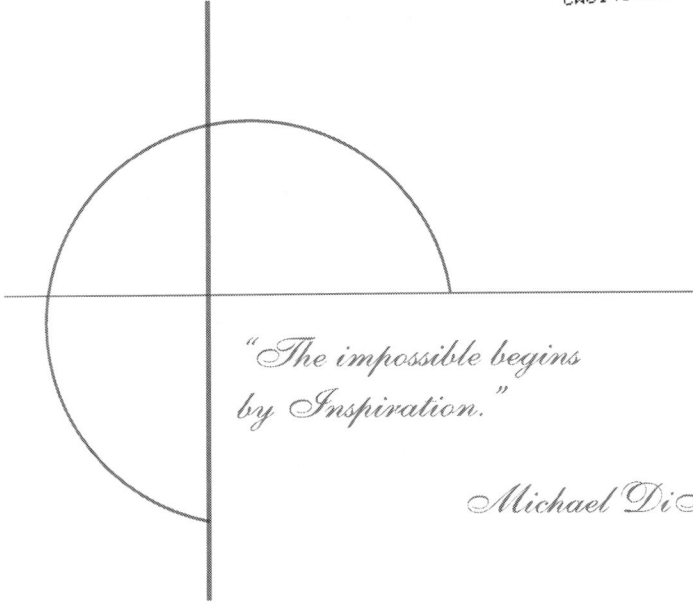

"The impossible begins by Inspiration."

Michael DiMuccio

The Science of the Nikken Business

a p.h.d. in nikken (platinum heading for diamond)

NAME: _____

Nikken's Mission

To inspire individuals to DISCOVER a whole new way of life and provide them the opportunity to LIVE IT by changing their lives through improved health and financial well being.

To order additional copies of this book, contact:
Xlibris Corporation
1-888-795-4274
www.Xlibris.com
Orders@Xlibris.com
92288

Contents

The Science of the Nikken Business

INTRODUCTION

This book can stand alone or you can follow along as you watch the DVDs. It is intended that you use this book as a working manual to build your Nikken Business . . . write on it, highlight it . . . On the top of each paragraph, we've made reference to time (in minutes) as it exists on the DVD, making it easier for you to locate a specific paragraph or segment on the DVD.

The purpose of this book is to provide Nikken Independent Wellness Consultants with a written source of the Nikken business plan developed by Royal Diamond Michael DiMucccio. Michael put together four sets of videos (which now have been formatted to DVD) to help Wellness Consultants better understand the Nikken Business.

About 2 years ago I approached Michael and asked him a question about the business. His reply was simple, "Watch my video The Missing Link." After watching that tape, I was so taken by the information it contained I was literally bouncing off the wall with excitement. I approached Michael once again as I felt there was more and, sure enough, I found out about the other tapes. Needless to say I purchased them and watched all of them.

In all the time I've been a Wellness Consultant, I had never been exposed to this type of information. I was so inspired by it that I decided to transcribe these tapes word for word and turn them into a manual that I could use to build my business . . . as well as help others do the same.

During a meeting with Michael in the summer of 2004, we decided to package the book and the DVD's as a kit. What you hold in your hands today represents over 10 years of business experience from Michael DiMuccio. He has built a very successful International business and has helped others do the same. After all its about duplication . . . it's comparable to building franchises all over the world with a proven plan—a written plan.

Presently there is no other book like this in existence.

I would like to take this opportunity to formally thank Michael for sharing his plan and developing the videos.

Antonio Mario Raimondo
Keynote Speaker/Independent Wellness Consultant

What I've Learned—Part 1

:08

The **Purpose of this** program is to provide you with some information for the benefit of the people who are going to be reading this or viewing it on video tape, wherever they may be . . . some ideas that can have a major impact on your business, simply on the merits of the belief that it will build. Let me start with a diagram that will be the foundation for this session.

:40

It is in the shape of a triangle and represents a process. Let the top of the triangle represent **Purpose.**

Below that is **Vision**

Below that is **Results**

Below that is **Behavior**

Below that is **Beliefs**

Below that is **Structure.**

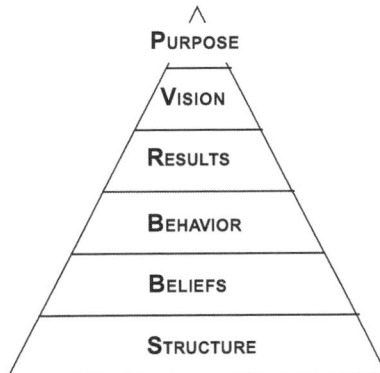

PURPOSE

VISION

RESULTS

BEHAVIOR

BELIEFS

STRUCTURE

1:27

How this works:

Structure could be a corporation, the compensation plan within a corporation, government, education, the family unit or organized religion. The structures that we are born into, become associated with, or become a part of, build our beliefs and these beliefs cause us to behave the way we do.

1:56

This is an absolute fact and has been clinically validated. So, if your beliefs control your behavior, then clearly, **your behavior controls your results.**

2:42

How do you know a good result from a bad result?

Results lead you in the direction you want to go, represented by your vision. So, let's say your vision is: "I want to have a house on the beach with a tennis court and a hot tub looking over the ocean." You have a vision of what it is . . . there is a materialistic side to it and you can actually see it. **The realization of your vision leads to the fulfillment of your purpose.** That's why Silver training is such an important concept. It really starts to help us to connect our operating system with the outcome we desire. What is important is to know where it is you want to go and how it is that you want to live. Purpose is an existence; it is a state of being . . . there is no end in mind. It is a state of "ism," you are happy; there is not an ending point, there is just existence—a state of being.

3:36

Vision

Vision on the other hand can have an end in mind. It is more concrete. Results are finite; these are things that you can measure and help you understand whether you are on track to realize your vision. The behavior, or the actions and the attitude give you the results. The beliefs are what cause you to behave

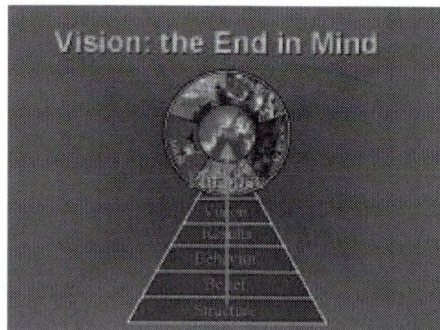

Vision: the End in Mind

Diagram 1

The Science of the Nikken Business

the way you do, to produce those results, and it is the structures that give you your beliefs.

4:14

Now this concept is exceptionally important because this is what can happen if you don't understand this concept. People will get results, unquestionably they get results. But how do they interpret those results? If those results are not consistent with a person's vision, then we assume the results are bad. At this point, they turn to the structures and blame them.

As an example, suppose you were in Nikken and you were doing what you were told to do to become successful. The people who told you how to do this believe that's what you have to do, whether they are right are wrong, but that is what they believe because the structure suggested to them that's what they should be doing. You go ahead and follow, but the results are not consistent with the vision, so you ask yourself, "What is wrong with this picture? I am doing everything they are telling me to do but I am not getting the results that I think I am supposed to be getting." At this point you start to "point the finger," you start blaming the structure (company), and if you are not wise enough to evaluate the structure, to modify the structure, then what you might end up doing is modifying your vision instead.
5:27

For example, what if your goal is to become a Silver distributor? You try to do all the things that people tell you that you are supposed to be doing, and then you are not a Silver distributor in a time frame that you thought you should be. All of a sudden you start to blame the people who taught you, who are part of the structure, or you blame the company or you blame the products or you blame network marketing. Blame, blame, blame . . . you can see why network marketing has the problems that it has in terms of interpretation. People are misinterpreting the results.

6:09
Change Your Strategy

Instead of blaming or pointing fingers, what you need to do is change your structure. Change your strategy, don't change your goal. There is nothing wrong with the goal, change the strategy. We will relate to Diagram 1 a number of times but clearly we do not have an end in mind. Then, how do we know if what we are doing is on track? Many people spend an entire lifetime behaving according to their beliefs, both conscious and more significantly unconscious beliefs . . . getting results that are usually inconsistent with their desires.

In fact 80% of the population hates what they do for a living. So, what do they do? They blame the government, they blame the companies they work for, they blame their parents, they blame . . . blame . . . blame. Instead of taking charge and accepting responsibility to change the structure, they go on living within the structure. They feel insignificant that they can't change the structure. It would be like trying to change the government . . . you can't, because that is the way it is.

7:25

Two things are certain in life—death and taxes. I happen to believe those things are not certain. We just believe they are; therefore they are, because we act according to our beliefs and we create the outcome. I am going to be talking mostly about structure because it is the structure that leads to beliefs.

7:47
The Structure that Leads to Beliefs

I have studied this network marketing industry for a little over ten years now and I think I have identified one of the things that causes inconsistent beliefs; in other words, beliefs that produce results that are inconsistent with people's desire. I have always been an advocate that this is a business, not a hobby. Treat it like a business and it will treat you back with respect.

The first picture I want to illustrate for you is one that I like to use when I am talking to somebody, either in a business briefing or a "one-on-one," to help them understand the nature of our business and the relationships that we have in our business.

8:27
Career Plan Launch Strategy

I did a Brochure called **Career Plan Launch Strategy** a while ago. It was packaged with a video tape. The very first page of that brochure explains the structure that someone becomes a part of, because if you don't understand the structure, then

Manufacturer ⟷ **You** ⟷ **Public**
Nikken Inc.   Inc.   Customer

you don't know exactly what to believe. For instance, some of you might actually believe your up-line is responsible for your success, but if you believe that and if you don't become successful, who are you going to blame . . . your up-line? If your up-line thinks they are responsible for your success, their belief that they are responsible for your success will result in them doing things for you that you should be doing yourself. They do not do it in a conscious way; they do it unconsciously and do it out of a sense of obligation. They do not even understand that they are actually penalizing you, hurting you instead of helping you.

It is the same situation when raising a child. Sometimes we can be overprotective with our kids, much to their detriment and ours, and so you can see how this plays a role in every facet of our lives, not only in our business.

Let's start with our first picture.

The Structure
In Business for Yourself ~ Not by Yourself

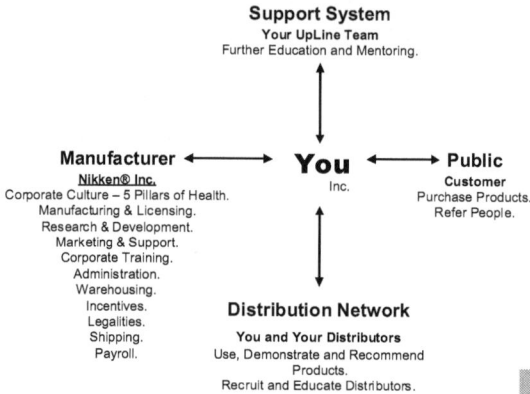

Support System
Your UpLine Team
Further Education and Mentoring.

Manufacturer ←——→ **You** ←——→ **Public**
Nikken® Inc. Inc. Customer
Corporate Culture – 5 Pillars of Health. Purchase Products.
Manufacturing & Licensing. Refer People.
Research & Development.
Marketing & Support.
Corporate Training.
Administration.
Warehousing.
Incentives. **Distribution Network**
Legalities.
Shipping. **You and Your Distributors**
Payroll. Use, Demonstrate and Recommend
Products. **Diagram 2**
Recruit and Educate Distributors.

9:37
YOU Inc

This is the picture I like to draw when I am
explaining the business we are in. The first thing
I like to talk about is YOU Inc. Why even make
a distinction between YOU Inc. and you? You
are a person, YOU Inc. is the identity of your
business . . . mine happens to be called Good
Vibrations International Inc. You Inc. is a concept,
it is not a person. It's the opportunity for a business
to become something.

You Inc.

10:20

You, on the other hand, are the CEO of YOU Inc. You are the one who
has to make the decisions on behalf of YOU Inc. that will help it become
what you intend it to become. I like to talk about that because a lot of

people come into this business and they think of their business as them. They don't make the distinction. They sign a distributor application form which is usually in their name, yet what they are signing is an independent contract. They have actually signed and registered to own the license, the right to distribute Nikken products. That's an entity in itself. That is worth money; you can sell that right later on in life to whomever you want. You are not selling you. It's the license; it's that entity unto itself.

Now let me talk a little bit about money, because every business has to be profitable or it will not survive. So, the first rule of business is to make some money.

11:25
First Rule of Business is to Make Some Money

$ People come into this business for various reasons, but ultimately what is going to keep them in business is profit. Money is a funny thing; a lot of people have weird ideas when it comes to money because they were born into a structure that taught them to believe certain things to be true about money.

What are those things that we believe to be true about money?

11:56
When I say the word money, let's say lots of money, what are some of the things you hear in your head. Perhaps . . . the root of all evil? That's a **belief**. What spawned that belief? What **structure** gave you that belief . . . family? Where did they get it from? Historically or perhaps somebody in the family had money, and they were not pleasant to be around so they were evil and so forth.

Religion is considered to be a structure. It's inbred in certain religions where they are taught that the meek should inherit the earth, suggesting that the meek, meaning the poor, and usually they throw that in with a few other supporting beliefs to suggest that it is the poor who will inherit the earth. Meanwhile, the richest of all structures on the planet is the church. The contradiction reveals itself if you follow this equation right through. We are living with many contradictions in our lives because the results we get in our lives contradict our beliefs. However, we rarely challenge our beliefs, we challenge the structures. We interpret the wrong thing. We think it is the structure that is to blame. As long as we are susceptible to structure we are susceptible to the belief; it is the belief that must change and so too the structure will change the consequences.

13:32
What Does This Business Do?

I want you to believe that You Inc. is a business. I don't want you to believe that your business is you. I want you to believe that you are the cause that makes this business happen, that the business is a business. What does this business do? Well, it must perform some function in society, otherwise there is no reason for this business to exist. If it does not add value to society in some way, then it will have no reason to exist and will have no purpose.

14:06

Let's look at society as a whole, and how our business exists to perform some function of value in society. Does our business exist to make money? This is a very interesting question, isn't it? Your structure is telling you that the business exists to make money because you believe that's what you are here to do. As long as that's what you are here to do, then what's on your mind . . . making money?

Your business therefore has no purpose, **because making money is not a purpose, it's a consequence of the fulfillment of the purpose.** Do you see how important that distinction is? I hear the highest of ranks in this industry whining and complaining that their pay check is not as big as they would like it to be and I say who are you blaming for that? Your pay check is exactly what it should be because there is a **universal law** in this world and that is, "**you get what you deserve.**" . . . you get in response to what you add, and if what you are adding is not valuable or it lacks value, then it is going to show up in your pay check. If you want to increase your pay check, then you must **increase your value.**

15:56

But if your focus is on increasing your pay check, and not increasing the value, how are you actually going to increase the pay check? What will happen is that you will be thinking about making more money, not doing anything differently. You are behaving according to the beliefs that you carry. So, you're thinking . . . make more money, add more value! And, the consequences . . . lose more money. So, you come back to—it does not work. I thought I could make more money! There is nothing wrong with making more money but you are operating with the structure and a system of beliefs that was not about adding more value, it was about making more money.

16:52

What can I get rather that what can I give? This is very fundamental to your success in this business because if there is a truth in this business, it is this: **this business operates according to those universal laws** better than anything I have ever seen.

17:00
Trading Time for Money

Let me just add to this concept. When most people think about money they think about time. Why, because they are trading one for the other and, generally speaking, they never end up with both. They have either had all the time and no money or all the money and no time. How do you get balance? Well, they believe something

to be true based on the structure. What is the structure? If I look around me and I look at all the people who earn money, how many of those people are earning money in proportion to the time they put in?

17:38

The answer is 97%. So what does that tell me? That you could only make more money by investing more time? The structure supports that belief. The belief supports that structure and so if you believe that time is money, what kind of a structure are you going to be involved with?

18:03

Trading time for money—you create the outcome yourself. You would not even think about looking for something where time and money was unrelated, you would not even associate money with anything other than time. In fact, usually it is not just time, but time usually means labor, and labor usually means hard work. And so if we really look at the belief system, what do we relate money with? Hard work! **So you come into a business of unlimited opportunity, unlimited possibilities and you limit it by your own beliefs.** Proven day in and day out because you go at it without a belief and therefore you create the structure to support it. You start working hard.

19:01

And you start to do all the things that prove that work is hard, you actually create the work. Have you ever seen that? Somebody who has two or three hours in a day and they are not quite sure what they are going to do with that time but they use all of it to do whatever it is they decided to do. And because they never allocated a certain amount of time, they take all of it. In other words we find the work to fill the time. Have you ever seen that? They make work. You know people who make work on a make-work schedule. Well that's what happens. If you believe it is hard work, you make sure it is hard work. You end up finding ways to make it hard, you create the outcome. And of course the results are, it is hard, because you act like it. This idea is a very important concept.

19:55

Now this is what 97% percent of the population associates with money, so when you come to them about Nikken and you start talking to them about unlimited opportunities, what are they thinking? They are thinking according to their beliefs not yours. They are thinking that this person is involved in some illegal structure; this person is involved in some scam. They start challenging the structure because their results are not consistent with what you are suggesting. So the first thing they point their finger at is the structure. It must be illegal; it must be this or it must be that, everything but what it really is because it does not support their model. How else would you justify 45 years of hard work to make the existence that you make and have somebody come along and say "I have the opportunity of a lifetime here." Think about it.

21:02

This plays an important role when you are presenting the Nikken opportunity to people. You must understand where they are coming from, that they are going to have a hard time swallowing these crazy ideas, because to them—they are crazy.

21:13

What kind of structure could produce those results? I have never seen one that could do that; therefore, it does not exist. It is too good to be true . . . it probably is. Let's talk about how we really make money. How does money come about?

21:34

How Does Money Come About?

Why am I telling you all of this? I am actually saying this to a prospect; I am actually talking to a new distributor this way . . . why? Because the very first thing I have to negate so we can start anew is . . . I've got to change their beliefs because their beliefs are going to tell them whether this structure is true or false. And so I have to zero their beliefs so that they can be accepting of the structure and new beliefs about that structure. From there, they will create certain behaviors which will produce certain results.

22:22

I have to get them to accept the structure. I know I am paralyzed until I change their beliefs because their beliefs support a different structure. Competition—is that a structure in the corporate world? Competition is a reality of the corporate world; the corporate structure spawns competition by virtue of the fact that there is limited room at the top. Everybody wants to be at the top and so the consequence of that structure is to produce competition. When they come into this environment and hear that somebody is going to help them and not even get paid to help them . . . immediately they are challenged with things they can't buy into, so you have to soften that blow!

23:12

You have to start working on their beliefs, you have to start talking to them about the possibility that what they think is true is not necessarily true. If you have heard me speak, whether at an executive lunch, a Wellness Preview, or one-on-one, the first thing that I start to attack is people's beliefs. I start to talk about what they believe to be true and then I show them evidence to the contrary.

23:38

I might suggest that once upon a time the world was flat. Was it? It was not flat at all, and yet if I asked that question 500 years ago, you would have believed it was, even though it was not. You would not dare go around the world if you believed it was flat because, as far as you could tell, it was flat and everyone believed it. Your vision was limited by the fact that you believed it was flat and yet, it was never flat. See, that's how our beliefs can affect the outcome of how we live our life. So what is the true equation?

24:24
How Do We Earn Money

Once upon a time I had a bunch of eggs that I wanted to take to the market because I did not want eggs for breakfast. I needed a loaf of bread, so I brought the eggs to market. Let's say, you make bread and I have eggs. "How many eggs can I give you for a loaf of bread? You could sure use half a dozen eggs, couldn't you? I'll give you half a dozen eggs, you give me a loaf of bread and we'll both be happy."

Next day I come to market, I still have the bread from yesterday, but I need lettuce. "So, how many eggs do you want for that head of lettuce?" You tell me you could sure use half a dozen eggs, so I give you half a dozen eggs and you give me the lettuce. I come home and I have a salad. Perfect!

Next day I come to market and you have eggs, so you don't need any more eggs. I don't need lettuce because I still have some left over, but I need bread. So I come to you and say, "I'll give you half a dozen eggs for a loaf of bread. I know you might not need any more eggs, but I need a loaf of bread. So, how about this? I will write you an 'IOU' on this piece of paper.

25:39
I will give you this note, "I owe you a half dozen eggs and you will give me a loaf of bread now." Fine. Now I go home. I have a loaf of bread and you have a note, and that note became legal tender. That was money. It was representative of what? It was an exchange of value. How did we decide that six eggs were worth a loaf of bread? It was arbitrary, we just decided it was, and from that day forward that's the standard that was set and so the standard of money and all of that stuff was simply **an exchange of value**. If we understand that **money is an**

exchange of value, then if we want to make more money we must add more value.

Who decides what is considered value to both? Society decides what is considered fair value and it changes all the time.

26:34

A hundred years ago buggy whips were considered valuable, but today they are not so valuable. Society determines what is valuable and as long as we are providing what society considers valuable in greater amounts, we earn money as an exchange. That's how it works. Bob Proctor taught me that if you want to see the difference that someone has made on society, look at the difference society has made on that person . . . by virtue of their wealth and so forth. Guess what else he showed me? It's not a moral issue.

27:07

The law that controls the universe, the universal laws, God's laws are absolute, they are not man-made judgment calls.

27:16

For instance, a drug dealer can make a lot of money by the same law. If they are adding value to society, they make money, and the better they are at adding value, the better distribution they have. The better distributor of drugs makes the money. I never said whether they are legal or illegal drugs. The same is true for both sides of the equation. It is not a moral issue. Money and morality don't have any business in the same sentence. It is a question of adding value to society and money is simply an exchange or means to distribute value.

28:03

Money makes it possible for us to get what we want when we need it. It is a convenience tool. So now, are you limited to the value you can add relative to the time you have? Well, if you are an electrician like I was, then the only time that I was being valuable as an electrician, was when I was punching the clock. But if I said to you, "Can you figure out a way to add more value to society without having to add more time," do you think you might come up with a few ideas if you spent the next six months to a year trying to figure out a solution?

28:41

Yes, but you would never look at doing such a thing if you did not believe that this was true. Do you see what I am saying? Now we are talking about adding more value without adding more time. How do we do that?

Let the "Growth of Business" arrow on the next page represent the value that we add to society. What we want to do is add more and more value to society without necessarily adding more time. Not only that, but we have to figure out what is considered valuable so we can actually offer it to society. So there is the dilemma. Can we come up with a solution? You bet we can.

EXAMPLE: Network Marketing is a complete change to the structure of how the economic world works. This leads to a different set of beliefs about what is possible. People reject Network Marketing because it challenges their beliefs.

CORPORATE STRUCTURE: The old structure was designed to serve a few: the ones at the top of the structure. It doesn't work for the rest.

THE STRUCTURE OF OUR BUSINESS:

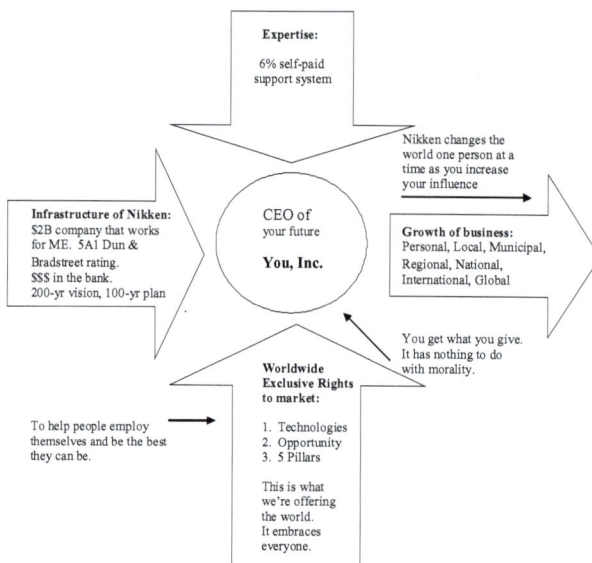

Expertise:

6% self-paid support system

Nikken changes the world one person at a time as you increase your influence

Infrastructure of Nikken: $2B company that works for ME. 5A1 Dun & Bradstreet rating. $$$ in the bank. 200-yr vision, 100-yr plan

CEO of your future

You, Inc.

Growth of business: Personal, Local, Municipal, Regional, National, International, Global

You get what you give. It has nothing to do with morality.

To help people employ themselves and be the best they can be.

Worldwide Exclusive Rights to market:

1. Technologies
2. Opportunity
3. 5 Pillars

This is what we're offering the world. It embraces everyone.

SUCCESS IN NIKKEN:

1. You have to add value to society. Adding value is the basis for earning money.
2. Decide how far you want to go (right arrow of the structure) because that will determine how much you will need to use from the other 3 aspects of the structure (the support system, the company infrastructure, rights to market the opportunity, 5 pillars, the technologies).
3. Imagine your business at the beginning being like a snowball. As it rolls along, it gets bigger and bigger. You need to embrace the products, the 5 Pillars, the support system, the internet, and so on and share it with lots of people for your business to start to grow.

Diagram 3

29:34
Something of Value to Offer Society

First, let's find something of value to offer society. Do you think Nikken's technologies are valuable? As a matter of fact, at this part of the presentation I could be introducing the person to the products. They have not seen them yet, but I can demonstrate some real value. A few demonstrations . . . and all of a sudden they are looking at this and they are saying, "Wow, these technologies are powerful. I can see how people start to believe these products make a difference and can really add value and make a huge impact on society and therefore the consequences of that would be more time and more money."

30:17

There is something beyond the technology, and that is the opportunity. When I got started in Nikken in 1992, we would sell a pair of magsteps. Today we sell a pair of magsteps, but their value is so much greater than the value when I first sold them. Do you know why?

30:52

Society has decided recently that because of the aging population, one of the most valuable things is health, not disease! So, all of a sudden, everything Nikken has to sell is more valuable today then when they were first selling it. One thing we have to look for is a way to add more value. **Can you imagine having a product that is actually worth more with every day that goes by?** The product that we provide increases in value every single day. As more and more aging baby boomers realize how important their health is and start to explore wellness solutions for which we are the premier company, you realize that the value of the opportunity is increasing every day. But if your results were not consistent with what you believed you should be getting, you might think the opposite.

31:54

We offer an opportunity. Is that valuable? Well, I look at myself. I was a member of society when my sponsor told me about this technology. Had they limited the discussion to the technology, today I would be a happy consumer of Nikken products and my back would be feeling as good as it is feeling. But would I be where I am? Would I have the lifestyle? Maybe you would not even be in Nikken? Perhaps I've sponsored you in this business by virtue of the network that I have created. By giving me this opportunity did this person add more value in my life? Did this person add more value in the lives of the people I've touched in this business? Did this person add more value to society in general by virtue of the organization that was created and the many millions of customers that are sure to follow?

32:42

Absolutely! So, just by this person offering me an opportunity above the technology, they themselves have added more value in society; therefore, they are worth more. **That is why we must become very efficient at talking about this opportunity and not just the products.**

33:03

The Five Pillars of Health

The Five Pillars of Health—is that all we talk about? Is there something else that we can share with people that might give even greater value in someone's life? **The philosophy, the five pillars.** What is interesting is what that philosophy represents. When you look at the 5 Pillars of Health, **isn't it that philosophy in a nutshell . . . the purpose of every human being is to become balanced.** The purpose of every human being is to be well . . . which leads to human beings more.

33:57

Human being more *is complete and totally in line with the purpose as human beings.* To be healthy: physically, mentally, within our families; to have relationships with healthier involvement; to be a healthier producer in society and to have healthier finances. It's an ongoing state of being. There is no end in mind, so in fact, Nikken's five pillar philosophy is one and the same as our ultimate purpose in life, therefore would it not be the greatest gift? The greatest thing we offer is the philosophy itself. And wouldn't that spawn people to be interested in the opportunity? Wouldn't they want to know how this philosophy could become a reality? In fact, how do you turn this into a reality? What is the vision that turns this into reality?

34:48

What are the results that turn the vision into the reality? Would a person not want to know the opportunities that make this possible? It's the structure which includes the products and the opportunities that make this possible. So if you talk about the philosophy . . . the five pillars, you can't help but talk about the opportunities and the products. But if you limit your discussion to the opportunity, you many never talk about the philosophy and it might just be the opportunity and the products, but **if you only talk about the products, you may never end up talking about the opportunity. So you need to become more, as the CEO of You Inc. You need to build your presence, build your beliefs, build your confidence in all three aspects of what we offer. And, the better you get at articulating that, particularly with the end in mind, the more people you are going to attract.**

35:42

This is exactly what is going to happen. You talk about the product . . . you attract the customers . . . you talk about the opportunity . . . and you attract customers and distributors. But, if you talk about the philosophy, you will attract leaders or visionaries, distributors and customers. You get them all by virtue of talking about the end in mind. And so, the **top notch distributors** in Nikken, the top notch distributors in the world of network marketing **always begin with the end in mind** and the products are the means to that end, thereby creating more value in the lives of every human being they touch. Some become customers, some become distributors, and some become outright leaders who make a huge difference and therefore the difference is made in your life.

36:50

YOU Inc. was in reference to you as a leader. Now let me talk to you as a prospect. **YOU inc. has been given the right, the worldwide exclusive right to market these products.** Let me ask you something. What would be the use of being given the worldwide right as a distributor, if you just kept it to yourself? Imagine you are the only human being on planet earth who ever knew about some amazing product, but didn't have any idea how to get it to market. It would be so frustrating, knowing the significance of the product and having the right to market it worldwide, but not knowing how to get it to market.

38:20
How Do I Get the Product to Market?
What a frustrating thing that would be, trying to get money from people every day, selling shares just to keep the dream alive because you did not know how to get this product to market . . . as good a product as it was. Do you know how many products have been lost because they could not get to market . . . not because they were not good products?

38:41
So here you are. **You have been given worldwide exclusive rights to one of the amazing discoveries in the history of the human race concerning health and wellness.** What good is it in your hands? What are you going to do about it? Well if you have never done anything like this before, let's think about this. I have to manufacture the product. That is going to take money and manufacturing. I will need to have order entry operators to take orders. I will need to be licensed, so I will have to go through the red tape of bureaucracy and government just to get licensed to be in the market for this product in any one particular country, never mind the world. Then I have to figure out how to physically get the product from the manufacturer to the consumer.

39:27
Educating the Consumer
Bigger problem, I've got to educate the consumer that this product exists. How I am going to do that? What kind of dollars is that going to

take to advertise and so forth. Do you see the problem? Just because you have the greatest product in the world, it means nothing if you don't have the means to get the product to the people who deserve it and decide whether it is a good product? Our problem is not our products; our problem is we don't have the distribution.

40:00

We have a tidal wave coming of 50+ year olds who are in desperate need of these solutions and we don't have enough people in the field talking about this for them to even know that we exist? <u>Less than 2% market penetration</u> in 11 years in North America. That's remarkable. What do I want you to believe? Why I am telling you this? If you think that you are still in that "Suzie Homemaker" business . . . well, your perception is your reality and nothing I say will change that.

40:40

You need to understand the business you are in. You need to know the scope of this business. People tell me I'm the top guy in Canada. What makes you think I am the top guy in Canada? It is because I have the biggest check in Canada? I know there is probably someone sitting on my sixth level who is going to build a bigger down-line in Canada than I have. Would that not make that person the top guy in Canada or top woman in Canada? Why am I? By virtue of default because, everybody else has suggested beliefs that I am, therefore I am. Understand this: I am . . . because you let me be . . . but I am ready to relinquish that role to anybody who wants it. You have the opportunity to go and build a bigger business than I have. Remember, you are only going to get paid on the business you build, not the business I build.

41:39

It's not like there is no room in society for you . . . less than 2% market penetration. They counted the number of distributors who have ever signed an application form, and only one in one hundred distributors own a sleep system. These are real numbers. One in three distributors own a pair

Our Population is growing faster than our ability to penetrate the market we have already reached. The Nikken opportunity is **never** going to be **"saturated."**

of magsteps. These are Nikken's stats. Ask yourself this question. Have we really done anything with this incredible technology that we have been given . . . that we are so embarrassed to talk about to our neighbors and friends? It's up to you and You Inc. to make a difference in the world with what you have been given . . . and Nikken gives you the opportunity to do so.

42:25

You might think, how can I have the worldwide exclusive when everybody else in Nikken has the same worldwide exclusive? OK, so let's take the population of the world . . . 6 billion divided by everybody in Nikken and let's figure out how long it is going to take for you to talk to these people. In fact, in the last 25 years, more people have been born on planet earth than all the people we've ever sold the product to. Our population is growing faster than our ability to penetrate the market we have already reached.

42:58

This opportunity is never going to be **"saturated."** That's a phantom, a fiction and it's created by people who don't know what they are talking about. Since you don't have the infrastructure and the money to go ahead and take this worldwide and actually market it worldwide, the benefit you have when you become a Nikken distributor is that you have a 2 billion dollar company that's very busy creating an infrastructure—that represents the products, the value, if you will, that you are going to add to society. This is the infrastructure that's being built to support your distribution of that value. Here is a 2 billion dollar giant called Nikken that is set up in 25 countries with intentions of being in 200 countries by the year 2100. They are going around the world setting up an infrastructure to make it possible for you to pick up the phone and have a product delivered to a consumer anywhere in the world Nikken is doing business.

44:08

Nikken is actually bringing the world to you in incredible ways—the internet. Right now they are madly working on a solution that by July, for the World Convention, they can announce that you will be able to have a customer in any of the 25 countries Nikken exists—by virtue of your web page. In any one of these countries you can have a customer walk to your door, to your web site, and buy a product in their language. That is amazing! It's remarkable. They are bringing the world to you, giving this "world wide exclusive right" serious treatment.

44:41

What does this company believe to be true? What do you think their purpose or their vision is? I received this information through a friend of a friend who made me a photocopy. As a result of my friend giving it to me, the President's Club is going to receive it too. But here is Nikken's business plan and an agenda for us.

The main events. Do you know they are going to be opening up a head office in Tokyo? Wait a minute. Haven't we been there 25 years and they are just now opening up a head office?

45:22

Do you think it is saturated? They are just getting started; it is just starting to get fun for Nikken. They have a big vision! Huge! Bigger than any one of us can imagine, but is it real? The only question I ask is—what is your role in it?

45:35

Everyone thought when Nikken came to Canada it was not a very big deal but do you know what that meant? It meant they came into Canada and they set up the infrastructure necessary to be able to accept applications and create distribution to sell products to consumers . . . but they didn't actually sell any. They didn't put big announcements in newspapers . . . NOW YOU CAN BUY YOUR MATTRESSES HERE! They just waited for us—one of us, or a group of us to say, "OK . . . we are here now! We are going to sign up this person. Can you take care of it now?" That's exactly how Nikken begins operations in a new country. They don't do anything—other than facilitate. It's us who distribute, not them.

46:23

Nikken just facilitates the process. You need to know that with less than 2% market penetration, the market is waiting for you to do something about it. In fact the market is not even waiting. Listen to the tape by Paul Zane Pilzner, *The Next Trillion Dollar Industry in North America.*

46:40

If you haven't heard that tape, get your hands on it and start marketing that tape to your people. It is powerful!

Understand, the **next trillion dollar industry** in North America is the wellness industry, a word I think Nikken invented nine years ago! I actually believe that Nikken invented that word. I never heard of wellness before that time, yet today, it is an industry in which we lead the way. This 25 year old company has set up an infrastructure to make it possible for you to take this thing to the world.

47:11

You do not have to worry about doing that. If you have never done that before, where do you begin?

Most businesses fail, do you know why? Not because they do not have a good product or a good idea, not because they do not have a great purpose, a great vision to make a difference in society. They fall apart because they run out of money that is necessary to keep the dream alive until they get the thing working. So they do this thing called trial and error. Trial and error . . . you go around fumbling here and there and hopefully you do not run out of money before you figure out how to make it, how to carve your niche, how to find your place in society so that you could offer that value that no one else can like you can . . . and it becomes profitable so that you can keep doing it. Most people run out of money in the first 18 months, 9 out of 10 companies will go bankrupt in 18 months for that reason . . . trial and error. And then, of the one tenth that survive, nine tenths of them will go bankrupt within the next eighteen months for the same reason. They just have deeper pockets and it only took a lit bit longer for them to run out.

48:19

Do you have time for trial and error? How do we solve this problem? When you become a part of this organization! By the way, I keep hearing people say, "I joined Nikken." Relative to the structure (Diagram 1, page 8), where do you see me joining Nikken in this equation? Are you now a CEO in Nikken? Do you own shares in the company? How did you join Nikken exactly? We do not use the right language because we are still thinking like a person in the corporate world. I joined IBM; I am now an employee of IBM. I'm sorry, you cannot join Nikken. So, if the arrow points to you, what actually happened? **(See Diagram 3 on Page 22)**.

49:18

Nikken joined you. Do you understand that? I am telling you the way it is because **if you don't understand the way it is, your beliefs are going to paralyze you and you are not going to see the kind of results you want to see.** The truth is Nikken joined you. This 2 billion dollar company is sitting waiting for you, the executive of You Inc. to make the next decision. That's a fact! They will do what you need them to do to facilitate this process. Now, they will you give you some suggestions. They have a thing called a **compensation plan** which suggests, that is all it is, because it is not a business plan. It just *suggests* what they would like you to do to facilitate them in making their dream a reality.

50:00

They are waiting for you to tell them what you need to do. I will tell you how factual this is. Just before the convention, Royal Diamonds were invited down to Nikken's home office. We were sitting in a boardroom meeting in their huge hall auditorium, discussing things because Nikken just shared with us their rhythm of the business. It was amazing for me to hear. It was music to my ears. We started to ask about the convention, thinking that they were supposed to set this thing in motion and that we would follow what they wanted us to do. So, the question from the Royal Diamonds was: "What do you want us to do?" A very legitimate question we thought.

Larry Profit stood up and said, "What do you mean, what do you want us to do? You need to tell us what you want to do." Well, all of us just about fell off our chairs!

51:18

Can you imagine we, Royal Diamonds, are being asked by the company—what do you want to do? They (Nikken) were there to facilitate us in creating what it is that we have a common . . . a vision to create. Larry asked again, "What do you want to do? You tell us and we will follow." So we started talking and the next thing you know we get handed a calendar. You would think a distributor wrote this. This is the first collaborative effort I have ever seen in the network marketing arena, where both the field and the corporation are working like a real business does, hand in hand. You need to become a part of that if you want to be a part of this vision.

51:47

Expertise—do you think you have expertise? Do you think that if you really want to know how to build your business in a hurry, in a big way, in a significant way, in a quality way . . . do you think you could resource that information? Is it available to you? Is it good information? Could you rely on that information? Talk about expertise. You've got some pretty hot experts: your sponsor, your up-line, and an organization called Team Diamond.

52:30

Team Diamond is comprised of the most successful distributors in the company who freely share their information with you. Have you been to a Team Diamond event? Was it free . . . in terms of the Diamonds freely giving out information? In fact, every one of those Diamonds paid their own ticket to be there. They paid their own airfare, their own food and hotel rooms. So, what are we doing? Basically, we're paying to educate you! Where in the world do you see that? You don't see that anywhere in the world, but you do see that in Nikken. I just love this six percent because it means no hidden agenda. (See Diagram 1 on page 8).

53:19

You never have to be concerned about whether you are getting good information, because then we would earn six percent of what—zero! So, why would anybody want to give you bad information? It would make no sense at all. And again that is not necessarily true in the corporate world where it spawns competition by virtue of the structure that it is. The higher up you go, the more misinformation there is to keep you on your perch so you don't push on anybody's heels. Not in this situation. The higher up you go, the MORE you get. It's amazing and this is the business that you're in. If you want to make a big impact in society, because you want society to make a big impact on you, then give what you want to get! Give . . . give five pillars to society and you get five pillars in return.

54:16

Give a little bit, get a little bit. Give a lot, get a lot! If you are going to give a lot, you are going to need a lot in the way of resources. You are going to need to get as much of those resources into your head as possible, into your business as much as possible.

You are going to need to tap into, not just the order entry department or the customer service department but you are going to start dealing with distributor services and the executive branches and so forth. **Because the more you are going to create an impact with the public, the more you need to know and be involved with the company.**

54:54

In Nikken, it is one thing to read your sales kit, it is another thing to get on your internet site and start educating yourself to the tool that Nikken is providing you with, to make it possible to manage your business, and your growth. If you do not want to make a big difference, you are not going to be interested in what Nikken is doing but if you are making a difference, and you want to make a bigger difference, you want to get to know how you can do that by utilizing Nikken.

Nikken does not want to waste time or money; they do not put things together for the sake of having things together.

55:37

They are doing everything because they are on a mission. And they know that the internet is so important to our future that if they don't do it, we do not have a future and they are trying to get us to understand that as distributors. They do everything possible to make it a "no-brainer" for those of us who are computer illiterate. They want it to be so easy that you do not have to have a computer to have a web site. Do you know that? You do not have to have a computer to have a web site. In fact, every one of you already has a web site, did you know that? What are you going to do with that knowledge? Pretend that you do not know? Well, if you don't know you have it, you can't use it.

56:22

If you don't know how to use it, you won't. Since they work for us, Nikken must have created it because they think it is important for us to be successful. Understand what I am saying. What I believe to be true is based on this structure.

The Structure
In Business for Yourself ~ Not by Yourself

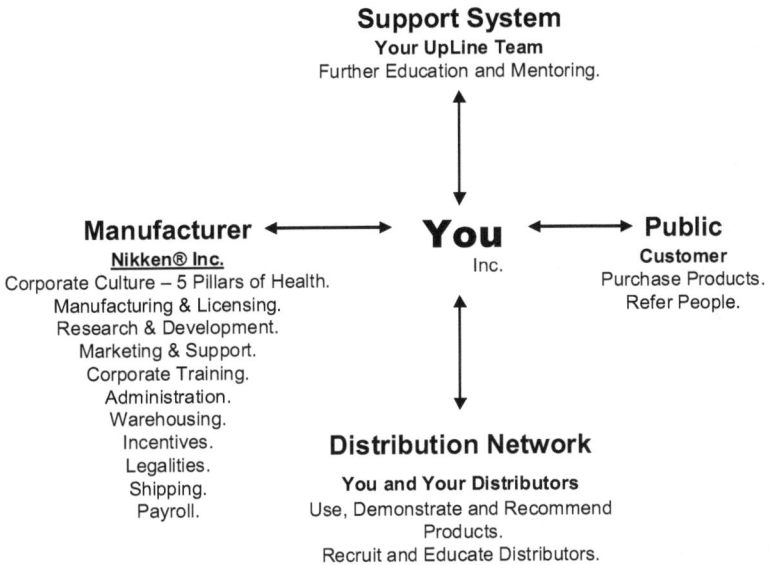

Support System
Your UpLine Team
Further Education and Mentoring.

Manufacturer ← → **You** ← → **Public**

Nikken® Inc.
Corporate Culture – 5 Pillars of Health.
Manufacturing & Licensing.
Research & Development.
Marketing & Support.
Corporate Training.
Administration.
Warehousing.
Incentives.
Legalities.
Shipping.
Payroll.

Inc.

Customer
Purchase Products.
Refer People.

Distribution Network

You and Your Distributors
Use, Demonstrate and Recommend Products.
Recruit and Educate Distributors.

Diagram 2

This is the structure upon which you are going to realize your potential. Understand this structure because this spawns certain beliefs and it is those beliefs that will empower you. If you don't believe you are the CEO, you will not act like a CEO, you will act like a dependant, instead of an independent distributor . . . dependant on everybody and everything to give you what you think you need rather than searching it out for yourself. So, this is one big concept.

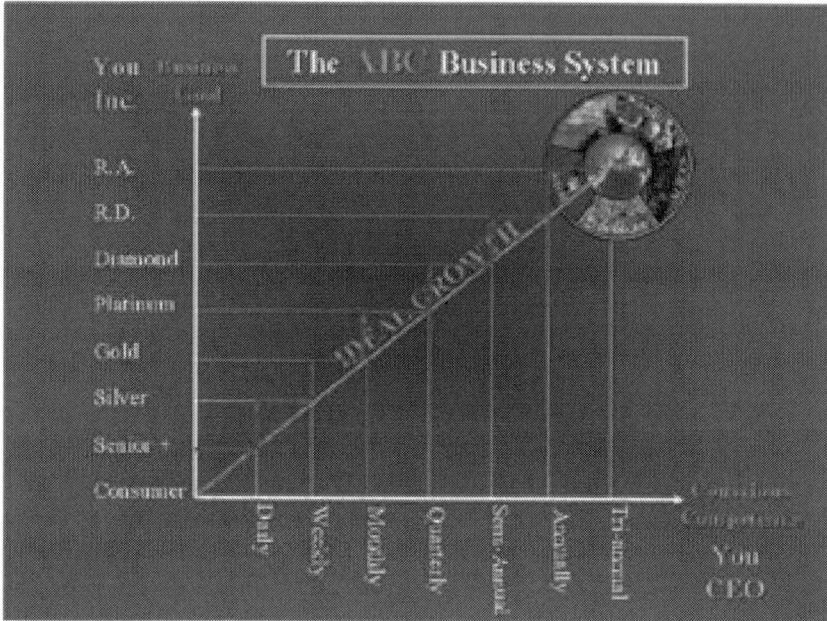

The ABC Business System

Diagram 3

57:24

The Vision—Beginning with the End in Mind

Let me talk about another structure . . . again, starting with the end in mind. What is it that we want to create for ourselves and what is it that we want our company to create? What we want to get is what we want to give. Do you want what Nikken has to offer in a big way? Then you've got to have it in your heart to give it in a big way, because you can't have it both ways. You've got to be able to give it to get it. You've got to give it in a big way in order to get it in a big way.

58:04

And so, what is the ultimate gift of Nikken?

Is it the product, is it the opportunity, or is it the life that can be generated by virtue of the opportunity and the products? So, let the 5 Pillars of Health diagram be represented by this one happy person, YOU . . . because you made a big difference in the lives of many, not only physically but mentally, through family, through the society pillar and financially. So, that's the end in mind.

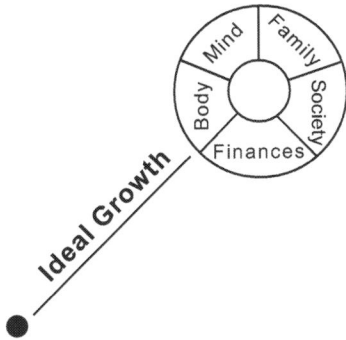

58:52

Let's say this is where we are right now. What is the shortest distance between two points? A straight line. So let that represent the ideal growth; call it a curve, the ideal growth curve. So we all start here and the idea is to get to here; balance, the fulfillment of life, our purpose. Now that seems like a mighty long road. We call it the Nikken highway and you'll hear people talk about success on the Nikken highway. Well let's start working backwards, because you have to, you start with the end in mind and work backwards from there.

59:36

What is the vision?   **What's a vision?**

Let's set some results. Results would be goals for instance. So, for you to fulfill your purpose to the max, what is the vision? Remember,

The Science of the Nikken Business   37

© 2005, Good Vibrations International + Success8

vision is something you can actually see. Now relate it in terms of Nikken, let this represent Nikken, your Nikken business, your YOU Inc. What is the biggest picture you can have in Nikken? Royal Ambassador. It is the biggest PIN with the largest affect. Now let this over here, this axis represent you, the CEO of YOU Inc. Would you agree that at the level you become a Royal Ambassador, and having made a huge impact on society, things are going pretty good in your life? But now what do you think?

1:01:13

Would you consider yourself pretty confident? Would you say, "Wow, do I ever understand health?" I am involved in it, I am doing it, I am utilizing the products and beyond. I've become **an expert in the area of health.** I am on the leading edge of all this technology. That's who I have become by virtue of becoming a Royal Ambassador. How about mentally . . . would you also say, "Boy, do I ever have a positive attitude? It takes a heck of a lot to get me off track, but I can get back on track pretty quickly. I have an amazing recovery." **Great attitude!**

1:01:36

Family—have I discovered the importance of that? In giving people the gift, I've discovered and rediscovered it back in my life. **Society**—I feel like I have contributed in a big way. **Financially**—not only do I have a lot of money, but I know how to keep it and put it to good use. **That is a competence**—isn't it? You have to learn how to deal with the money you earn.

Do you know that 85% of people who win the lottery, lose everything they've won and more, within three years because they did not develop the capacity for the wealth.

1:02:23

They get wealthy so quickly that they do not develop inside. They do not change their beliefs and so they go right back to what they know, and produce the results that are consistent with their beliefs . . . poverty. They found brilliant ways to get rid of the money and don't take any responsibility for it because they are blaming.

You have become very competent. So, now this CEO is somebody who has become very, very competent. Then what would a Royal Diamond be? It's someone who is on the Nikken highway but not quite as far along. A Diamond is someone who is on the Nikken highway, but not all the way along. The same goes for Platinum, Gold, Silver, Senior, or a Distributor. They are just people somewhere along the Nikken highway (Refer to Diagram 3, Page 36) with varying degrees of success in terms of measurable success, goal-oriented success . . . varying degrees of accomplishment in terms of their capacity for success or competence, which is a function of their beliefs.

The result of the two together however, is someone who is existing, living a purposeful life.

1:04:01
Your Business "You Inc." has 3 Sides

Your business, You Inc., has three sides to it. There is a **retail side** which is the *sale of the products*. There is a recruiting side, and that is the *sale of the opportunity*. Then, there is **a residual side**—and that is the *sale of the vision*.

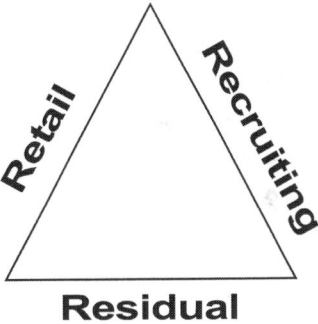

Retail / Recruiting / **Residual**

1:04:35
Goals

Retail leads to immediate sales and income, recruiting leads to growth of your business and leads to residual income through leadership. So these are goals that we want to set for ourselves, and a goal is something we can set that has a time frame. It is a specific tangible thing. Goals are results-oriented . . . but we need actions to make those goals a reality. To make actions possible, we need to develop competence.

In a recent meeting I asked a group of Silvers if they felt competent in being able to duplicate Silvers. Very few hands went up. How are they going to go Gold? My point: this is not something to be embarrassed about! I will tell you that until I recognized this, it was a problem! I did not understand the results, therefore there must have been something wrong . . . but, there wasn't anything wrong—I just did not understand the results.

1:06:01

Here is what I have discovered. If you have a half decent up-line, you are going to reach Silver before you ever become competent at being Silver. This is what I figured out. This is the only industry in the world where somebody can get a promotion and be a complete incompetent. It's absolutely true! It **is the most incredible thing about this opportunity,** and it also could be the most frustrating thing about this opportunity. But, it definitely is the most incredible thing, because it really gives a person hope. Think about it. If you have a capable, competent up-line who knows exactly what they are doing, they can put you in situations and circumstances without you even being aware of it. The next thing you know you've sponsored 5-10 people and you are a Silver Distributor wondering what happened. That happens to me a lot. In fact, my biggest problem in winning Nikken's contest is my people go Silver right away and I can't get the open volume to be big enough. That is a problem, or is it?

1:07:28

On the other hand, in the corporate world, you don't get a promotion until you have proven yourself to be twice as competent as the person above you, especially if you are a woman. Can you see the difference? That is why our industry can lead people to misinterpret the results, even though they are getting results. They get to Silver, they reach the PIN and get paraded on stage and they feel really awkward. They're thinking to themselves, "What am I doing here? I don't even know how I got here?" It's true. I've had this conversation with Golds, I've had it with Platinums, I've had it with Diamonds.

Can you imagine being a Diamond and not feeling competent? It is the most frustrating thing in the world for them, because these people really want to make a difference, and they feel somehow their arms are tied behind their backs. Not that they haven't been making a difference, it is what they feel, and if they don't believe they understand, how are they going to act? What kind of results are they going to produce if they have a feeling of inadequacy? Here they become a diamond and they feel inadequate. Think about that! Why? Because of this one idea, this one concept. There is nothing wrong with it. We just have to understand that's the industry we are in. We have a structure that actually creates this, but it's the best part of it. A person can get to Silver and be incompetent, but that does not mean they are going to get to Gold. It does mean however, that we have to recognize that they are not yet where they need to be to get to that next place.
1:08:25

1:09:08
This is an opportunity. It is an opportunity for us to educate and to work with people to get them to where they need to be, "back on the highway." Now they feel like they can do something. Then, what happens . . . boom, they go to Gold. Once again they feel incompetent, but that is not a reason to stop; it is another opportunity to get them back onto the ideal growth curve where they become a competent Gold. The next thing you know they are duplicating like crazy to become Platinum and they feel incompetent, so we need to get them back onto the ideal growth curve (Nikken Highway). And so this continues all the way up.

All of the deviations from the ideal growth curve simply represent an opportunity to work with, to teach, to educate, to motivate, to stimulate those people who are feeling inadequate at that rank, those people who are a little incompetent or maybe don't have the strategy or they

are frustrated. You may be wondering how I know all of these things? I know because I have made the last 9 1/2 years of my life a study of Nikken—a study of this industry and I will tell you something. If you study one thing long enough, you are going to figure it out. Keep asking the right questions. You will see it for yourself.
1:10:40

This was a real eye opener for some of the Diamonds I was talking to. I got a phone call from a Diamond. This is someone who went right through the entire medical system, graduated as a doctor and practiced medicine in a successful family practice. He felt competent and capable of helping people. Then he joins network marketing and he ends up a Diamond . . . yet feels totally incompetent.

1:11:19
What's wrong with that picture? There is nothing wrong. He was competent to a point, he just did not understand how to get to the next point.

If this is true, then we also have Senior Distributors who are incompetent. I will say we have Seniors and above—which can represent Senior, Executive or Bronze, who are incompetent and need help to get to a degree of competence. For example, what will make a Senior Distributor a competent Senior Distributor? What do they need to know to become Silver? They need to know how to sponsor Seniors, Seniors and above. That means sponsoring, recruiting. So, **they have to learn the competency of recruiting,** and that is a competence **that means learning how to get someone interested in what it is you have to talk about.** It's getting that person to a point where they want to hear what is it that you have to say and learning how to take them through the **process** so that they can **discover** what's there for them.

1:12:37
Once this new person makes a decision, or you help them make a decision to work even more, the Senior needs to learn how to work with

an "A," which is another competence. You actually have to work to let yourself be helped. **Many people are not used to being helped.** We come from another world and letting an "A" in . . . well, sometimes we have to pull teeth to make it happen. But, **that is a competence**, because if you don't do it, you will not duplicate. You disempower yourself. You may not see it yet, because you do not have any distributors, but if you want to have some, you better learn how to duplicate and duplication is a competence. It's the recruiting competence.

1:13:51

What is the **competence that a distributor** must have? Signing an application—they need to know how to write. If they don't know how to write, how are they going to **sign their name to an application form?** That seems a little simple, but the truth of the matter is that it is a competence; they need to know there is such a thing as an application form and they have to sign it.

1:14:45

What must a distributor do to become a senior, let alone a competent senior? How does a distributor become a senior? What **competence** must they have? A **credit card** . . . they have to have a credit card or some means or access to money. You might laugh, but I was in Italy working with some distributors and I spent almost an hour debating with one individual who believed that it was in their best interest to give product to their new distributors to help them get started. I said to this woman, "You're going to be very effective at doing very little in this business because you have just penalized them."

1:15:26

The First Competence

You haven't even given them the **first competence,** the one that says, *you* **are responsible for your success, nobody else!** You stripped that person of that by giving them something for nothing. You are creating a dependent distributor and you are violating the highest order of what we're doing. Make sure you understand this. Do you think

I believe it? You bet I believe it. **The greatest miracle workers on planet earth have always been those who gave people their power,** not those who took it way.

1:16:03

'Leave it up to me!' 'It's OK. I will take care of it!' We don't need to be taken care of; we need to **learn how to care.** That is the difference, and so that's what this business is . . . when you really put it to the test. **The ultimate drive and purpose of this business is to give people their freedom,** their freedom to be and to choose. You give that person choice, that opportunity to decide.

1:16:34

I will tell you a story. A young French Canadian man by the name of Silvaine Simard wanted to sign up but he did not have the money. He had just lost $11,000 dollars in a business venture. He owed money and he wanted me to sign him up and work with him. So, I told him what I was taught by Larry Profit: "This is about you, not about me, and if you really want this bad enough, you will do what you have to do." I didn't think I would see that person ever again. Honestly, I never really expected to. **Three months later he called me, he had the money.** In fact, he had enough to pay his debts, buy the products and get started. Eight months later, he was the first Gold Distributor in Quebec. Within one or two months he was Silver, now he is the top earner in Quebec. And how did that happen?

1:17:36

Giving Your Wellness Consultants Independence

If you were to ask Silvaine what was the one thing Mike taught him that has made the biggest impact, I know what his answer would be. **What I gave him was his independence and it was on that, that he built a business.** It is like a snowball. I really love this analogy. Nikken is like a snowball. How many of you want to build a **big snowman?** So, how do you do it, how does it start? You pack a little snowball and you pack it really good because if it is all lopsided it is not going to roll very well. Take a healthy cell for instance, if you want to grow a healthy body what do you need? Healthy cells! Each cell has to be individual, independent and healthy! What does a healthy cell look like in Nikken? What does a healthy snowball look like—one that can be rolled and will become a gigantic snowball? What does it look like?

Well I think one of the first things it looks like is at least a **demo pack and a career pack.** Let's not forget there is a sponsor bonus that we want them to get when they duplicate that. They have to think beyond who is going to benefit.

1:19:11

Every decision you make is on behalf of everyone in the organization, because you cannot possibly expect more from them than you give. By the way, I failed to mention this, but you can make a personal impact just by using the products and make a difference in your personal life.

You could take it to the next level and make a **local impact.** Set up a little Wellness Preview in your community once a week . . . do Wellness Previews and trainings and become a Wellness Consultant. You'll be servicing the community in a small way.

1:19:45

You can go beyond that and make a municipal impact on **a municipal scale.** A municipality is something like a city and you can become known as a leading edge wellness expert in the city. Now, not everybody in the city is going to know that, but on a municipal level you will become a leader, inside of the organization called Nikken.

And then there are **regional leaders.** These are people who make a difference in the lives of people and impact several cities within a 3-4 hour radius of one another.

Then we have **national leaders.** These are the people who have contributed to the health and welfare of the country. They have created distribution and distributors across the country by virtue of the business that has been created.

We then have **international leaders**. They are in multiple countries and expanding. And then we have those on the very leading edge of the global revolution working right along side of Nikken . . . The Vision of Nikken, Global Wellness.

1:20:57

So what is the impact you want to make? That is the decision you have to make because that is going to determine what you are going to draw in as far as resources. It all begins by starting with you. Personally, what are you going to do, what are you going to embrace that you are going to share with others? A magstep? Wow, you'll make a HUGE difference.

1:21:27

What Should I Buy?

When people start to compromise and ask, "What should I buy?" My answer is—everything! What do I believe? I believe that if you want to make the greatest impact in society and the tool you have been given is the distribution network, if you don't know what the products are, how are you going to use them. It's like trying to be an electrician with a screw driver, without a set of pliers, without wire cutters, without . . . How are you going to be an electrician if you only have half a pouch of tools? You are not going to be a very good electrician. Think about it! How you see yourself is going to determine how you interpret this information.

1:22:35

I believe you ought to have everything. Does that mean you have to start with everything? No, but I believe you ought to have everything, so you have to make a point of getting everything. I do believe you have **to start with something, something that's duplicatable,** something that others can do, should do and would benefit them if they do. Thinking on behalf of my organization, what I want *them* doing is what *I* must

---

do. Demo pack and career pack and on top of that, personal products to use. **That's duplicatable.** If you are going to add something on top of that, it's just more of the business use and personal use products. Simple, duplicatable. There are products for the business, products for you and you need both. The more you can have the better it is.

Decide how big a snowball you want to start with. You may ask what that is going to determine? Think about it, because this is a great analogy. If you start with a little tiny snowball and you go out there, is it hard to push? No! A little tiny snowball? You obviously have not built a snowman lately—it is hard to get that thing going and it's so small you really have to handle it.

1:24:03

You start with a big one, pack a big one, you can push it with one hand. That is the same analogy. If you start with a little bit of product, it is going to be a hard thing to get started. But, if you **start with a lot, the easier it becomes. These analogies are realities. I can save you a lot of time.** If you don't believe me try it, duplicate it. See what happens.

What else does a person need? They need to be at HBT (Humans Being More) Training and that ought to be a prerequisite, not an option. It isn't when *I* sponsor somebody. Clearly understand this: Silver Training isn't an option when I sponsor somebody.

1:24:35

Nikken says very clearly that it **does not require you to do anything,** because you don't work for Nikken. You are an independent contractor, and that is why, by law, they can't ask or demand that you to do anything.

I am the expert and you come to me for expertise and I don't tell you the truth, what does that make me? Well, it certainly does not make me somebody who is reliable. What will the expert give you as information? Whatever they need to help you create what you want to create.

1:25:31

So, the answer that I give you is going to depend on what it is you tell me that you want to do. If you tell me you want to do this in a small way, I will tell you how to do it in a small way. If you tell me you want to do this in a big way, I will tell you how to do this in a big way. If you can tell me the timeframe you want to do it in, I will show you how to do it in that timeframe. It is a function of what you want to do. That's the advice I give. But I will you give you advice according to what it is that you want to do. If you want to do this as a business, then you must go to Silver training because you won't understand the business you are in until you understand the company you are working with. What is it that they have in store for others and what it is that they want to give as a gift? If you have not received it yourself, you can't give it . . . very fundamental to the equation.

1:26:41

So, we have products, we have Silver training, what else? How about a **list of names.** A basic list; we call it a million dollar list. If your new person doesn't have a list, who are you going to contact for them? Whoever comes to mind, whenever they come to mind? Does that sound like a good business plan? Personally speaking, **I want to know who I am going to talk to, when I am going to talk to them and exactly what I am going to talk to them about before I talk to them.** If I bump into somebody unexpectedly, I will defer speaking with them about the opportunity until I am prepared to talk to them. I will gather information and then I will go back to them when I am ready to talk to them. This way, I know what I want to talk about and know how to talk to them professionally.

1:27:10

You want to be somebody who is perceived as someone who is a professional? You want to behave like a professional. You don't want to be looked upon as somebody who is unprofessional. It goes back to—what do you want to create? What do you see yourself as?

OK—so we've got a list, products, Silver Training. What did I miss?

1:27:35

Time—time to do what? Well, nobody said it was going to take all your time and you know it's not going to take some time . . . so, we're going to add value with a little bit of time. We are going to learn how to multiply that into a lot of time—not our time. So again, the little snowball—we have to give a little bit to get a lot. A little bit of money, a little bit of time and a little bit of vision is going to grow into a whole lot of money, a whole lot of time and a lot of vision. I cannot give it to you any simpler than that; that's as fundamental as it gets. You have to start with a healthy cell, a healthy snowball. If you are not doing enough for your people because you are timid about asking them to do what is right, what kind of upline are you?

1:28:27

Tell it like it is. What kind of expert are you? They are relying on you for good information and you are too afraid to tell them like it is. Think about it. Do you have time for that? Do you have time to make mistakes? You know I have heard people say, "Why didn't you tell me I should have started as an executive?" "Well I didn't think." That's right! If this scenario occurs, you didn't think! You didn't ask the person what they wanted to create. Remember—act professionally, be professional!

1:29:15

The Structure of our Business

Let's start moving into a new concept. Let me put these two pictures together for you. (The Structure—Diagram 2; The Ideal Growth Curve—Diagram 3—see pages 35-36). This is the difference you want to make, the value you want to add. If you look at the Nikken distributor, if you look at the structure, what you will find is that a Senior Distributor is really somebody who has made a contribution to their life on a personal level. They start to use the products, they have started to understand and embrace the philosophy of Nikken through the five pillars of health that they discovered through the process of Silver training. They have made a business decision . . . they got their products and they generated a list. They allocated the time to work with somebody, to create a business plan. Did I say a **business plan**? That almost sounds like a business. **(See Diagram on Page 22).**

1:30:13
Network Marketing Is A Business

What is network marketing? It's a business. It is a business that has been treated like a hobby by a lot of people . . . at the price of a lot of good people and a lot of dreams . . . because the person didn't take the responsibility, or weren't given the responsibility. They were sold a promise—an empty promise because someone didn't have the courage to tell them how it really is. It is **NET-WORK** Marketing. It is going to take some work, but the fruits of this labor are a heck of a lot better than fruits of any other labor. I can tell you that you are going to have to climb a ladder one way or another. Make sure the ladder you are climbing leans on the right wall.

1:30:53
Let's look at somebody who is making a personal impact. They just bought some products and attended training. They really did not go out and make a difference yet. They have made a personal impact.

RANK	IMPACT
Silver	Local
Gold	Municipal
Platinum	Provincial
Diamond	National
Royal Diamond	International
Royal Ambassador	Global

The next plateau is Silver. This is somebody who obviously has made an impact locally. When you think of Silver, that's someone who has gone out on purpose, talked to people on purpose, shared their feelings about these products and the opportunity with people they know, friends and family—on purpose. They are making a difference locally, not necessarily beyond family and acquaintances.

1:31:42

Then we have the Gold Distributor. They're someone who has pockets of business . . . a little bit of business in Kleinburg, a little bit of business in the city, a little business in Mississauga. They have touched lives on a municipal scale, so their impact is reaching further out.

Then comes the Platinum Distributor. What I find with Platinums is that their business is spread out across Ontario maybe stretching out to a few adjacent provinces. They are regional leaders who have made an impact regionally because their business touches the lives of people on a regional scale. That does not mean they control the region. Let's understand the difference. If somebody is the Regional Manager of Toyota, that means they control the region. There is no one else who controls that region, but that is not how we live in Nikken. It means a Platinum Distributor has influenced a Region. Yet, if you take all of the Platinum Distributors who have influenced that region, to this day we still haven't influenced more than 2% of the region.

1:33:12

A Diamond distributor is national. When I look at a Diamond Distributor's reports, their genealogies, you will see 70% of their income is generated from distributors within one nation and so they are someone who has made a national impact. But if you take all the diamonds together in one country, all the diamonds together have not made a national impact of greater than 2%, but they have touched lives on a national scale, meaning they can pick up a phone and call people in an organization that might be somewhere in that country. They have friends around the country.

1:34:05

A Royal Diamond is international, and an international distributor clearly is somebody who is in multiple countries. I am a Royal Diamond pushing Royal Ambassador. Correction—I am a Royal Diamond in qualification for Royal Ambassador. I have four Diamonds and it would follow that my business is fairly international. Nikken is in 25 countries and a person would think I should be in a pretty good cluster of those countries. I am in 15 of those 25 countries and climbing which means that in my organization there are distributors within 15 countries. That does not mean that I control 15 countries.

1:34:43

Then there is the Royal Ambassador who we see as somebody who has made a global impact. Certainly that is what Nikken sees and so they send the Royal Ambassador around the world as an ambassador of good will. When they hit the rank of World Ambassador they do two trips around the world going to the various countries and just sprinkling a little bit of their stardust to give people some hope and vision about the purpose of Nikken. They are the reality; they are the realization of the vision of this company—the manifestation of the idea and that is somebody whom we respect on a global scale. Very exciting!

1:35:44

Now, if you take all the world ambassadors in Nikken and put them together, two of them so far, and you ask yourself, **"What impact have these global visionaries had on the global wellness of the world?" You would conclude that we haven't even started yet.**

You can now start to imagine what it must be like for Tom Watanabi who was the President and CEO of Nikken globally and what he is thinking about on a daily basis. As big as we are, we are nothing compared to what we can be and what can be done and what needs to be done. So, where is that going to come from? Where is Nikken going to fulfill its realization? How is Nikken going to realize its vision if each and every one of us is not doing our bit, contributing in our own way to our communities and our countries? This is something that is worth talking about, something that is becoming more and more valuable every single day. These products that we are selling make more sense to more people every day . . . globally.

1:36:54
The Rhythm of the Business

I am going to tie in two more concepts. Have you heard the expression, "rhythm of the business?" What does it mean? It means that each of these people is contributing to the structure in some way to keep people growing in that structure . . . to keep this thing expanding outward so that each individual contributes and as a whole we contribute . . . more market penetration, if you will . . . more Platinums, more Golds, more Silvers, more Executives, more Seniors, more Diamonds, more Royal Diamonds. Wave after wave, penetrating a little bit deeper into the wellness state of the world. When are you going to start your waves?

1:38:12

There is a rhythm to this and **everything has rhythm.** All life, all structure has rhythm. Structure has rhythm . . . the sun comes up, the sun goes down, the moon comes up, the moon goes down. We revolve around the sun, the earth itself spins, the moon spins and so forth. There is rhythm in everything—life has rhythm. Everything has rhythm and for every structure there is a rhythm. In fact, do you realize this appears to be a solid structure when, in fact, it is all atoms and vibrations and there is a natural rhythm? It's called resonance frequency and that means that it has a signature and if I hit it with a pea-shooter at the resonance frequency, it will actually collapse before your eyes. There is resonance frequency to every structure.

1:39:25

If this is a structure, there must be a rhythm to this structure. And if we can get into the rhythm, the amplitude is going to be greater and greater and this thing will explode. There is a huge movement taking place right now in Nikken—from the corporation through to the field—to get the corporation and the field in harmony, so that Nikken can build in amplitude . . . in greater amplitude and make a deeper impact each and every time. This is how it works.

The Science of the Nikken Business   53

1:40:16

A **Senior** Distributor is involved in a rhythm everyday. What are they doing? They are using the products. And, what are they doing when they use the products? It raises their belief! And since **we act in accordance to our beliefs,** what does somebody who believes in the products do? They talk about them. Every day they are talking to new people, so the **daily rhythm is to make new friends,** new acquaintances and contact with new people to explore the possibilities that Nikken might have in store for them.

What comes after the daily rhythm? How often is a Wellness Preview used? Weekly! So, there is a **weekly rhythm. The Wellness Preview** serves not only as a Wellness Preview but basic training. In fact, if this person is making contact daily, then usually they are doing it through ABCs which means they are being trained at the same time they are making contact. So, weekly we have a Wellness Preview basic training to help recruit and get them going. And who puts that on?

1:41:28

Well, if they are competent, the Silvers would be doing it and if they are incompetent, they would have someone else do it for them. So here is an opportunity for a Silver to step into the world of competence by beginning to participate in the actual presenting of the Wellness Preview.

I was the first Silver within my group. When we started conducting one of the first Wellness Previews, we would **break up it up into three sections:** the **introduction,** the **product,** the **business.** The host would do the introduction. The products would always be presented by somebody new.

1:42:13

Why would we choose somebody who is relatively new? Because what does a Senior who is competent do? They talk about the products. And because they are familiar with the products, we put them in front of the audience to talk about what they are already comfortable talking about. Now all they have to do is to deal with the fact that they are talking to a larger group and so that helps them become more comfortable.

The first time they present, they are obviously nervous. So we put them on stage with somebody else. But you know what happens after that person does his or her first Wellness Preview—the person starts to come out of their shell. They love to talk. And all of a sudden you have them talking in front of an audience. Can you imagine a global leader who can not stand in front of an audience and talk with confidence, with capacity, compassion and credibility? I don't think you can imagine a global leader being like that. This business will cause you to come out of *your* shell. You are going to become a global leader . . . which means you will have an opinion. And, your opinion is going to be worth a fortune.

1:43:32

Having an opinion is going to become something very important and the sooner you get started having an opinion, and not worrying what everybody else thinks about your opinion, the sooner you are going to see success in this business. People are relying on us to provide them with factual information about things that can make a difference in their lives, like these products.

Silvers are conducting weekly presentations. So, when Seniors and Executives make contact and they get somebody excited, they want to bring that person to a presentation. If there is no presentation to bring them to, the excitement window goes away! So, you want to **make sure that there is a presentation going on every week . . .** whether it is a public presentation or it is in somebody's living room, it really does not matter, just as long as we have somewhere you can bring them to and where there are other people who have a similar story to share.

1:44:29

What happens monthly? **Gold Distributors host what we call a month-end event.** Some people in Nikken call it Super Saturday. It is a special event, a bit more prestigious than a weekly Wellness Preview. Usually it means **there are higher PINS present**. It typically involves more training, advanced training instead of basic training and it really features people.

1:45:02

What is it that you want to hear when you get to a Wellness Preview more than anything? **Testimonials** from new distributors and **new Seniors.** So, a Wellness Preview features the seniors and executives because they are new and they are exited. We want those other prospects to hear their stories, because we want the other prospects to want to be Senior distributors.

1:45:48

Every month we want people to make a decision to go from being a Senior to being Silver so we have to feature the Silvers, new Silvers, and this is why the Golds host a monthly presentation that features new Silvers. Why? We want those Senior distributors to hear the stories of those new Silvers, so they understand. Let them hear from new Silvers, those who have just become Silvers . . . their excitement, their enthusiasm, the things that they did. I want a Senior to make a decision to become Silver, so let me put them into the mind of the Silver so they can see it is not that big of a deal. It's exciting, it's going to involve challenge, it's going to be work and so forth but it is going to be fun. Involve the Seniors in the process of being a Silver rather than keep it a mystery. The talk goes, "What does it mean to be Silver? Could I ever be one?" "Sure, I can show you what it means to be Silver!" So, we feature Silvers. If you've heard the tape, **"Silver's a Blast,"** that's what that tape is all about!

1:46:47

We also have a **quarterly event** and it's a bigger deal. We have higher ranks and the **Platinums** are the **hosts. We feature Golds** and we even have **Diamonds** and **Royal Diamonds** who are going to present to you. We have special guests and so forth. Why? We want you to think bigger, we want you to be moving beyond where you currently are and where you think you can be.

1:47:20
Every once in a while we have to prompt you. Even the Silvers get stale. We need to prompt them to become Gold and on it goes.

Semi-annual events are hosted by **Diamonds.** In other words, Team Diamond. And, that event **features the Platinums** because we want to encourage people to move up to Platinum. So, each of these events happen on a bigger scale, and they attract people from larger areas, so we attract from a larger audience. This is a national event.

1:48:32
PLAN to Do What it Takes to Get There
Internationally . . . we have Nikken's International Annual Convention. Every three years Nikken puts on a global convention and that is like being at the heart of the United Nations. It is impressive! Many distributors will plan to win their trip for free. Notice that I use the word *plan*. What would the CEO of a business do? Hope and pray? Or do they plan to go? They plan to do what it takes to get there.

There is one other concept I want to go over. At a Wellness Preview that happens weekly, who is "A?" "A" is the speakers, who are the Silvers. Who's the "B?" . . . the Seniors, the people who brought the "C's," who are the guests. A's job is to present. B's job is to learn but also to validate. So, there's a presenter and then there is the validation. You must present and validate if you ever hope to get "C" to want to be a "B." You present and then you validate; you present the information about the products and you validate the efficacy of the products . . . present the information about the business and validate the business.

1:50:10
So, your testimonials should be product testimonies. Business testimonials should have a lot of validation, **because even if a prospect**

didn't quite understand the facts, they will understand the emotion, and that will cause them to want to become involved. Have you ever seen that movie "When Harry met Sally?" Remember the scene, "I'm having what she is having!" They did not know what she was having but they knew how she felt about it.

1:50:41

So that's the ABC's, technically speaking, about the structure of Nikken. The advancement of the distributors in Nikken is all about the ABC's . . . whether it is one-on-one, which is misnomer since there should never be one-on-one. We always have an "A," "B," and "C" or an ABC **Wellness Preview.** It's an event that we call a month-end regional event where the "A" is the Gold distributor; "B" is the Silver distributor; "C" is the Senior distributor. And even though we might have prospects there, we're really talking to the Seniors. We are featuring the Silvers with their stories and Golds are presenting the information. So, this ABC concept goes all the way up the ladder. Depending on what event it is, there is always an "A," a "B," and a "C." The "A's" are the presenters, the "B's" are those people who validate what the people are presenting and the "C's" are the people who we are hoping to motivate into action. Does this make sense? That's **the structure of our business** and how do you learn it? One step at a time.
1:52:16

What I've Learned—Part 2

Before I leave this chart let us turn your attention to the CEO. We talked about the three aspects of your goals.

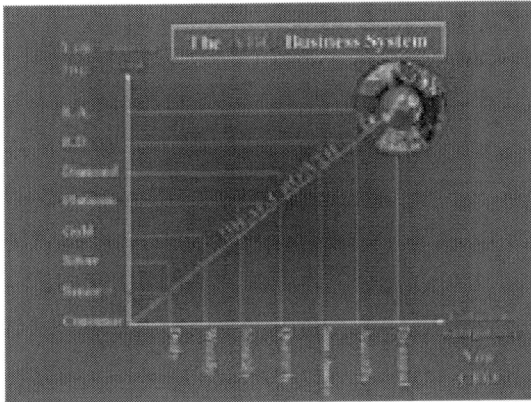

Diagram 3

0:10
Your Goals
We **start with a purpose** and then we break that purpose down into some goals. At this point, we look at what we need to do, what we need to learn, how to do it and how often do we need to do it to achieve those goals. There is a strategy. Competence is our strategy and by learning how to do it, we actually create it. This is on the job training at Nikken. You actually become and realize what you become simultaneously. So what is it that a CEO needs to do?

0:50
What are the Three Aspects of a Good Healthy CEO?
Your CEO would be "A" for attitude. Develop your competence. A is the development of your attitude. Jeff Van Blaricum strongly

advocated and still does advocate affirmation tapes, because what an affirmation tape really works on is your attitude. You really start to look at your beliefs and start to work on your attitude. If you believe you can succeed, you start to act like someone who succeeds. Your attitude leads to a change of your beliefs and a positive attitude changes your beliefs about what you can do. Your beliefs then change your behavior, or the commitments you make for the choices you make. It is attitude, belief and commitment or attitude, commitment and choice.

A CEO is someone who is always working on their attitude, their beliefs and their choices, correcting their commitments and realigning themselves so that they begin to realize their goals. Their purpose is always their purpose; their goals are always their goals. They work on those things that they need to develop in themselves in order to realize their goals.

2:18

For instance, back in the early 60's, the United States had a vision that they would lead the way into the space age. And, when the Russians demonstrated that they knew how to put a sputnik into orbit, that was a call to action for the Americans to make their vision more clear, more distinct. So, from a vision they set a goal and it was held by the President of that time, JFK, who said, "Before the decade is out, we will have put a man on the moon." This was a huge goal based on the vision or the purpose of them leading the way into the space age. By having a statement of that goal, people started to take stock of where they were, and look at what they needed to develop in order to move toward the realization of that goal. They did not yet have the technology but they knew they could discover it if they were committed to the goal. They never changed the goal even though they did not have the capability, what they did was to develop the capability and realize the goal.

3:18

Do you realize how that works? Never change the goal. What if you do not reach your goal the first time 'round? Never change it, change the strategy. Change you. Change what needs to be changed in you in order for that goal to become a reality. As long as one person has done it before you, you can learn what they have done and that you can be sure of. Everything that anyone has done is teachable and learnable, provided you are teachable and someone can teach you. Based on this equation, I think you will agree with me that at least we know how to get to Royal Ambassador.

4:06

We know that at least two people have become Royal Ambassadors, and we know that we can get to that information when that information becomes relevant to you. The information that is relevant to you right now is your next level. That is the information that is relevant to you right now, beyond that is not relevant to you now. Even though I am a Royal Diamond moving toward Royal Ambassador, I only work with the person who becomes a new senior very quickly or I don't work with them at all. Otherwise, what would they be doing in my business? I am not going to talk to them about what it means to be a Diamond or a Royal Diamond because that is totally irrelevant to them. That's way up here (referring to the higher ranks on the Nikken Highway)! The new distributor still has to do this (Diagram 3—Senior Level and daily activity), so we work on this (Diagram 3—Senior Level), and when we get that mastered they should be hitting here (Diagram 3—Senior Level). And then we work on this and on this. It is a step by step process.

5:09

(Refer to Diagram 3, Page 59) I take my Royal Diamond hat off and I put my Silver hat on and I work with them as if I am their Silver teaching them what a Silver would teach a new Senior. And when they get to Silver, I take my Silver hat off and put my Gold hat on and say, "Now that you are a Silver, let me show you what it means to go beyond." And when they get to Gold, I take my Gold hat off and put my Platinum hat on and I work with them as if they are Gold. I will teach them what they need to learn to get to the next rank, what events they need to be responsible for, and how they need to delegate the events they should no longer be doing. Isn't that interesting? Go figure! There are some people who should not be doing events?

6:02

I should not point fingers, but I was asked to talk to a group of leaders. I saw a calendar of events and was shocked that the featured speakers for the entire month in all the various Wellness Previews were three of four Diamonds. I asked them if they knew what they were doing by speaking at the Wellness Previews. They thought they were doing something good. There they were, trying to help out. But my thought is this: by virtue of the Diamonds presenting with the level of skills they have, they are implying that their Platinums, Golds and Silvers don't have the skills to conduct a Wellness Preview as good as they can, so they should never attempt it.

6:52

If you're at fault and doing this, you are harming your leaders before they get out of the gate. These Diamonds never realized that! How could a Silver sitting in that audience ever hope to be as good as them, that they would want to take over that Wellness Preview?

Do you know what happened? If that Diamond was not there to perform next week, nobody would come! And that is exactly what happened. They created dependency instead of independence, instead of delegating and encouraging people to step up, to have an opinion—even if it's wrong . . . at least you have an opinion and take your place. Be that leader, one step at a time, whether standing up and giving your testimony in the audience or standing at the front of the room and presenting what you believe in. You are beginning to become that leader and are making a difference. That's what it's all about. It's about putting these two things together (referring to Diagram 3—pointing to business goal line and competence line to becoming a Royal Ambassador), and the last thing you want to be is incompetent, no matter what rank you are at. You want to make sure that you are always working on YOU as much as you are working on your business, that they are separate and distinct.

8:08
To Loan or not to Loan?

Let's move on to another concept quickly. This is an interesting one. There is always this great debate in Nikken. When I got into Nikken, there was a great debate—"to loan or not to loan." What I realized was, it is the flip side of the coin. We are talking about the same coin, it is just the flip side, and there is no right or wrong. And then the debate became—do you do in-home presentations or do you do hotel presentations? The in-home presentation was really a "Ma & Pa" kind of thing, the retail kind of thing. The slick hotel presentation was the *professional* presentation and this image came to my head. I realized it was the flip side of the same coin . . . still talking about the same thing, just a different venue. So, I started to realize that the big paradoxes in Nikken was nothing more than the flip side of the coin and so this chart will help you see something.

Recruiting Blitz . . . Present what you believe is in their best interest and they decide

ABC IS THE MECHANISM	A	B	C	
Private	1	1	1	Reserve for top 10 people Use A's time wisely
Personal In-Home	1	1	Many	Great for new product Launches
Public e.g. Wellness Preview, Expo, Month End, and so on	1-3	Many	Many	For a bigger vision than you can present alone

WHEN IT ALL SHAKES OUT, HOW TO DEAL WITH ALL THE PEOPLE

What do you do with the:

LEADERS	A types
BUSINESS BUILDERS	B types
ACTIVE CUSTOMERS	C types
RETAIL CUSTOMERS	D types
NO'S	E types

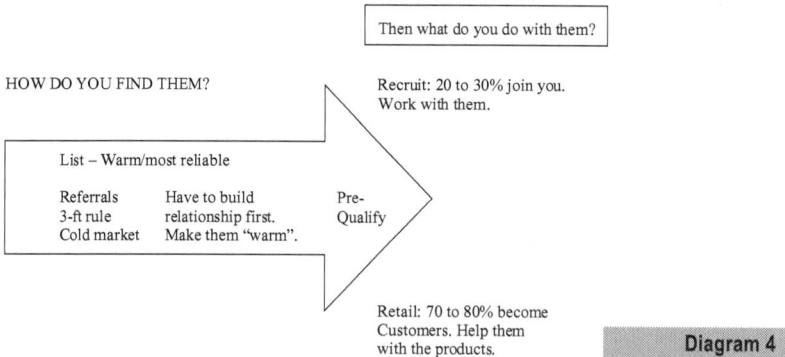

Then what do you do with them?

HOW DO YOU FIND THEM?

Recruit: 20 to 30% join you.
Work with them.

List – Warm/most reliable

Referrals   Have to build
3-ft rule   relationship first.   Pre-
Cold market   Make them "warm".   Qualify

Retail: 70 to 80% become
Customers. Help them
with the products.

Diagram 4

The Science of the Nikken Business

ABC is the key to everything that is the business we are in (refer to Diagram 4 on previous page).

10:31

This is a private gathering—**a private meeting. This is a personal one** and this is **a public one.** Each of these three environments is **distinct.** Which one do you think has more importance when you are meeting someone for the very first time? Which one would give a more effective impact? What is more effective? . . . taking a new prospect to a large meeting or sitting down with him and talking to him in private?

11:58

A private one is going to have a greater significance to that person. So, an example of a **private** meeting would be what we refer to as a **"one-on-one,"** which I really do not think is the right choice of words; it should be an ABC but some people call it one-on-one.

You can do this over lunch or coffee, whatever. There's one "A," one "B," and one "C." It's a private gathering. One "decision making unit" is probably a very good way of looking at "C," because it could be a couple—just as long as long as there is **one decision making unit.** "A" is doing the presenting; "B" is doing the validating, "B" validates "A," with the hopes that "C" wants to become a "B."

13:26

The Proper "ABC"—Is it Appropriate for B to Present?

It is never, ever appropriate for B to present . . . ever. An "A" could also be an audio cassette, or a videotape, an "A" could be a telephone call, an "A" could be a real person, any way you can get that person. But the "A" ought to be presenting and the "B" ought to be in the "A" person's corner. **It should never be the** "B" **presenting, because the second the** "B" **crosses the line, what the** "B" **becomes is selling.** The "B" comes across as selling. What happens when you come across as selling? How do they perceive you? Needy!! Understand, this ABC is a very powerful, powerful medium and we need to learn how to use it effectively.

14:30

Now, let's talk about **a personal scenario.** This is what I refer to as an **in-home.** Would you not agree that if I invited you to my home, it would be more personal and you would consider it a personal encounter? In that scenario, how many "A's" are there? One. How many "B's?" One. How many "C's" are there? There could be one or there could be many. Here is an opportunity to leverage time because now the "A's" can present to many "C's" on behalf of the one "B." There is still a focal point, the "B." So, this is the perfect situation if I am launching someone; it's through them I am helping them launch their business. This is very great scenario for them to learn and to encounter some of their top prospects.

15:51
Public Event

In contrast, let's look at a **public event.** A Wellness Preview, an event of any sort, is an example of a public event. The number of "A's" could be anywhere from one to ten, depending on the size of that event, perhaps even more if it is a Team Diamond event. There would be many "B's" and "C's." A public event is not very personal. So what impact can something like a public event have? It could have an impact that a personal event can't have. So, it is at the **public events where the real decision is made and the commitments are made and here is where there is closure and so forth.** Personal or in-home presentations are a great opportunity to present information, very distinct information, very personalized information. It is very directed and targeted information. You can extract information; it is a very interactive dialogue so it is intimate. Public events are not at all intimate.

17:29

But what is more powerful than a personal presentation? **Validation. A public event** is an excellent opportunity to validate; an in-home is a great opportunity to present **targeted** information. Your presentation is **very specific** very targeted. At the event, the validation can be overwhelming, so somewhere down the middle is where that personal in-home comes to mind. Because during an in-home presentation you have the **opportunity to do a little bit of both,** present and validate but you are still working through a more direct focal point.

18:14

I am going to show you how you utilize ABC's in building an organization. Question: is it appropriate to have more than one "B" (validator) at a personal in-home presentation? Well if you have more than one "B" (validator), then you are actually turning the in-home into a public event. Think about the point of view of the person who you are trying to really impress—the "C." You have a "C," they come to your in-home meeting and there is one "B." "C" knows that "B" and "C" was invited there with a specific thing in mind with an introduction and so forth.

19:00

They know that person and so they see somebody who is a stranger. What makes the "A" and "C" have a respect and a commonality is they both know the one person. Now bring somebody else to the equation they don't know. You do not know that person, I don't know that person, how do we feel? We will have you in common. Now there is this other person who is not even in common with you, not in common with them. Who is this third man out? If that person has their people whom they know, then it looks like there is another group going on. It is like there is another meeting going on because there are too many parties now involved. Do you see what I am saying? It is not as effective. It can still work for you but when you add more people to the equation you change the dynamics. So it depends on what outcome you want to get at the presentation, and that determines what you do. I say this on purpose because each one of these presentations can have a focal point.

20:16

We are going to be the presenter, but what are we going to present? Because what we present creates an outcome. What we present, our presentation, the way we present our presentation, creates an outcome.

What is the desired outcome? If you don't know what the desired outcome is that you are after, and you don't know what it is you need to do to get what you are after, then what is going to happen? You are going to get something, but it may be what you are not looking for. (Refer to diagram on page 70.)

20:57

For my presentation, **I have to know in advance what the result is going to be for me to know** what kind of presentation I am going to give. How many of you want to create customers? How many of you want to recruit distributors? Well, depending on what you want to create will determine what and how you are going to present. Would you agree?

So I refer to this as **the slant presentation** (diagram on Page 70). The presentation now has a slant and I can present in any of these three fashions (private, in-home or public). I can present with a **retail slant** or I can present with a **recruiting slant,** let me give you a great example of two.

21:54

How many of you have heard of a tape or of the work of Dave Stoltzfus. He is doing in-home Wellness Previews, home presentations. We use the word Wellness Preview to describe a public event. A Wellness Preview in my mind, in my vocabulary, a Wellness Preview is a public event with a specific presentation, and the presentation is on a flip chart. We refer to the flip chart presentation as the Wellness Preview presentation because it was designed for the Wellness Preview.

22:34

When I do an in-home presentation I never use the Wellness Preview flip chart because it does not allow me to be personal, intimate and responsive to the people I am talking to. It sounds too "canned." In my opinion, it is less impressive because it takes away from the personal touch. Now that does not mean I do not cover the same points. That does not mean that I do not have the same understanding

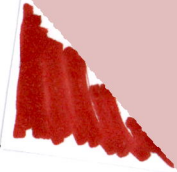

in my head when I go through my presentation, but I just use a piece of paper and I evolve the ideas as I talk about the same things. The difference—there is a greater slant, either toward the business or toward the product depending on what I am doing.

23:29

In the Dave Stolfus presentation for example, there is a greater emphasis on retail, a great emphasis on presenting the value of the products as an introduction. In fact, the invitation goes something like this. "Come on over, we are having a get-together to introduce a fabulous new technology that could make a huge difference in people's lives. Leave your checkbook and credit cards at home. We just want to introduce you to this new technology." Of course the anticipation is that they are going to come with their wallet anyway, and maybe somebody mentions an opportunity, just to see if anybody is paying attention. He then deals with those people who are interested in the opportunity while the rest of the demonstration happens and the retail takes place. So he uses the in-home much like most people perceive the in-home to be, with the retail edge.

24:19

I, on the other hand, use the in-home completely differently. **I do it with a recruiting edge.** I do it as ***an opportunity to launch a new distributor, to attract to their business, their nucleus, their key people.*** So that presentation is focused on the business, it is focused on **what** we are doing here, **why** they have been invited; it talks about the **potential of the market.** It focuses on why we, me ("A") and the host ("B"), have made a decision to do this. The presentation has a completely different angle, it talks about what we have decided to do without their permission.

25:00

This is what we are doing. (Refer to Diagram 3—YOU Inc., Page 22.) We are going to create this business with this remarkable technology and we are going to do it with the backing of this massive corporation. We have the expertise of a lineage that will impress the president of the USA and we are asking you if you want to become a part of it. See the difference? We have a projected start date and we need to know if you are going to be a part of this team.

25:31

So between now and that projected start date, what do you want to know? Do you want to know about these products? Take them home and try them. Do you want to know about Nikken? Get on the Internet, it will tell you. Do you want to know about the people I work with? Let me introduce you to some of these people. **I see the in-home presentation as an opportunity to invite them into a process,** a process that will take them through an exploration, to decide whether they want to join us in what we are about to do. We already know that we are going to do it, with or without them, and that is the impression that I leave at one of those presentations.

26:07

Leave The Impression I Want You to be Part of a Winning Team

My in-home presentation is an invitation to be a part of something. Part of a team that is going somewhere as opposed to being introduced to this wonderful wellness technology. You see how this works? There is **the retail slant and there is the recruiting slant.** Same venue, same in-home, the difference is who has been invited.

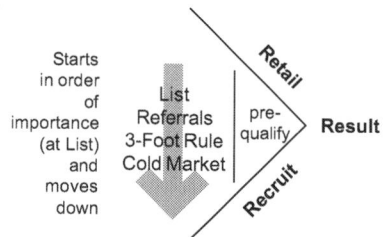

So now I have a list, which is **one way of generating prospects.** I could also generate prospects with referrals. I can also generate prospects with what we call the **three foot rule**—anybody within three feet you get to know.

Starts in order of importance (at List) and moves down

List
Referrals
3-Foot Rule
Cold Market

Retail
pre-qualify
Recruit
Result

27:07

Basically it is based on observation. You are at a restaurant and you observe somebody in your environment that impresses you and they are someone that you would really like to be in business with. Notice I use the words: who you would like to be in business with, not who you would like to recruit, not who would be great in Nikken, but who you would want to be in business with, and that's a very different thing. Why? What do I believe? What's the paradigm I'm operating from? (Refer to YOU Inc. diagram, Page 35). The structure I'm operating from is that I have a choice as to who I am going to invite into my space, who I'm going to spend the rest of my life with. I don't want to spend the rest of my life with someone who is whining on the phone. I want to make sure that before I invite somebody to be in business with me, they are somebody that I want to be in business with. I need to get to know them a little bit. This is the cold market.

28:06

In terms of these three methods (list, referrals, 3-foot rule), which one do you think is **the most accessible** and the most reliable? **Your list!** So it starts there (with your list—diagram, Page 70) and it works this way (downward toward the cold market) in terms of order of importance always. Besides this (list of names), this is readily available to a brand new distributor, (remember the snowball), I want to get them started right away, making that snowball.

They don't have availability to the cold market right away and I don't want them going here right away because they are not qualified, they don't even know how to make cold calls.

29:04

What must I do to decide which presentation is appropriate for the particular person I'm talking too? I must pre-qualify them. In the case of invitations to my retail presentation, it is getting too complicated with all the products. There are too many products to do in one sitting and so you almost feel a need to become a specialist in each category. There is the magnetic category, the sleep technology, and have you noticed how Nikken is starting to come out with incentives and so forth around each of those things.

29:58

That is because Nikken is starting to re-model themselves; they are taking a look at the structure. They have had a few of us pestering them long enough to say we need to look at it. So, they are starting to frame and package, like in the sleep promotion. You are going to see another one coming, and then another, and they are starting to direct their promotions. In fact pretty soon they are going to have a promotion very clearly identified every ninety days. **There will be a focus on retailing and recruiting every ninety days,** so you can choose which one of the two you want to participate in or how you want to participate in both, because **we need both.**

30:39

There is nothing to say that out of a list of 100 names, 80 who qualified would be retail customers. Why didn't they qualify over there (as business builders)? Well, just because they did not qualify over here! If they don't make it to this list (recruiting) they always get on that list (products). There is nothing to say that from my list of 100 names that these 80 people should not be invited to explore new technology that could benefit them and their family. **During one week, I can set up a number of in-home presentations, then personally invite friends and family to explore technology that I think could make a difference in their lives.** How am I going to communicate that?

31:24
Inviting Customers/Prospects to your home

What do I want them to do? I want them to come therefore what must I have them believe in, in order to get them to come, because that's why they will come.

31:50

That will be the result. They will come to my presentation. That will be the action they take because they believe a certain thing, therefore what must I say? What is the structure of the words I must use? The choice of words and how I say them is what will cause them to believe what it is that I want them to believe so they will act consistent with those beliefs and be at my house. If you thought of it that way then you can say to yourself "**What do I want them to believe**?" Let's just think about it, what do you want them to believe?

32:24

Something of value! Something that they cannot afford to miss! It must be something that's urgent, that there might not be another chance for them to hear about it . . . something that could be a life changing thing, something that becomes more valuable than anything else they could be doing that night. In fact, if they already have booked that night, if I really wanted them to believe that this was far more important than anything that they already have booked, then **I would tell them to change it.** I would be prepared for that answer, and then suggest to them that this is too important for them to miss. So what would I say if I wanted them to believe what they needed to believe to ensure that they are going to act like someone who is going to be at my presentation?

33:08

You can write any script according to this formula. If you just think it through; if you put yourself in the shoes of that person. I can do an in-home presentation inviting people to learn about pi-mag technology. "Water, is that a concern in your mind? Well I have the answer. There is no longer a need for you to have bottled water in your home, at your schools or at your job. The bottled water industry is finished when you see what we have! You cannot afford to miss this!" I will invite 80 people to my home over the course of 2 or 3 nights and I will put on 3 individual seminars on water—I might have the water video. I will do all of the things we are taught to do that work very effectively. They will come, they will learn and they are going to buy.

34:05

If out of 80 people 40 show up, and out of the 40 who show up, 1 in 10 buy, that's pretty reasonable. If 4-8 people buy and it's probably going to be a lot more than that and you know that because you know your numbers. What are 4-5 Pi-Mag systems in terms of volume? That's a nice boost in volume! What if every one of your leaders did that, one week, once, in the next 2-3 months? I think Nikken has an expression for this—they call it a 21 Club. You see, they have an incentive already geared around that. And what's to say these same 80 people aren't going to be interested the next time Nikken comes up with something new. Since they've never heard of MagSteps or the magnetic technology or they've never heard of the infrared or the nutritionals or the skin care line or the Pi-Mag line.

35:11

What's to say that we could not invite them over each and every time for a different product presentation. If, out of 80 people half show up . . . some one time, some another time. These are people who you know, trust and respect, and they appreciate the value of what you are offering and you are able to demonstrate that value and they become a consumer. What's to say that they are not going to be a consumer for life? Why not get some of these customers on auto-ship?

35:38

Why not put some of these customers on the C.A.P. program, so you have business every month? Now you are starting to think like a business person, but you do the numbers. What if 100 people in your down line did the same thing because you taught them to, beginning with you! What if 1,000 people in your down line did that because you taught them, beginning with you? What would your volume be? Never mind recruiting, what would your volume be? Every time you recruit new people, that would just add more volume. If I am interested in volume, I will do this (retail). What does it take to go Silver? Volume! A lot of people who go Silver employ this method—multiple 21 clubs and so forth.

36:40

Let's talk about recruiting for a moment. If my **presentation was geared toward business,** what would I say in order to get the people to believe what it is that they would need to believe in order for them to act like some one who is truly interested in becoming a Wellness **Expert in the movement of Health and Wellness as it grows nationally and internationally?** What would I say to get them to believe (refer to diagram, Page 7), in order to act like someone who is going to help me build this Wellness Movement? **Recruit people to help us,** not people who simply need our help. **Do you see the difference?**

I look to find people who can help us. If I say I want you to help me, or if I say we want you to help US? What do you feel? Joining a cause—a TEAM that already has a mission. Do you see the difference that one little word makes?

37:39
Helping Society in a BIG WAY

I start with a vision; the vision is to help society in a big way. Do you think I can help society in a big way one person at a time? If I start to recruit people I want to help, I am going to be busy for a long time and at best, how many people will I have helped? But if I truly want to be consistent with my purpose—to help society in a big way, Nikken has already told me what that means. They said, "Mike, you say you want to help society in a big way, well let me show you what that means! It's called **Royal Ambassador,** and having done that, not only will you have made a global impact on society but **you'll have moved up in rank on the Nikken Highway!"** (Refer to Diagram 3, Page 36.)

38:31
I think I like their plan better! Instead of helping one at a time, I should get some people to help me help other people. Instead of worrying about just how somebody may benefit where the products are concerned, maybe I should teach them what I am learning about the value of living a life worth living and adding that much more value in society.

39:00

So I look to find people who can help us. Who is US? Help us! Do you see the difference when I say help us? What's the difference? If I say I want you to help me, or if I say we want you to help US? What do you feel? Joining a cause—a TEAM that already has a mission. Do you see the difference that one little word makes? Help me or help US? Do you see the difference that it makes? The impact is huge because adding people already shows a change in the structure. **It's not about me, it's about WE**. You see the difference in the structure right there. What's the corporate world all about? If it's going to be, then it's up to me. Where does that phrase come from? In Nikken, if it's going to be it's up to WE, because you cannot build this alone, and so it's an immediate change in structure.

40:38

The first perception a person has is the change in the structure. It is on a sub-conscious level, and on the sub-conscious level they see something different which leads to what? A change in the way they see it—BELIEF! Very important! Very simple! It is very subtle, but it has a huge impact in the results of the behavior of the prospect.

I am back to my presentation. WE have invited you to hear about what we are doing and we want you to be a part of this, and that is why you have been invited. You have been pre-selected to be here, we could have invited anybody but we did not, we invited you . . . what's the impression I am giving that person?

41:18

I want you. I don't need you, but I want you. You are important. You are valuable. We see you as valuable in what it is you want to create. We believe you can be a great contributor to this. And, if we are right, you are going to get a whole bunch of fringe benefits. If we are right and this is viable, not only are you going to help us make a huge difference in the world, but you are going to become something you never imagined possible. That is, if we are right. Now I don't want you to believe us on first glimpse, so here is what we want you to do. We have an expected launch date and we want you, between now and then, to experience the total impact of what we are saying. We want you to understand the Structure; we want you to understand who these people are and what they have already done without us, but what we are capable of doing with them. We want you to meet the **people** who we are working with, who are giving us the information, the insights, the know-how. How they have set up internationally to support us in our organization as it grows, that is what we have the intention of doing!

42:44

Do you see the difference those words are making in your own mind? Can you see yourself being in a presentation by someone who is delivering those words . . . the impact that would make, the difference that would make? In recruiting, what you are actually doing is dealing with growth; the recruits are pre-qualified to be in that room, retail customers are not!

Recruits are people I present the opportunity to because I believe they are the kind of people I want to be in business with, who can contribute to the vision.

43:27

These people (retail) don't necessarily have those characteristics. I could be wrong, there might be one or 2 in that group who might very well surprise me and I will gladly take them on if in fact they surprise me. That remains to be seen. At least here (business), I'm going in already knowing who I am talking to, already knowing what I am going to talk to them about, and knowing pretty well how they might interpret that information. Whether they do join or not is not my business. That's up to them to decide, but at least I know that they will take me seriously. I know that they will take the presentation with credibility.

44:07

These recruiting meetings are pre-qualified. These retailing meetings (*products*) anybody can come to. There is a different slant. You can do this one at a time. You can do this in a small group in someone's living room or boardroom, but then what would I need? Validation. Now that I have presented, what would I want them to see next . . . the Wellness Preview! The Wellness **Preview is an awesome way for me to validate,** but I am talking from the point of view of the leader. What if you have someone in your down line who does not necessarily have a business plan?

Let's go back to the snowball. Have you attracted anyone into your organization, who has not yet packed that snow ball, who is a mutated cell? What do you do with them? If they are not willing to do the first thing the way it has to be done, what do you do with these people? Do you ignore them or do you give them a chance to grow? We are about growth and opportunity so I want to give them a chance to grow, but what do I do with these people?

45:39
Create an Environment That Encourages Growth
I don't have the time to deal with them on a personal basis because chances are it is going to be a waste of my time. If they are not willing to take instructions from me and do what they need to do, I can't help them, they can only help themselves. But what I can do as a leader is create an environment that encourages growth and is the best use of my time. If I have public events on an ongoing basis, for instance every week—a Wellness Preview and a basic training, then one week they might just get it. Which week I don't know, so I have to have it every week.

46:36
One week they might bring someone who is a pretty sharp candidate. I don't know, but I have to have the event. McDonald's never knows when you are going to eat, but they have to open the doors every day to make sure that they are open when you decide to eat. Well, we just never know when our distributors who are lagging are going to wake up. We just never know when those Silvers, who have been Silver forever want

to step up to the plate and go Gold. We just never know, so we have to make sure we are open for business **when they are ready. When they are ready,** we move into a strategy with their list of prospects in one direction or another. That's a business plan. Actually, it's not a business plan, it's a business idea. Now let's put a plan together.

47:46
Creating Volume Bursts

This is a great way to create volume bursts. Imagine you have 100 people in your down line, leaders or even people who are not necessarily the super stars, but they really enjoy Nikken and are excited by sharing these products. When Nikken comes out with a new product launch, they are the first to want to have an in-home or a party to expose people to the new product. That's a volume burst. Multiply 100 people by $4000-$5000 in volume, that's half a million dollars in volume. Can anybody make use of 6% of half a million? Doing what? Simply introducing to people they already know and care about a product that they believe in, in a way that they are very comfortable—in their home.

48:32
On the other hand, if they decide to advance in the marketing plan, that means that they have to build a team. Building a team is a different way of doing things. Building a team is focusing on the end in mind. What do you want? You want to recruit somebody therefore your presentation is going to have to reflect what it is that you want as an outcome. I don't like recruiting people by accident. **I like recruiting people on purpose.** I like going Silver on purpose, I like going Gold on purpose, I like going Platinum on purpose. I like going Diamond/Royal Diamond/Royal Ambassador on purpose. I hate when it's by accident because I don't feel that I was responsible, I don't feel like I know how to do it again. I don't feel like I can take anybody else with me. And, the last thing I want to be is an incompetent leader. With everybody looking up to me for answers and I don't have them and so I make them up, which leads them to believe what I say because I have the PIN, which

leads them to do what I say. If what I'm saying is not accurate, guess what the results look like? Different than the picture. Then who do you blame? Not all leaders were meant to be teachers.

49:46
Building a Business or Pushing a Rope

Here is a story about having a strategy. I had an interesting thing happen to me in Italy this summer. I went with the intent of helping a cousin of mine become a distributor and get his business off the ground. My cousin had a child in the two years since I had been there last, and it changed his whole picture of life, and now all of a sudden he realized he wasn't going anywhere. He needed an opportunity and at that point in time he started paying attention, started asking me questions. So the next thing you know I am going there to help him kick off his business. I quickly discovered I was pushing a rope; he wasn't really committed. I kind of knew it going in, but we were having a family reunion in Italy with my dad and uncles who had not been back to Italy together in 33 years so this was going to be a wonderful vacation.

51:16
In fact, there was a young man from a completely different organization in Naples who came over to Ischia because he learned that I was there. The next thing I know I am spending my time educating this young man, because I thought . . . this kid could be a star. He is 22 years old and he deserves the best education he can get and he took the time to come to visit me. So here is a guy who has no business in my business but I like the fact that I can help him. He has since broken 2 Silvers, perhaps he is Gold already, I don't know.

51:45
Anyway, I am there on vacation and my dad tells me that my cousin from Milan is coming down. I had never met him before, but the next thing I know he came with his wife, his best friend and his wife, to learn about the business, although they were actually coming to see me. The reason they were coming to see me is because one of my uncles had

taken out a back flex to let him try because his back was bothering him. The next thing you know his back feels much better and when he asks my uncle about it, he tells him to come and see me because I know more about it.

52:29

I really wasn't prepared, but I had a few supplies I had actually brought to help my other cousin. I started showing him and his best friend about Nikken. I taught him some concepts, but didn't know where it was going to go. In fact I didn't find out until after I presented everything to him, that he had come specifically for that reason. In any event, we had a nice couple of days together and he went of to Milan and then the phone started to ring.

53:11

Every single day, 2-3 times a day the phone would ring while I was in Italy. He was begging me to go to Milan because he had some people for me to talk to. How do you know when somebody is interested? Here I am in Ischia trying to push a rope, and I've got this other guy calling me constantly. Because of my family, I wasn't about to take all my kids and everybody and go up to Milan and change all my plans because I was only there a week. He kept calling and so I said I would come, but I couldn't schedule him in until the end of September.

54:07

I was so busy that I was squeezing him in between other commitments. I hadn't spoken to him, so as the time was approaching I started talking to him. By now he has signed up and he has ordered a career pack. That's when you know someone is interested.

54:49

They are doing things without you asking. He is already on top of this. He signed up because he wanted to get the sales kit so he could learn more about things. He ordered the products because he thought it would be appropriate to learn more about the products. Meanwhile he is doing his own due diligence. So we started planning. I am going to go there but what I need is for him to order the demo pack because I can't do the back rolls if I don't have the demo pack and I'm not going to cart mine from here to there. Besides (**remember the snowball**), if we are going to this, we are going to do this my way!

55:21

He gets off the phone and the very next phone call is to Nikken and he orders a demo pack. How do you know if someone is interested? They are willing to do what you suggest they need to do, because you are the expert, and because they are teachable. How would you like to say you helped someone go Platinum in 30 days? How would you like to say you were responsible for doing that at least 4 times? One went Platinum in 30 days, two went Platinum in 60 days, and one went Platinum in 90 days. All were designed to go Platinum in 90 days but some do it sooner then others. How would you like to say you had a hand in that?

56:18

I'm saying that's called **conscious competence** as opposed to unconscious competence. It's knowing your craft and knowing how to design things. But as good as a business plan is, as incredible as an opportunity is, with all the potential that it has . . . what good is it if you put it in the hands of someone who is unwilling to change themselves, unwilling to modify their beliefs, unwilling to change their perception of structure in order to take full advantage of it. It is a combination of two things—you have to know what you are doing and you have to find someone who is willing to do it. It happens once in a while in a big way. When it does, it's very exciting!

57:05

Back to my Italy story. I tell my cousin what he needs to do and he does it! Two weeks before my arrival in Italy I told him that I had these 2 days and that we would do a presentation each day. By doing it this way, the people who come to the first one can bring people to the second one and at least we can get something going. We talked about who he was going to invite, I told him not to put me in front of people who he thought he could help. **I wanted him to put me in front of people who could help us capture the Italian Market.**

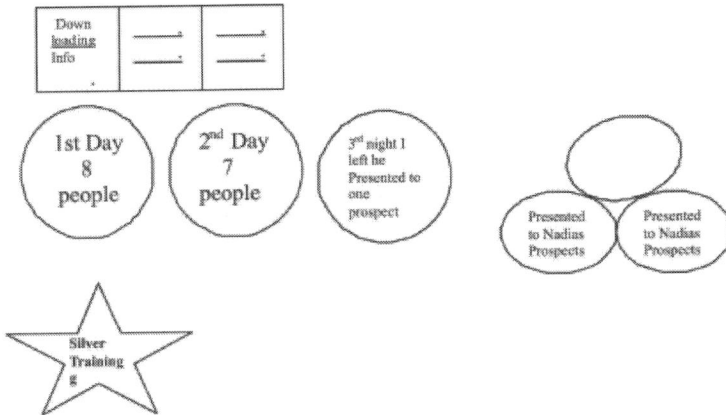

57:50

We wanted business-minded people, entrepreneurial, big vision people! I got to his house and there were 7 days left in September . . . that was it. The first day we did a presentation for 8 people, the second day we did a presentation for 7 people. Between the time that I got there and the time I left the next morning, no matter what we were doing, I was teaching him. Why, because I had to leave. If I did not leave with him having the basic competencies under his belt, at least theoretically, then I would leave and what would happen? Nothing, because he would not believe he had the ability to do it, and he wouldn't have the structure to do it.

58:49

I was busy trying to **give him the competencies.** I made sure **I rolled everybody's back,** so he could watch me. **I made his best friend watch me roll his back,** then **I had his friend watch me roll**

his best friend's back. Why, why would I do all those things? Because I had to leave and I had to make sure that when I left, he had the confidence and the ability to carry on, at least with the basics. I did a flip-chart presentation that was maybe 4-5 pages, it was so simple. Why? Because I had to leave, and I had to make sure that when I left he could at least do what I did. It was a very simple presentation. We had a dining room table, we had the products scattered on the table, we had brochures laid out, the sales kit, everything one would get. Remember the snowball; if they did everything we asked them to do.

59:47

At least they could physically see what we were asking them to do. I demonstrated the products, so they knew what we needed the products for. In those two days we had 8,000 points and 3 new distributors. Now that's not huge, but it's a good start. I left and that night he did a presentation for one. The next morning he called me and he said he wasn't doing that again because it takes too much time to do a presentation for just one person. He learned quickly and so he continued. In fact, one night he went to his sister Nadia's, who was recruited on a previous night and did the same presentation for her and her people that I did for him. DUPLICATION!

1:00:47

By the end of 7 days and 7 nights, they had done 20,500 in volume and they were Silver. In fact, he was doing a presentation when I called and it was minutes to go before the end of the night. His best friend was punching in the Internet orders, while he was doing a Wellness Preview. They were punching in orders to get the last of the orders in, because he had forgotten it was midnight. They went Silver in 7 days. Do you think that is impressive? It's not very impressive at all. Who cares about going Silver . . . that's not why we started this. In fact, he never heard me ask him to go Silver once until the morning when I suggested that with 8000 in the kitty, he could reach Silver by the end of the month if he kept this up.

1:01:57

He said, "What's that?" He saw me do the presentation and I talked about Silver but he never saw himself as a Silver. So it never occurred to him that we might actually be going for Silver. **But was it his responsibility to know that?** He is a new distributor. I was just busy trying to get him to learn how to do what he had to do in my absence. Whose responsibility was it to strategize his launch? Mine? His up-line? Technically speaking, I was his up-line Silver, and I was orchestrating his launch. He was just busy doing what he was doing while I shared what he needed to do. He did, and I orchestrated it so that it was done in a certain time frame. The result of which, he was Silver. Do you think he is competent Silver?

1:02:50

No way, but I will tell you one thing. **After 2 nights he was doing the Wellness Preview;** at the very least he was a very competent Senior or above! He was earning his title and when he got to Silver **by the end of that week,** he had done at least five presentations. **He was mastering his skill on a local level** because no longer was he doing it in his home. He was doing it in his sister's home. He drove 3 hours to do presentations in his sister-in-law's home. **He was already going regional.** Even though his rank was Silver, he was already starting to build his competence as a leader.

1:03:41

I had to go to Australia and so now there's this huge gap of time between my first arrival in Milan and me getting back to Milan to pick up from where we left off. There is always a tendency for momentum to be lost, **so I had to figure out what to do to keep that plane in the air while I was busy doing what I had to do.** I just set little goals—little goals to keep them moving. I told him that the next goal was Silver training. I found out there was a Silver training in Italy so I told him I wanted 20 people at Silver training, so **he took that upon himself as a goal.**

1:04:18

He kept doing presentations in homes and started getting many "B's" and "C's." What do we call that? **A Wellness Preview** . . . only it was in somebody's home. **He started doing Wellness Previews, the equivalent of a public event—building his competence**, really starting to be a Silver, defined by a true Silver, all the while directing people to Silver training. **He had 19 people including himself at Silver training.** Now, what happens **at an event like Silver training?**

1:05:09

People make decisions *about what they want to do with the rest of their life and* how Nikken may fit into that picture. They start evaluating those big issues and **they start asking themselves** if what I am doing is going to get me where I want to go or do I need to re-think **what it is I am doing?** Maybe Nikken is the means by which I can get to where I really want to be. Silver training is an excellent catalyst, so I bought the time necessary to get him to keep on going and his volume never dropped below 18,000 in those 3 months.

1:05:54

I kept him going with a goal and mini-goals. I needed to buy time between my first trip and when I could fly back which was 3 weeks. The next big event was the equivalent of Team Diamond, Team Europa in Germany. So I told him that **now is when we are going to find out who is really on the team**. I told him to tell everybody who had come through the turnstiles, since the day we started, to come to Germany. Now I knew what was going to happen—the **process of elimination.** Those people who can't see themselves as big players will eliminate themselves from the equation. "You mean I have to go to Germany, that's a 4 hour drive!" Seriously, and *some people thought, "I'm not going to drive for 4 hours."* **What did you say you want to be?**

1:07:02

How does a person act? **According to their vision, according to their beliefs.** If their vision isn't a big vision, they are being led by their beliefs, not by their vision. So *their belief is that 4 hours is a long way to drive*, but it is not a long drive, not for someone who's going to change the world, or at least the state of health in Milan or the state of health in Italy. They are driven by their beliefs, not by their vision. But I knew that the leaders, who are the visionaries, would quickly emerge when we put this carrot in front of them—asking who is coming with us to Germany. I set a goal for 15, and we had 14. We always seem to miss it by one, but that's still good enough. We had 14 people and that was the beginning of a team. **While I was there, I taught that group of people what they needed to** do if they wanted to be considered competent players.

1:07:59

By the time I was finished with them, Distributors who had not yet capitalized understood that you are either on this page or you are not on this page, there is nothing in between here. To the people who were Seniors I said: "If you are going to waste our time not moving forward, what did you get involved for?" I was the person who came in and took stock of the situation and presented the facts and presented the training. We did this one night with 30-40 people in the room, and then I knew that this group was going. He is shooting for Gold this month. His target is Diamond for June. But, then again, I would not be impressed. **I expected that to happen.** If it happens, I expect it to happen. I will congratulate them, because they did what they were supposed to do. If they don't get it done, I will try to figure out what went wrong, what has to be modified. How can I say that with such confidence? Because I built the plan and if they follow the plan, that is what should happen.

1:09:10

So what is this plan? Let's quickly take stock of what I just talked about! I'm going to show you this in terms of a picture!

There is an airplane on the runway. There is another airplane over here and it's taxiing. There's another plane over here and it's parked at the gate. Three airplanes (refer to diagram, Page94), one that's parked at the gate, one that's taxiing and one that's ready to go.

1:10:03

Let's talk about the plane that's parked at the gate. Let's give these people a name by the way. This is the potential "A," this is the "B" category and this is the "C" category. Whenever you present this opportunity, and you present it with the vision in mind . . . the big picture, here is what you will attract: leaders, business builders, distributors, retail customers and simply "No's" . . . which means not now. By now you should realize that you will get all of those people, you will get them all. I even get them all. I expect someone is a leader but they don't always prove themselves to be a leader. But every time you present the vision of Nikken, you will attract people and then the people self qualify; they sort themselves out.

1:11:17

When you recruit a distributor, what do you think that distributor is going to become, honestly? Every time, what do you think you've got? Oh this one is going to be a Diamond. Right? What are you thinking? I don't get excited. I never get excited when I hear somebody signed somebody up, because that does not mean anything to me, it just means they put their name on a piece of paper. Congratulations, they have proven that they can write. It does not mean anything yet, but what we now need to know is who they see themselves as being. We have to expose them to a little bit more of Nikken so they can start to size up Nikken and their role. We have to have some discussion and dialogue to determine what they want to do with this thing. If you get a "No" right now, that means follow up. We are going to follow up with that person because you never know when they are going to be ready. How many of you said no to network marketing once before? No, never means no!

1:12:18

Retail customers—what will we want to do with these people? We want to teach these people how to order direct, because you never know when they are going to order product. Get them on your website, get them on the C.A.P. program. Get them to stay plugged into Nikken because you just don't know when they might buy something again, and it will be a nice little surprise in your pay check. Teach them how to order for themselves because if they can't get a hold of you, they know how to order direct from Nikken. They don't need you, but that's still volume.

1:12:55

Then there's **the distributor.** This is the person who wants to buy wholesale. By the way, you don't have to sign somebody up to sell them wholesale. Did you know that? They can buy directly off of your web site at wholesale. You can go into your web site at e-Nikken, your personal website, in maintenance for customers, and you can punch in codes, one code for 5% discount, one code for 10%, one code for 15%, one code for 20% discount of the mark up price. You can give any one of your customers these codes and you can make the codes time sensitive. You could have a special for the month and tell your customers to go into your website, punch in a code, and receive a 20 % discount. You can create preferred customers. **I would rather you not sign them up as distributors, if all they want to be is a customer.**

1:13:46

Most people don't want to sign, up but they want to be customers. We try to force them to be distributors and then they don't want to be anything anymore. Quickly realize what they are asking you to do, and do it. You never know, they might turn around and become a distributor later, but in the meantime let's not throw these customers out because we think they should be a distributor . . . because we know best.

Listen and they will tell you what they think. A distributor does not necessarily have an agenda, they want to do it their way. I want to try Nikken! I DON'T THINK SO!! Nikken is going to try you and we will see which one survives. But they don't have an agenda, they don't have a particular business plan, so we need to entertain these people. **We entertain these people by creating an environment, an environment to keep these people plugged** in long enough to get them educated and to see something. So that maybe one day they wake up and smell the coffee and say: "OK, there is a business here. What do I do to make it work?" These are what I refer to as the "C's."

1:15:02

Then there is **the business builder.** This is a person who really likes the business idea. They see themselves making a business out of this, a part time income, maybe even a full time income $2000-$3000, $5000, $10,000 a month. These people are business builders. They recruit and they retail, doing both things simultaneously, and they really are the heart and soul of the business. We want to give these people a good start, so we need a launch strategy to start them in the business properly. We teach them what they need to do; they have to pack that snowball like everybody else! And we are going to show them—one step at a time. These are the "B's."

1:15:40

And then there are the "A's." These are the visionaries. These are the people who see Royal Ambassador—there is nothing in between, and so we also need a strong launch plan for them. These people are going to be developing the environment; they are going to be the ones who create the environment. They create the support system that everybody plugs into. The "A's" are always the people who put on the events. The "B's" are those who utilize the events. Keep that in mind. If you want to become an "A" in your own little respective way, locally, municipally regionally, plug into the people who are making things happen and you will become competent.

1:16:37

Take Guido Paniccia for an example. Here is a guy who is a Gold distributor. I think he is one away from Platinum, and he asked me when there was an opening for the team of Gold's and Platinum's—Team Toronto. When they were looking for someone to step into the role as the chairman, he asked me if I thought he should do it. I said absolutely! By accepting the responsibility and becoming the person who puts on the events and takes on a leadership role, leader of leaders so to speak, **what does he get out of it? Competence! Confidence! Credibility!** All of that is going to translate directly into the way he acts, which is going to translate directly into his results in his business. Absolutely! Definitely you want to take on that role. Plug in and get involved, that's what these people do, so we need a launch strategy for these people and here is how it looks.

1:17:28
Launch Strategy

Somebody who becomes a distributor who is really not quite sure about network marketing may not be very confident in talking to people. We need to build their confidence, so we need to build their belief. It's all about building belief in you and in others. Leaders build belief in others, but first they have to believe in themselves. Here is somebody who maybe likes the products or maybe they're not sure. What does an airplane do at the gate before it gets going? It has to fuel. So, when I refer to fueling the engines, I am talking about building belief in the product. The "C" is building belief in the product and we know that because when they believe in the product they start acting like a "B" and they start talking to people about the products.

1:18:24
They start bringing people to Wellness Previews and what ends up happening? The "B" starts building a business; they are starting to taxi. What they are doing right now is building belief in the business and I can facilitate this process. If I know I have a "C" on my hands, I encourage them to buy products. I encourage them to come out to Wellness Previews. I encourage them to use the products to build their belief in the products. I encourage them to listen to tapes about the products and so forth. If I have a "B" in my hands or the "C" is becoming a "B" what do I do?

1:19:05
I want to encourage them in building a business so I want to help them build confidence in the business. The best way to do that is to sponsor somebody. I may take that "B" under my wing for a few days

and we, if I personally sponsored them, will go out together and do some presentations. I am helping that "B" get their confidence, by telling them to listen and learn. We may even sponsor somebody, or get somebody interested and what happens to that person's confidence if they actually sponsor somebody?

1:19:36

Better yet, if they sponsor somebody and that person buys something, according to the ABC, because I suggested they do that, what happens to their confidence in the business? It just revs them right up. That "B" might be transitioning into an "A," so what I need to do is encourage them with an event. Similar to the event I had with my cousin's group (Silver training). Encourage with Silver training or an even bigger event, the Team Diamond event or an Expo. What that event did for me as an "A" was help me move those "B"s into the launch position, to determine who was ready to fire up. Pull all the engines forward because they catch that vision and they are ready to go.

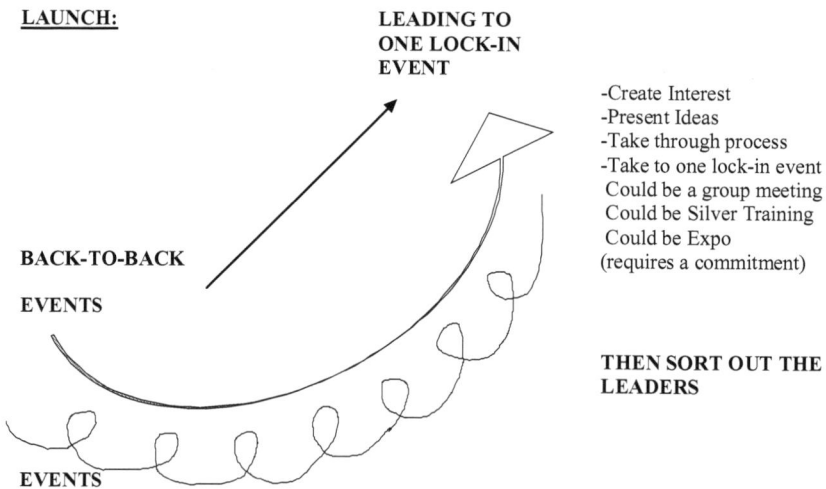

LAUNCH:

LEADING TO
ONE LOCK-IN
EVENT

-Create Interest
-Present Ideas
-Take through process
-Take to one lock-in event
Could be a group meeting
Could be Silver Training
Could be Expo
(requires a commitment)

BACK-TO-BACK

EVENTS

THEN SORT OUT THE
LEADERS

EVENTS

Diagram 7

SELF-QUALIFYING CATEGORIES → ACTION PLAN FOR UPLINE "Program"

SELF-QUALIFYING CATEGORIES		ACTION PLAN FOR UPLINE "Program"
"A" Type LEADER	Recruits Builds InfraStructure/ Support System →	Launch Plan A
"B" Type BUSINESS BUILDER	Retails / Recruits →	Launch Plan B
"C" Type DISTRIBUTOR	Wholesale Buyer / Retails →	Plan C - Plug into Support System
RETAIL CUSTOMER	Purchases / Referrals →	Teach to Self Purchase
"NO" = "NOT NOW!"	Referrals →	Follow Up

ACTION PLANS (PROGRAMS)

LAUNCH PLAN A

List (108+ names / Top 20 Business)
Products (Residual/Business)
90 Day Business Plan (Time)
Next Silver Training

→ 1 on 1's and series of back-to-back In-Homes with recruiting slant. Public W/P **only** as follow-up for **Validation.**

LAUNCH PLAN B

List (108+ names)
Products (Personal/Business)
Business Plan (Time)
Next Silver Training

→ Series of In-Homes with Retail slant, i.e. 21 Club and Public W/P for Business Prospects with 1-on-1 for Follow Up, i.e. Paragon.

Diagram 8

ANALOGY
New Silver's transference of
point of view

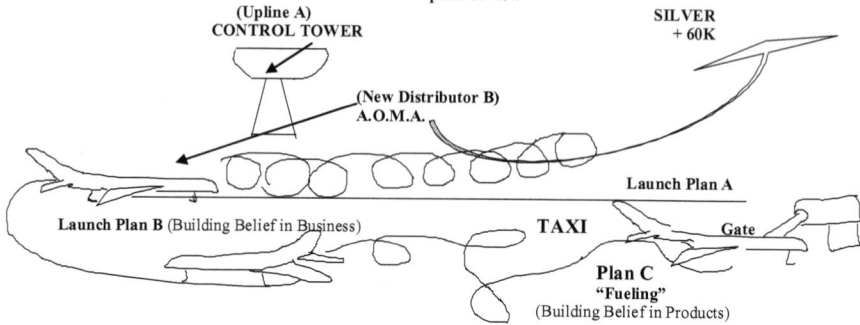

(Upline A)
CONTROL TOWER

SILVER
+ 60K

(New Distributor B)
A.O.M.A.

Launch Plan A

Launch Plan B (Building Belief in Business)

TAXI

Gate

Plan C
"Fueling"
(Building Belief in Products)

MAINTENANCE PROGRAMS (RESIDUAL)

RETAIL DRIVES
(Focus on Volume Boosts and
Customer Accumulation C.A.P.)

⟶

(Product Launches)
In-Home with Retail Slant
To expose retail market to
new technology.

Focus on 1 main technology, i.e
21 Club = Sleep Systems.

Nikken must create these complete with
Tools / promotions to facilitate hosts
(a good example is what
Partylite Candles is doing)

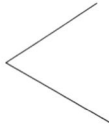

Themes:
"Sleep Clinic"
"Nutrition Clinic"
"Living Water Clinic"
"Makeover Clinic" etc.

RECRUITING DRIVES
(Focus on Growth/Rank
Personal/Group/Organisational)

⟶ Personal: i.e. Paragon

⟶ Downline Group: Launches Of
A and B types

⟶ Rhythm Of The Business

**Events designed to prompt advancement and transference of point of view at all ranks of
organization**

The Science of the Nikken Business

1:20:28

The launch phase is about making sure they **have their list,** making sure they have done their **Silver training** or registered for it, making sure they have a career **pack, a demo pack,** and their personal use products. That they have whatever tools they might need and above **all a business plan that requires their time.** Did it require my cousin's time to do those presentations? Yes, he had to be there! In one way or another he had to invite people so he was involved. His time was involved, even though he is a very busy person. That's time with a business plan, with an agenda, and that is what distinguishes a "B" from an "A."

1:21:25

It was my business plan; I was the one who was running the show. There is still someone else in this picture, the person inside the control tower. The real "A" is the person in the control tower, and the person in the control tower sees all three planes. He calls instructions to all three. Hoping and waiting and working with these people to move to the next level, and the next level, creating situations and environments to encourage that progress. When you know you have somebody ready to go, YOU GO! You launch them and get them in the air, don't worry about the small details, get them in the air. They will figure it out. Get them in the air. Full pedal to the metal, get them in the air.

1:22:28

That's a launch! It consists of a series of presentations, multiple presentations to expose multiple people to a presentation. That presentation is already **defined.** You already **know how you are going to conduct it, who** is coming and what you are going to be saying, with the **expectation to recruit new distributors.** When this thing gets off the ground there are going to be new distributors coming on board. Those distributors will take shape. Just like it was happening at my cousin's in-home presentations, all of a sudden he was having groups of people, distributors coming to the presentation. Somebody was hosting it in their house, so you know they were involved.

1:23:20

Some of them were bringing people and some of them were just coming to the presentation. So, right there within that presentation, there were "A's," "B's," and "C's." I came into the situation, created the situation to quickly help my cousin separate the group.

1:23:48

Why? Because we want **to launch the "A's" appropriately with their own launch strategy,** with their **own business plan,** with their own key prospects and not clutter the audience with people who should not be there. I did not want those "A's" doing in-home presentations cluttering those presentations with people who did not have a specific agenda or a reason to be there. I needed to take the "A's" aside and start a launch campaign here, a launch campaign there. And what do we do to deal with everybody else?

1:24:35

Let's put a calendar together and we will publicly announce when the Wellness Preview or the Business training is. That way, all the other distributors can do their "onezee's" and "twozees" in that public venue. They need each other to create an event, so we use the synergy of the group to create a Wellness Preview. Now what they are conducting is Wellness Previews for people who are the "B's" and "C's" and they are **doing in-homes for the people who are the "A's."** This is really important.

1:25:20

When my cousin finally got that airplane in the air (he is Silver), how do I keep it going? If there is anything that I have identified as the biggest shortfall, it's right here. Most people think that now that you are a Silver, you are OK. What new Silvers really are is incompetent Silvers. Now is when you really have to go in there and help them by taking them out of the driver seat of the plane and putting them into the control tower. You need to help them understand that not everyone in their group is going to be a Diamond, not everyone in their group is acting like somebody who even understands what the heck they are doing.

1:26:28

You need to get them into your head space so they can see that there are some parked at the gate, and here is what you do with them. There are some sitting here in taxi mode, not quite sure, and here is what you do with them. And, there are some that we have got to get behind now before they lose the momentum, before they get tired and blow their energy dealing with people who don't know what they want.

1:26:50

Let's get behind these new Silvers. Let's set a calendar of events together in their home and let's get a public event for these people now that they are an "A." They are looking for the next person to launch, and they are dealing with the group as a whole in a public agenda. That's what my cousin has done. He has just broken his first Silver and is on his way for the next two to break this month.

Tap Rooting
A good Tap Root is 3 levels in a row
First Level Leaders

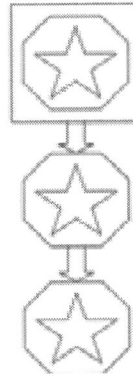

Diagram 8

1:27:22

Who do you work with? You work with who you want to become a Leader. How many of you have heard of **the tap root strategy?** What does that mean? Whichever person you want to become a leader, you want to mentor them through the ranks, whether it's first level or the next leader down . . .

whomever that might be or the next leader down, whomever that might be. I see a good tap root as three leaders in a row beginning with your first level. If it doesn't start with your first level, how are you going to go Platinum and Diamond and Royal Diamond. Nikken's marketing plan is very clear. They say they want you to have first level leaders, we don't care after that, but we do care at the first level. Do you understand that? How do you ensure you have first level leaders? This is the last thing we are going to do and then I am just going to tie everything together with what Nikken has got going as an incentive program.

1:28:40
How do you ensure growth?

How do you ensure the last component—residual? Remember, there are three facets to your business. There is **retail.** How do you ensure that? By you taking an initiative to do things like a **21 Club** or to do in-home presentations about the products, **basically to take this product to the people you know**. Each and every one of us can come up with a list of names of people we know and that we would love to share this product with. If you are embarrassed to share these products with the people you know because you are worried about what they are going to think, what good are you to society?

1:29:29

What good are you to this movement, to this cause, that you have become a part of if you are not willing to share this with anybody and everybody? Really, what good are you? A mouth that is zippered closed and that has a technology and an **exclusive right** is not worth anything and you are going to get exactly what you are worth. You want to be able to be comfortable talking to people about these products. If you don't **know the product well enough, then learn about it. Use it. You are always the first customer** of your business. Always! Nikken expects that. I would expect that!

The Science of the Nikken Business

1:29:55

Get to know the products, Share the products with people who you feel are people you would like to share the products with. **You control your recruiting activities and you can control maintaining your recruiting activities by things like the Paragon.** Paragon is about **adding 2 new (Senior) distributors monthly.** Early in the business you should be doing that. I will tell you what I always did and I always teach and never will stop teaching. **If you want to have residual,** if you are serious about having residual, then you **must find leaders**—you cannot create them. They either want to be or they don't want to be. They either are or they aren't. You cannot do anything other than provide them with an environment that allows them to make those decisions, because if you think you can, you are denying your budding leaders of that very thing we are trying to give them, the authority to choose!

1:31:13

You can only encourage them to choose, you can't make them choose. You can only provide an environment that's conducive for them to take the initiative. What also happens whenever you create a situation where someone can choose, they can also choose NOT to! They can also reinforce their current position, but that's the beautiful thing that God gave us—**FREE WILL**. I am not going to steal that from anybody. If you want to be sure **to have residual** income then you must **develop leaders,** because leaders are people who don't need you, who are glad to be around you and all, but who don't need you.

If you have to develop leaders, what does that word mean? Develop leaders? It gives you the impression that you actually have to fabricate them. Let me share something with you. If you decide you are going to be a Royal Ambassador, then the four Diamond distributors who are going to get you there are already walking this planet. <u>**Your job is to find them**</u>! You will not create them! Who are they? You've got to find them. What does it mean to find them?

1:32:43

It means, **if I do enough recruiting then I am going to get leaders!** If you talk to every Royal Diamond Distributor you will find that each one has at least a certain number of Seniors or above. You will find that they have at least a certain number of Silvers or above. You will find that they have at least a certain number of Platinums or above.

1:33:14

I will give you an example. His name is Wolfgang Sonnenburg who, by the way, loves this so much that if you go to Germany what you will see is this—it's a calendar from Team Europa. They have the events for 2001 and 2002 already set and what they all come down to is just one date. It means that everywhere in Germany and the neighboring countries that have adapted this, they will all conduct an Expo on one date, not whenever they feel like it. **All the local leaders are on the same rhythm.**

1:34:02

He has been able to actually successfully implement it. I was told in December that his organizational volume was 8.3 million dollars and his check in just 3 years of being in Nikken was a little over $200,000 US. He is a Royal Diamond and this year, only his fourth year, he will qualify as a Royal Ambassador—twice as fast as anybody has ever done it. Why? **Because he came to North America, learned how to do this as a business and started a whole group with a structure, that created beliefs, that led to behavior, that is producing results.**

1:34:42

This is the structure (Diagram 1 page 8 and Diagram 3 page59). Wolfgang Sonnenburg has 16 front line Silvers or above. He's got seven who are Platinum or above, of which four are Diamond or above. At this point, how many seniors or above did he sponsor? This number I don't have from Wolfgang, but I could probably figure it out, and I am sure it would be not too far off. In terms of seniors and above I am one of those rare breeds. I came into this business early in the curve when a good business strategy had not yet evolved. So when there is no business strategy what do you do?

1:36:09

You fire enough at the wall and you hope something sticks, and that was my strategy. Fortunately, I fired enough at the wall that enough stuck. But in the nine years I have been in Nikken there were about 70 people I have sponsored, so probably a realistic number is 60 Seniors or above. What do you see there? What is 60 divided by 3? Twenty. What is 20 divided by 3? That is 7. **We refer to it as the rule of thirds.** We see the same things on Wolfgang's numbers—one out of three. The rule of thirds is very real; it means that **you can reasonably expect that one third of the people you sponsor will get to the next level.**

1:37:05

If you want **to have leaders in your down line, you have to have leaders in your frontline.** Let me repeat that. If you want to have leaders in your down line, which is your six percent, your residual income, you have to have leaders in your frontline, which makes you a leader. A leader sets the pace. This business is something you are going to do for however long you want to do it. But, in that time you are doing it, you are always **going to be recruiting.** Always! Even at the Royal Diamond level. If you think that when you get to Royal Diamond you can sit on your high horse and command people, you have lost sight of what we are doing. Remember, **everyone is their own person;** they are not your people.

1:38:09

We (leaders) are not Moses parting the waters. None of you are *my* people. You happen to be in my organization, but none of you are my people. **You all have your own business. You are independent of me,** you are **independent of Nikken** and the best thing I could ever do for you is to remind you every single day that **you are the CEO**

of your own business and it requires your attention. Remember that a strong front line leads to strong leaders and you can expect the rule of thirds to always be the rule of thirds. This is how I look at the rule of thirds.

The Rule of Thirds

The rule of thirds is very real. It means that you can reasonably expect that one third of the people you sponsor will get to the next level.

1:39:00

One third of these people (Seniors) become these people (Silvers). One third of these people (Golds) become these people (Platinums). **That is the rule of thirds**; one third of these people (Diamonds) become Royal Diamonds. Now, it does not mean that they all can't be there. If you said, "Mike, in the next 90 days, if **I put a business plan together of a bunch of activities, events and I sponsored 12 people** at the Senior level or above, in 90 days what could I realistically expect to have happen?" I have state that you have a business event, you have calendar events . . . and for the people you sponsored or presented to . . . you shared with them what you expected them to do and invited them to do it. And you told them, if they decided to do it, this is what they would be involved. So if they made a decision to do it, you didn't have to ask them again because they were already doing it in the first place. You have to **recruit them with a purpose in mind.** I thought that's what business people do when they are recruiting people—they have a purpose in mind for why they are recruiting those people. If you did all of that, **what could you reasonably expect? To be Gold in 90 days;** that is what you reasonably could expect.

HOW TO DESIGN A CALENDAR WITH
A GOAL OF PLATINUM IN THREE MONTHS IN MIND

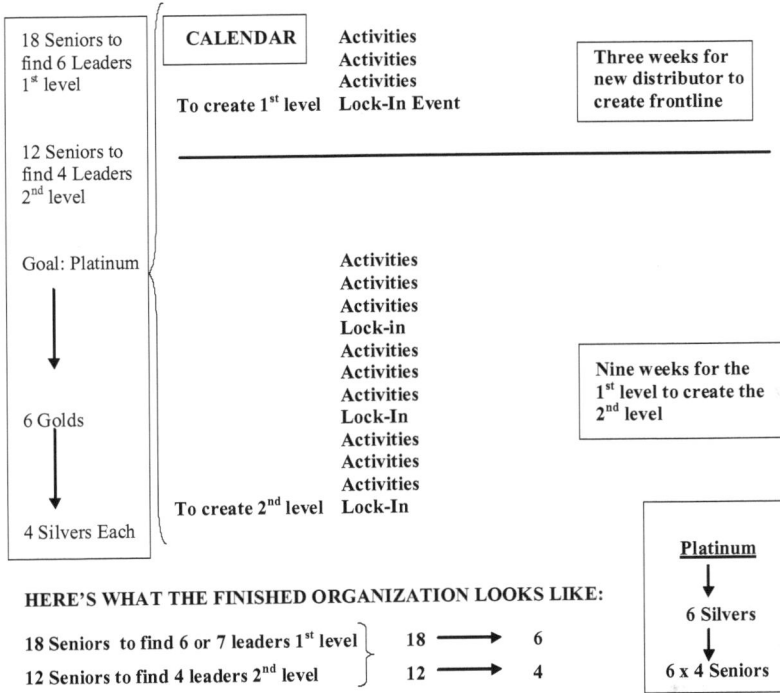

18 Seniors to find 6 Leaders 1st level	**CALENDAR**	Activities Activities Activities	**Three weeks for new distributor to create frontline**
	To create 1st level	Lock-In Event	
12 Seniors to find 4 Leaders 2nd level			
Goal: Platinum		Activities Activities Activities Lock-in Activities Activities Activities Lock-In Activities Activities Activities	**Nine weeks for the 1st level to create the 2nd level**
6 Golds	To create 2nd level	Lock-In	
4 Silvers Each			

HERE'S WHAT THE FINISHED ORGANIZATION LOOKS LIKE:

18 Seniors to find 6 or 7 leaders 1st level   18 → 6

12 Seniors to find 4 leaders 2nd level   12 → 4

<u>Platinum</u>
↓
6 Silvers
↓
6 x 4 Seniors

1:40:29

Why could you expect that? Out of your 12 Seniors, one third are going to go Silver. That gives you a spare. If you did it again, 90 days later, what could you reasonably expect? You do not even have to do that, because you would only have to have six.

1:41:45

So if I were building a business plan to help someone go **Platinum in 90 days,** what would that business plan be? **18 Seniors or above would have to be found in a certain time frame.** Give those 18 people the opportunity to distinguish themselves as to what category they fall in, so that we could identify the six and enough time to get those six rolled off the launch pad.

1:42:27

When the 18 who started are done, we have six who are Silver. If I anticipated them going Silver, then what else should I have been anticipating before I began this agenda? That if each of these people are going to go Silver, each of these six, are going to go Silver, then **what would their business plan be?** It would be 12 seniors or above, if they are going to go Silver. Twelve seniors and above and they are going to go Silver why? Well I thought you said 12 seniors and above is going to get them the Gold, and it is. If **12 Seniors and above** is going to get them to Gold, then 12 Seniors and above is going to get them to Silver. Because you can't get to Gold without getting to Silver this is an absolutely surefire way of guaranteeing that's going to happen, isn't it?

1:43:27

So if you are going to help somebody plan a business launch to go Platinum in 90 days, then what you are actually seeing is **them plan the launch of 6 individuals who each sponsored 12 Seniors and above within a certain timeframe.** They would have to first find these individuals or a bunch of individuals and then present them with a plan and then help them execute that plan to as great a degree as possible, **the result of which would be Platinum in 90 days.** Now, if you didn't plan this, then you are the kind of person who hopes and prays this is going to work for you.

1:44:12

But if you decided to **plan it, thinking with the end in mind,** what could you do? **I have been testing this theory** for I don't know how long and it works, it absolutely works. **The best launch** that has ever happened was 300,000 in volume in the first month. **That person came to this restaurant,** filmed a presentation, sat down for two hours at lunch, took notes, went home and applied it. That's what could happen if you find the right person and you give them the right information.

The Science of the Nikken Business

1:44:47

There are a lot of people with the wrong information and there are a lot of wrong people with no information at all. So **find the right people and give them the right information. The two together are magic.**

Hence the Science of the Nikken Business AMR

I have given you what I believe is the right information and I am demonstrating that. Let me leave you with this one last note that should really help you understand and crystallize this. I have a business plan, an agenda that my cousin is on for going Diamond. He has specific target dates. He must get the 18 and above Senior distributors in position within 90 days, which by the way, his first 90 days proved that you can count on these numbers. After that these numbers change. It is 90 days that is the magic number.

1:45:54

That is why Nikken's plan is every 90 days. It is proof beyond a shadow of a doubt; it is based on the people who were sponsored, one went Silver in those 90 days. When he saw that and I said to him, "Remember when I told you three months ago? Now you see with your own eyes." I was saying remember what I was teaching you; now you can see it with your own eyes. Look at your group, isn't it exactly what I said it would be, and that it would be according to what you did?

1:46:39

The rules are the rules based on what you did. Here is how the rules produce an outcome. He was amazed. Then I said, "Are you going to do what I tell you, the way I want it done?" "Yes," he assures me, "by the end of this month, this is done." I said, "I don't care if you have to stop working with every one of those people, this has to get done or the rest is not going to get done. This must be the first priority." So that is the agenda he is on. Now I know what to do from that point on. I am going to visit at the end of March to shake out the six. We already have one or two more, so we shake out the other three. What we will be doing then is to put a plan for those people to go Gold in 90 days. What does that make him? It makes a Diamond out of him! Here is what you think about, when you think about stuff like this.

1:47:32

Have you ever **broken a board?** Have you seen anyone break a board? What is the first thing they are taught how to do after they are taught how to stand properly? Focus. Focus where? **Focus beyond the board.** In fact if they do not focus beyond the board their hand ends up touching the board and actually stopping! They won't break the board; it is the most amazing thing to see.

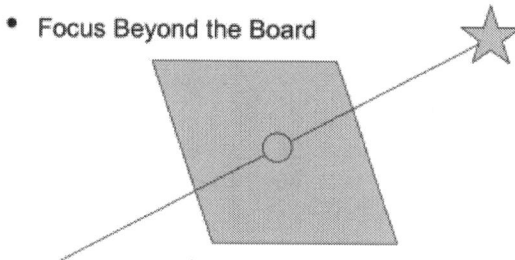

- Focus Beyond the Board

1:48:14

Your hand knows exactly where your eyes go. It is called hand-eye coordination. If you are driving and you look to the side of the road, where does the car go? Automatically your eyes and your body respond. Your vision and your behavior are tied together like a steering wheel. You actually behave according to your vision. If you have no vision how you do behave? According to your structure and the beliefs that structure has taught you! **The vision is what causes the structure to be modified,** because as soon as you see the results are inconsistent with the vision, you go down to the Structure and you change it, if you have been guided by your vision. **If you are not being guided by a vision, you blame the structure.**

1:49:11

Do you see the difference? One is **paralyzed and one is in control.** How do you want to live the rest of your life . . . thinking that you are a victim or thinking that you are a co-creator in the outcome? So now, the vision is beyond the board. Now, if I want someone to **absolutely be a Silver distributor** what must I have them focus on? Gold, absolutely, Gold and above!

1:49:28

So now, let's understand the outcome of that if I am looking to go Silver. If Silver was the target, then what do I need to find to meet the **requirements** of Silver? 20,000 points, which means what? **Anybody with a credit card!** That search would have me looking for volume. That search would put me in front of anybody. I would not be thinking qualified or not qualified, I would just be thinking of selling product and getting people interested in the product.

1:50:23

But, if I was **planning on going Gold and above,** in fact if my big picture was Royal Ambassador, then **what am I thinking?** What does it take to be a Royal Ambassador? 4 Diamonds and above. **It takes leaders! So, the hunt would be a different hunt.** If I was looking for leaders instead of looking for volume, then that's a different hunt. **My behavior, my beliefs** would be very different. **My structure, my presentation, how I would be communicating** would be very different, wouldn't it? **I would get a different outcome based on the way I was acting.** If I was looking for volume I would get one result. **But if I was looking for leaders, I would be acting differently.** Volume—anybody will do, PIN level (which is the goal beyond the board)—not everybody will do. In retail—I can expect a person to make a decision right away—you like the product or you don't like the product.

1:51:12

You need to take them through a process of investigation and therefore they might need time to process information. The difference in the way you act depends on the outcome you want. If this is what I want people to do (find leaders), because ultimately where is that six percent, where does that freedom come from? Leaders. Guess what happens when you look for leaders? What happens is you get everybody!

1:51:43

Which includes volume! But if you are only looking for volume, you will not necessarily find leaders, and so your plane gets off the ground and then goes straight back down. That is why a lot of Silvers fail. They did not have their eyes focused in the right place. It is very important.

If I want someone to go **Platinum, my business plan is** six Golds. Why would I ever recruit somebody and tell them I want you to go Silver?

1:52:29

So if you would anticipate somebody going Platinum, you would never talk to this person about going Silver, because IF you talk to them about going Silver, they may never go Silver. They may hit that board for a few months and then die. You are going to talk to them about going Gold and beyond. You are going to put them on the same regimen and the same program.

1:52:55

What ends up happening is they go Silver anyway as a consequence of what it is that we intend to do. Find the leaders to build the business. Nikken did not bring them into the business for them to go Silver. What purpose does that serve? **I am bringing them into the business to build a business, so that is the vision** . . . going Gold and beyond is the exercise. **Nikken has a quarterly rhythm** and that means that every quarter they are going to announce **through the Neat system, through their newsletter** and so forth, **specific agendas** that are targeted at helping us **facilitate this process of retailing and recruiting.** The **21 Club** for example. Breaking Silvers should not be important to you. **Focusing people on launching their business** to Gold and above is going to cause you to break Silvers.

1:53:48

If you learn anything, what I would like you to learn is Nikken's agenda. Nikken's quarterly programs are designed to facilitate us. **Figure out a way you can incorporate Nikken's incentive program into your launch strategy,** so that when you are presenting the opportunity to these people to get involved with you, not only are you presenting an opportunity to build a business, but they are also getting a huge benefit. Those people who are going Silver and beyond are going to go to the Nikken conventions with you in other countries. How many would you like to take? Forget about going there yourself!

1:54:22

How many are you going to take with you? This is a huge incentive. Go ask people, "Do you want to go to the Convention in Germany for free?" and then explain to them how they are going to get there. There is this thing called Nikken and tell the story.

1:54:53

That is the means; this is the vehicle, the means to the end. The end is what you have to start with. Figure out how you can turn Nikken's program and business plans into your business plans. That will motivate and excite other people. Think of other people; always think of other people ahead of yourself. Think about where you are going and where you are going to help those people go, and you will build a huge business. Get outside of you.

The Missing Link—Part 1

:06

Many of you have seen the first edition of the "What I've Learned" video series which I believe will answer a number of questions that you and I get on a daily basis. **I've made it a rule, if you are a Wellness Consultant in my organization and you haven't watched those video tapes, we have nothing to talk about.** If you want my advice, there is four hours of it. It is the best that I have to offer and this session will add a dimension to that.

Let me explain why we are here.

:36

As you probably know, **I make it a point of studying this business.** I travel here and there. I have businesses at various stages of development, so I am not just a Royal Diamond sitting in an ivory tower. I have businesses at all levels of development . . . Silvers . . . brand new people who aren't Silver yet, Golds, Platinums, Diamonds and soon to be Royal Diamonds. I am involved in building various aspects of this business with the people I work with.

1:04

So, I am very **familiar with the issues** that you are all familiar with, and since we're addressing Silvers and above, you may have already probably hit the wall. You've come to a point in time **where you are trying to figure out some things that just don't seem to be working for you** and you cannot quite understand what's going on with your business. So this is a great opportunity for me to exercise some teaching, because honestly, if you do not have the question, giving you an answer is pointless. There are a lot of people thinking they need more information than what they really need in order to build this business.

1:46
A Rule of Thumb

Let me start with a basic rule of thumb. **If you are a Silver Distributor or above, it is your responsibility . . . not your brand new distributor's responsibility . . . to put a plan together for them to go Silver and beyond.** It's not their responsibility.

2:10
YOU 3

One of the biggest mistakes I think I made in the early days with Marty Jeffery when we created the YOU³ system was releasing it to the general public. **It was actually a system that was designed to be the "teacher's notes."** The teacher being someone who had already succeeded at executing that plan and subsequently had documentation as to what they did, so that they could impart that information, one piece at a time, to someone new they were working with. Instead, we handed it over; it was your business in a box expecting the "**B**" to be the "**A**."

2:42

You cannot be an "A" if you have not been a "B." If you have not yet been a "B," if you have not been launched, if you have not gone through that experience and understood those dynamics, it would be ridiculous to even expect you to be an "**A**." You cannot launch yourself! And, a lot of you have down-lines that you are expecting to launch themselves. You are not taking charge of that responsibility; you are not initiating the launch of their business. That has never happened with me; I've never done that. When I sponsor somebody who I'm interested in helping, I am right in there calling the shots.

3:26

I don't expect them to tell me what to do. I expect them to ask me what should be done and how that is one of the things that I think is fundamentally different in how I do business and a lot of people do business. **I don't wait for people to make decisions; I make**

decisions for them that are in their best interest, because I know what I am talking about.

3:45

I have done it before. I've done it a number of times and so will you when you **become consciously competent** at launching a new distributor . . . you will realize it is your responsibility, not theirs. How can they possibly know what to do? They're not able to promote themselves. They need you to promote them and they will promote you. **That ABC concept is what causes the business to explode quickly,** so I just want to add that, as a footnote, before we really get to the main thrust of what we are going to get into. I see it time and time again and it's got to stop. You cannot launch yourself . . . therefore, it would stand that nobody in your organization can launch themselves.

4:25

They can start . . . they can buy products . . . they can sign up . . . but don't expect anything and don't you expect the business to erupt from nothing. These people may be savvy business people but I tell you that even the smartest business person I sponsored came to me and asked me what they should do. Even though they were making three times more money than I was making at that time and were operating seven businesses, very successful businesses . . . this savvy business person was savvy enough to realize that what they needed was help. This is going to be a **fundamental theme** to our program.

5:00

How do you really attract people who will skyrocket your business? Remember, you cannot promote yourself, you cannot be an "A" until you have been a "B," so don't expect anybody in your down-line to be an "A" before they have had an opportunity to be a "B." You must be the "A."

5:28

The person who needs to understand how to create that strategy for launching your new recruits is you! It needs to be you

---

The Science of the Nikken Business   113

and if you don't have that, if you are not competent or confident that you are competent, then you can acquire that knowledge. From where?

Up-line . . . <u>somewhere in your up-line there is competence that you need to resource.</u> In other words, you need to get into the habit of being a "B."

5:53

You need to get into the habit of being a "B" because you will always be a "B" and you will always be an "A" once you have launched into this business. You will be an "A" to the people you have, you will be a "B" with the people you are working with . . . forever more, regardless of your rank. If you are not a "B" and not in the habit of asking for help, you must learn to ask for help. I believe this is our fault, in part. Perhaps in the beginning we said: "If it is to be, it is up to me!" Do you remember that expression? Only a person who does not understand this business would say such a thing, because this is not the case.

6:36

Nobody has ever reached the top of any organization or business of any monumental success alone. Ever! And, since you need to be a "B" before you can be an "A," it means that you need to resource help when you need it. You need to ask for help when you need it. When you are working for somebody new and you don't think you know what you are doing, that's when you really need to ask for help and you will get it.

7:05

Don't expect someone to launch themselves! I really want to make that point because we have a videotape that is going across the world of Nikken. Let's create the mindset here and now . . . that you cannot be an "A" until you have been a "B" and you have to be a "B" forevermore.

7:28
Attract Anybody You Want in this Business

The reason we are doing this program is that it has become apparent to me that there was a missing link. As much as I was doing, something was not clicking, something was not connecting. I believe the information in the "What I Have Learned" tape series was as good as it was going to get, but there seemed to be a missing link.

I got a call from two Gold Distributors who wanted to visit me. They wanted to do a bit of strategizing, pick my brain, so to speak. In the first few minutes of that conversation, what became very apparent to me was that they had no perspective of what it was that they were doing and all of their questions they asked did not have a context. This will be clearer to you as we go along.

8:22

I was in a training in Cincinnati after the Team Diamond Event and we spent almost two hours trying to define what it was that we were about to create. We were very excited about the business opportunity, we saw great speakers, we got a lot of information . . . but how does a person put this information to use? If it is just information, what is the context of that information, because if you don't know the context of the information, you wouldn't know how to apply it?

9:02

What is becoming obvious to me is **that this is the missing link;** people do not yet fully understand the context because we are in a new paradigm. You walk into this business and there is a lot about this business you do not understand. And, to make matters worse, we, as experienced networkers, do very little to understand. We continue to propagate the paradigm of network marketing.

9:34

We continue to talk the "network marketing language," which is a foreign language to most people. So, half the time we end up trying to get people to understand things in a language they are totally unfamiliar with. You almost need a network marketing school to learn the language of network marketing, just as there is "computer lingo" when someone is starting to learning about computers. The first thing you have to learn is the language of computers before you learn how to operate the computers! Yet, we have not considered that in our business.

10:06

I know there is a lot of information being circulated, but it is not being understood and it is not getting applied because there is a filter; there is a lack of interpretation.

We are going to start with a book that I recently read, that I am going to suggest, on video, on record that it be an absolute "mandatory read," as the first read in anybody's life in networking marketing.

10:37

Robert Kiyosaki does not know that I am saying this, so I should expect a call sometime in the future! Here is a guy who is saying what I have been saying for so long, only from the point of view from somebody who is not in the network marketing business. And, because of this, he is able to use plain old English. I had to unlearn my network marketing language.

I have been studying business in general to learn how to communicate to business people. Would you like to know that? Would you like to have the keys to be able to attract anybody you want into this business, regardless of how high they are on the totem pole of success?

11:16

Would you like to be able to go out and be able to put it into words and present it in a way that you could literally attract and have the confidence to go and ask just about anybody to be on your team? I'm sure you would!

11:39
The Context of Networking Marketing—The Business of Network Marketing

That's what you are going to get. In a haphazard way, we are going to get at those things, but again, you will not appreciate the words until you understand the context, so let's start by understanding the context of networking marketing, the business of network marketing. This book is called "The Business School for People who Like Helping People," subtitled "The Eight Hidden Values of a Network Business Other Than Making Money."

12:05

It's very interesting, very powerful! Business people like making money but they don't build businesses for the sake of making money—there is more to it than that. The title again is: "The Business School for People who Like Helping People," subtitled "The Eight Hidden Values of a Network Business Other Than Making Money" by Robert T. Kiyosaki, author of *Rich Dad, Poor Dad*. Here is a guy who is raised by two parents through marriage (both fathers), one wealthy and one poor. The father in Hawaii, I believe, was the wealthiest man in the state of Hawaii.

12:40

The story goes . . . here's a young man growing up. On one hand he had a rich dad who definitely took an interest in his son. He would make comments and make suggestions to give that son the values that he believed in, as it related to money and business and so forth. On the other hand, he had the poor dad who was not exactly poor, but struggled to make a living, which is what most people do in life. He, of course, was interested in the son's success and offered suggestions to instill his values and advice in terms of money issues.

13:12

So, you have a young man, a son, who is hearing two opinions about the same subject, both opinions being valid, because every opinion is valid. Valid to what context is another issue. If this young man decided he liked to live like his 'poor dad,' then he takes the advice of poor dad, but if he wanted to live like his 'rich dad,' he would have to take the advice of 'rich dad,' which he subsequently did.

13:37

To give you a simple example, this fellow made and lost two fortunes on his way to his third fortune. Each time he went bankrupt after losing millions.

Rich Dad would say: **"Keep going, you will get there eventually. You are learning."**		Poor Dad would say: **"Haven't you learned yet?"**

Same scenario with two very different opinions!

The 'poor dad' would be much more conservative, and say: "Haven't you learned your lesson yet young man. Why are you doing this to yourself and your family again?" However, 'rich dad' would say: "You are well on your way. You've made two mistakes and you are probably going to make a few more. You are going to get there. Keep on going, mistakes are how we learn."

14:22

We were designed to make mistakes; that is how we learn. The more you make, the smarter you will get. It would be a sin not to learn from your mistakes. 'Poor dad' would say: "Avoid making mistakes."

In the educational system, of which all of us have been a part, what happened when you made a mistake? How did you feel? How were you made to feel? You and I have been born and raised in a structure.

14:46

This structure inevitably led to generating beliefs. And, those beliefs became the operating system, the software with which we operate and so we make decisions based on that software. You wonder why people struggle when they get into a business themselves, let alone this business. We are operating from old software and we are operating from software that does not apply in this business. It is like buying an advanced computer and trying to plug in software that does not work any more.

15:19

That's what 95% of the Nikken and networking organizations in the world are doing right now. They are trying to build network businesses without realizing that the software for the people coming into the business is malfunctioning, and there are two different operating systems.

One of the first things that I think needs to happen is each person should receive a lesson in the business we are in.

E B

S I

15:45

And that's what this book will do. It will give you a true understanding of the difference between this as a business and just about anything else you are doing, whether you are a business owner, a professional or an employee.

16:05

Robert Kiyosaki's 4 Cash Flow Quadrants

Let me start by defining what this is called.

16:41

He talks about four cash flow quadrants, "E," "S," "B," and "I." The "E" quadrant represents the employee quadrant. This is somebody who is an employee, someone who punches the clock and trades time for money. We all understand the mentality of an employee. In fact, it is a mentality because for someone to be and remain an employee, they have a mentality and they are driven by certain hidden values, certain core values that were part of their beliefs system during their upbringing.

17:14

The "S" quadrant is the self employed quadrant, a small business owner, even a professional who works for themselves could be considered to be in the "S" quadrant. This is someone who has created their own job.

17:35

The "S" quadrant mentality is slightly different. This is somebody who wants to be their own boss, but they only know a certain thing. They are often are so involved in that belief system that they will perpetuate that believe by hiring people who are less competent than them . . . to prove to themselves that they are the only one who can do it. This is the person who creates the expression "if it is to be, it is up to me."

18:01

It is an absolute fact that this is a person who is often the smartest person at the place they are at, but they can't entrust anyone else to do anything. This is proven through the people they hire. What they have on their radar screen is their belief system, so they will attract according to their belief system. If their belief system is, "if it is to be, it is up to me," then their software program will make sure whomever they are hiring is somebody who is incompetent and incapable of doing the job they are capable of doing.

18:41

They create a dependent for themselves and by virtue of having a dependent, it makes them feel like they are worth something. In fact in these two categories ("E" and "S"), these two people identify who they are as a person by what they do. I am a doctor. I am an engineer. I am, and so, by what I do, I define who I am. Isn't that an interesting fact! What drives these people to either work for somebody else or to hire people less competent than them, so they can have this little dictatorship?

The Science of the Nikken Business

19:32

There are some hidden values that drive them and what they are looking for here is the need to be important, the need to feel important, the need to feel recognized. "E" and "S" quadrant people are security based. Security is their underlying value. **Their core value is security**, and so to have a sense of security they need someone paying them. If I do this and if I know I did what I had to do, then I have that guarantee of the money being there.

20:16

They create a sense of security in themselves, that if I am familiar with what I have to do and I do it, then there should be a pay check at the end of the day. In the case of "S," they are also security driven because they have a sense of security if they stay in control. These people have to stay in control of the situation to feel secure; they can't delegate, they can't give it up.

20:40

These people never take a vacation because it costs them too much. Can you relate to what I am saying? So, what kind of a business would these people get involved in? Furthermore, if they were to get involved in a huge opportunity . . . a business that had unlimited potential . . . but their hidden value is security, how would they perceive that business? They would not see the sense of security; in fact what drives this group is fear. Fear is the underlying emotion that would cause somebody to feel a need for security—it is a sense of fear.

21:26

That's the vibration that "E" and "S" quadrant people were exposed to and the structures that they were a part of supported that—fear driven. How many of you need to be saved? I love what Bob Proctor says, "There is only thing we need to be saved from and that is ignorance." Fear is merely lack of understanding and when there is a sense of insecurity, there is a need for security and hence they find themselves immersed in these structures. A lot of people who start as an "E" manage to get themselves to move into the "S" quadrant and so a lot of you joined this business thinking—I need to be my own boss. So, you joined the networking business because it was a cheap way to be your own boss. Guess what? You are that person I was talking about who needs to be in control, therefore you've never been a "B" because you always thought you had to be an "A" from day one and that is what you have been. How well is it working for you by the way?

22:31
A Small Business Mentality
Obviously, "E" and "S" quadrants are of a small business mentality and you can't develop a big business with that kind of mentality, security based and fear based. You don't build this business to get out of doing something, or to replace your sense of security in your job. That is not why you build this business and that is not what's going to attract people to this business . . . not the kind of people who you are looking to attract, the individuals who make it go quickly and painlessly.

23:06
Let's move on to another quadrant—the "B" quadrant. There's a very different mentality moving from "E" and "S" to "B" and "I." The "B" quadrant is the big business builder, the big business owner. What you will find in the "B" quadrant is that the people who are in this quadrant, generally speaking, are not the smartest. That may surprise you because all of these people have an education. The university system, the educational system teaches you how to be a good employee or a professional, which is a self employed person in these two quadrants. That's all it teaches. I don't believe anyone has gone to an educational institution of any sort and got an education in this quadrant.

23:53
In fact, ironically, if you avoided school, you had a better chance of being successful in life than someone who went through the entire educational system. The more you get educated, the more you think you are educated, and remember what I said . . . you associate who

you are, with what degree or label you put on yourself . . . which means you can't move out of that.

24:18

Imagine how a doctor would feel if he or she decided not to be a doctor anymore? It's hard for them to break away. The more educated you have been, the deeper the hole you dug for yourself. That's the irony of the whole thing, but we've all been brought up in the same place, the same system.

Quadrant "I"—this quadrant represents people who recognize that they can't do it alone. As I mentioned earlier in quadrant "S," these people trade time for money. They can't take time off because their time is in direct portion to money, in fact this person can't take time off because they have people around them who would drain them of everything they had if they took the time off, so they are trading time for money at a different level.

25:06

The "I" group of people doesn't work for money but they make lots of money. In fact, they make money so that they can invest money. This is the investment quadrant, the "I" quadrant. This is the income you earn from investments—it's the income you earn from business. So, what happens when you put money into an investment? You create cash flow and that cash gives you more money to invest in another business or to expand the one you have. The "rich get richer is the expression," while the poor have their sense of security which is an absolutely false sense of security.

25:50

Who is more secure? A person who can make more money or a person who has their hand out hoping and praying that the economy does not have a bump in the grind? "I" quadrant people make money no matter what the economy does. "B" and "I" people are independent. However "S" quadrant people do what they do for a sense of security. "B" quadrant individuals are those who are secure. In fact, the motive they operate with is liberty, freedom . . . they do what they do for freedom.

26:10

Looking to Recruit a Superstar: What to Ask!

If I was looking to recruit a superstar in this business, one question I might ask is: **"What is your core value? What is the most important thing to you, freedom or security?" That is the only question I ever ask to determine if I want to sponsor somebody.**

26:39

Isn't that interesting. Why? What is this "B" quadrant person about? Creating. This person is about creation. They need to be involved in some type of creative activity. They need to be building a business, acting out on their desires and their inspiration and so forth. They are not necessarily the smartest one and they know they are not the smartest one. Generally speaking, they are a little bit more humble about themselves, and a lot more humble than "S" quadrant, because they know they need help.

27:12

Quadrant "I" know they can't do it alone; they know they need expertise and they position themselves and create for themselves an opportunity or presentation to attract that expertise. I'll give you a simple scenario. Bill Gates was not the smartest guy in his organization. He still is not the smartest guy in his organization but he gets all the credit, why?

Let's take Dave Johnson. I can say with confidence that Dave Johnson probably doesn't have the highest IQ in his organization, but he certainly gets a lot of credit. So what is the key? He got help. He attracted the necessary help to make what was possible, to make the vision a reality. That makes Dave a very smart person!

27:58

They were working toward a vision. They are working toward this thing out there that is driving them forward. "S" and "E" people are just

The Science of the Nikken Business

looking. You know—what do I have to do now. Whereas "S" and "E" people are more concerned with what I am going to do, to make what I make. "I" and "B" people are more interested in what I am going to build and if I build it I don't have to worry about making, because what they are going to build has some sense of value and worth.

28:19
The Business Builder Mentality

"S" and "E" quadrant people are just looking to see what they have to do. So when you hear people down-line asking "what do I have to do" instead of "what do I have to build," realize that's an employee mentality talking as opposed to a business builder mentality. Now, how is somebody going to build this business with an employee mentality? Let me give you an example.
28:52

MONEY/TIME CHART

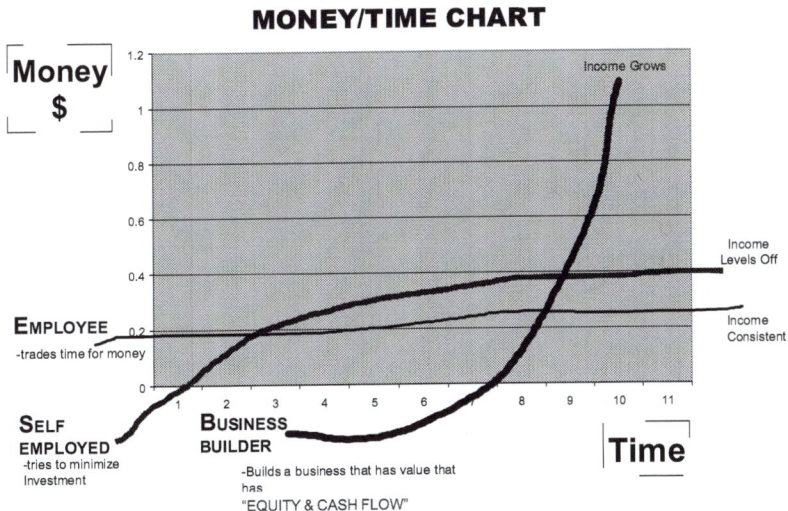

Let's refer to the chart on the previous page and say this represents money or success (which is the measuring stick) and this is time. If you are an employee, right now you earn your money in proportion to your time. You know if you put in "X" number of hours you make "X" many dollars and once in a while, you get a little bit of a raise. It usually goes like this. There's the employee, now they *know* based on the presentations we have given them because we build our presentations based on our mentality.

29:42

Many of us who build presentations have still not created the ideal presentation and that is what we are working on. You are going to read about parts of it in this program.

So, a person who is self employed, what do they expect? The "S" understands that they have to invest. So, if this is positive and this is negative, then this is zero . . . and they will never have enough money to get the business off the ground. What does an employee mentality think . . . minimize the investment? Why do I have to buy a demo pack and a career pack, why not just start with magsteps? You can now see what's directing their language. Are you going to encourage them to stay in their quadrant?

30:31

Are you going to say, "Oh sure, you can start anywhere you like." Is that the person you want to invest your time, energy and resources in? Or do you want to help that person shift out of the mentality of "E" quadrant over to "B" quadrant where everybody needs to be?

30:48

How are you going to shift that mentality? By denying them? By sending them home and telling them, "When you are ready to build a business give me a call?" That's exactly what I told Sylvain Simard, who became one of the first leaders in Quebec. You have to have the guts to stick to the plan and to your vision. You don't need these people. What you need to be is specific, what you settle for is atrocious. **You settle for people not doing what they *should* do, just so that they *might* do something.**

31:24

Personally, I don't. I never will and I never have. That is the difference between the people who make it quickly in this business and the people who struggle and bump along. You have a sense of responsibility for everybody you sponsor. I know that, because you probably come from the "E" or "S" quadrant, so you feel responsible for their success. And now, because of that, it's a little string that's attached to you and you can't go forward without feeling that string tugging at you. And, all of a sudden what you are carrying around with you is this mighty load of dependent people who aren't willing to break out of the quadrant they are in, because becoming wealthy is not doing the right things, it's changing your mind.

32:12

You will attract the right people when you change your mind about what you are doing and what this business is for. Let's look at the "S" quadrant. This is the self employed mentality. They think it's going to cost some money, but that they will make it back really quick. And usually, because of their self employed mentality, they are limited by their time because they don't involve themselves with people who can take the idea beyond themselves . . . so, they flat line . . . they hit a maximum income.

Sometimes it goes up a little bit more, but it is still there, still a flat line. This might be three to five years, but eventually the self employed person hits a maximum where they cannot earn more than what they are earning, without having to put more money in, or whatever. Usually they do not trust anybody with their money, that's if they have it, so that's the self employed "S" quadrant.

33:11

What is the mentality of the "B" quadrant? The "B" quadrant does not care how much money it is going cost to get started, because they do not care about the cost. What they care about is the result. If they build what they have in mind to build, then where they are going will far exceed the cost and so they do not barter with the price of success?

33:36

"B" quadrant people will start the business and will pay whatever it costs. They understand where they are going and they know there is a period of time that is involved in getting to their goal (i.e. Royal Ambassador) and they are willing to do it. They are willing to pay the price; they are not working for money. They are not saying, "I put in "X" number of hours. Where is my pay check?" The typical person who starts out in Nikken is of the employee mentality. They start out wherever they start and they haven't broken even yet. They're saying things like, "Well, I put my hours in! I might as well keep doing what I am doing. At least I know how much I am going to make if I put in ten hours." So they are competing with this equation (being on a fixed income), meanwhile they are in this business (of unlimited income).

34:22

How can you compare these two businesses (self employed vs. business builder)? One is a job, one is a business. With one, if you stop working, it stops—period. The "I" and "B" quadrant's business is such, once it is built . . . will continue to operate without your involvement. You can even sell it to someone else for a big chunk of money. A business builder is not looking to trade time for money. They are looking to build a business that has worth and value and in the end, equity. They are looking for **equity . . .** and **cash flow**. Those are the **buzz words** to the business builder.

35:07

If we are looking to attract some of these business builders into our business, people like Bruce Black and Marty Jeffery, how do we attract these people into our business when we come from an "E" or "S" quadrant mentality? We would probably use words that turn them off . . . our phrasing would be all off. We don't know we are doing it. They have no interest in this little thing. They are not interested in helping you be somebody. You see, "E" and "S" people—they want to be somebody and "I" and "B" people—they want to build something. I ask you, who would you be attracted

The Science of the Nikken Business

to? . . . somebody who wants to be somebody, or someone who wants to build something?

36:10

So, what does this have to do with network marketing? Well, if you want to be a Royal Diamond . . . you just proved my point. That was not a trick question. In fact, I was sitting at a boardroom meeting at Nikken's Head Office with Nikken's President, Kendall Cho and Larry Profit. I relayed to them that I thought Nikken had **an identity crisis**. Larry thought that was interesting. What I was referring to is the fact that **we have people who are *trying* to be a Royal Diamond, instead of building a Royal Diamond distributorship.** We have people waiting for Nikken to make decisions for them, rather than making decisions for themselves.

37:06

We had an interesting conversation amongst the Royal Diamonds that went on for about an hour and a half. And Larry simply kept pushing it back to us, until I realized what he was doing. In essence, he was saying, "You are the president and CEO . . . you decide. What do you want from us?" That's when it occurred to me, it's our problem . . . we have an identity crisis. In fact, we are all responsible for having created it and so has Nikken. I explained the fact that I'm called a Royal Diamond. But I am not a Royal Diamond. In fact, nowhere on paper, does the word Mike DiMuccio, Royal Diamond exist. I am not legally a Royal Diamond. I asked why do they keep referring to me as a Royal Diamond?

37:56

I further explained how I am the CEO of Good Vibration International Incorporated. *It* is an independent Wellness Consultant that has created a "Royal Diamondship," a Royal Diamond organization. It is a specific thing. Even Nikken's compensation plan tells you exactly how specific it is, what must happen. But everybody refers to me as a Royal Diamond. So now everyone wants to be one. In fact, if I asked you to close your eyes for one second and imagine Royal Diamond. What do you see? What images come to mind? What images? Thousands of people? Mike DiMuccio? Did you see a lifestyle—fancy cars, beach, and stuff like that? You can build it. If I asked you to close your eyes and imagine a dog house, how many people do you think would want to build one? Interesting difference!

39:10
Royal Diamond as a Structure?
Because Royal Diamond is a concrete structure and you can see an end in mind, you can assemble the things necessary to make that structure a possibility. But when you think Royal Diamond, what do you think? You don't think in terms of structure. You think in terms of what you want to be. That's "S" and "E quadrant mentality, trying to be somebody. Out the door you go with your hot prospect list . . . who can I invite to help me be somebody? And the words you use, "If you join this business you can be somebody too." Some people really come across that way!

39:50
A prospect, if he or she is thinking, should respond, "Wait a second. If I join this business so I can be somebody that means that you need me to join this business so that you can be somebody. Aren't you somebody yet?"

People make the mistake of saying, "If you join this business you can make a lot of money" Naturally, they're met with, "How much money are you making?" Now you understand why that question comes up. If you get that question, who's does the selling? Ever wonder why you get that question? Is it possible that maybe that's the question we create because we do not explain our business in a way that's comprehensive.

40:40
I'm referring to a complete shift in how we think about what we are doing . . . a total shift in what is it that we are trying to do. Are we trying to be somebody? Is that what this is all about? Because if this

exercise is all about you, I take full responsibility because I have been a coconspirator in this process? From day one, we have all been brought up and born in this organization from the structures we've come from and we continue to perpetuate this language barrier and these concepts in the way we dialogue. Let's stop that. Let's change it. It is high time. That's what this program is all about. I'm fine tuning what I am doing. What you are doing?

41:27
Putting a New Face on Network Marketing

It's about putting a new face to network marketing. What is network marketing if it isn't just a word? It means nothing; it is a business. It is one of many types of businesses. Recommend Kiyosaki's book to your prospects. And, by the way, it is a fabulous prospecting tool . . . and comes with an audio cassette. You can order it from Team Tools, 1-800-667-0198.

42:00
Let's take a look at this. Think! The "E" quadrant person is trying to be somebody versus trying to build something. When they come into this business, they have their hand out, they are waiting. If they don't make money right away for the little time and effort they put in, you start hearing them whine. They are starting to compare their effort and their results compared to their effort because they are doing it for money!!

42:40
These people are doing what they are doing for money. I put "X" amount of time in, I expect "X" amount of dollars out. It cost me two or three thousand dollars to be in my own business so I could put "X" number of hours in. What is their fantasy? Being a Royal Diamond is a complete abstract thought that means absolutely nothing and has no basis for reality for these people. Their expectation is "the moon" and it's a false expectation, because their belief system does not support it. They go about doing their business and try to compare their current

activities with results, saying "I make more money being in real estate. Why would I keep on doing this?"

43:28

They have not been sold the truth and what is the truth? It is bigger and better than what we have been sold. That is truth. We just never sold it properly; no one has ever explained it to us in a context outside of the network marketing context. We are all out there trying to sell a business, for the sake of selling a business. We hear things like, "Get into this thing so that you can be somebody too, so you can make me somebody." We are trying to sell what we want, which is like Bill Gates going out and saying "Hey, if you come and help me build Microsoft, I will be the richest man in the world and have the biggest company in the world. Wouldn't you like that?"

44:12

I don't think Bill Gates would have done very well if that's how he went out and presented his vision . . . his vision was who he could be and what he could become.

"Guess what? If you join me, you could become a Royal Diamond too?" And, then they bring this person to a Wellness Preview and see all kinds of "wanna be's" from every walk of life. And somebody who already is somebody, walks in and says, "You want me to join this group? They don't know if they're coming or going? And you think this is where I am going to find my place?"

44:53

Think about it. Think about what we are doing and the impression we must be giving, hence the reputation we have earned as an industry. I think we are so much better than that and we could do so much better and I think all it takes is a fundamental shift in how we perceive ourselves and what we are doing. When we figure out what this business could really be for us, it is going back to the idea of what the "B" quadrant is in business.

The Science of the Nikken Business

45:26

A "B" quadrant business is a business that will create cash flow for certain. Why? Because it is a business that has something to offer the world . . . value. And what you want to offer the world that is considered valuable is a vision. That is what a business vision is. You have something in mind that has never been done before, something in mind that is powerful and can make a difference. That is what a vision is. And the first person to acknowledge that you have something powerful and so big that you can't handle . . . has got to be you. In fact, you should be the first to say to everyone you meet . . . it's big, it's way beyond me. I can't possibly do it alone, that is why I am talking to you.

46:23

Isn't that a different perspective than . . . if you are broken, I can fix you. I am here to fix you, just tell me which part of your five pillars of health is broken and I will help fix you. Think about how we are coming across. I tell you, we've been around this issue a million times, 'round in circles, and we keep coming back to it. I can't even imagine how I actually communicated this business to Bruce Black . . . way back when!

46:59

People ask me where I found that point of interest that got me in the door with Bruce . . . what did I do to get to him. Well, that's the first thing. Many people have a tough time seeing somebody, never mind getting an opportunity to present to them. What on earth was it—what was that attraction? What was it that got him to stop and say, "Come on over and show me what you've got kid." I must have had some vision that he saw and it was sufficient in quality and quantity that he could see himself in some small way, maybe helping me realize my vision or contribute in some small way as a generous person would do.

47:47

But if the words that came out of my mouth were, "Bruce, here is a business you could make a bunch of money." At the time, Bruce was a multimillionaire and I had a zero bank account. So, how do you talk to these people? And don't you want to be one of these people; don't you want a business that runs itself? Do you? Do you want a business that runs itself? Do you want to attract people who run their businesses instead of waiting for you to make all the decisions and make all the moves and so forth? Don't you want to do that? I can tell you, it's so much fun. It's hard to see all the suffering I see all around me. It drives me nuts and it is all self-induced.

48:40

There are so many people out there who could contribute to this cause. Ask yourself this question: Is this cause worthy of people's time and energy? Is this world not in need of what it is we are doing? Not just in products . . . but philosophically? What we are doing is shifting the way we think about wellness, health issues, life in general. We're shifting the perspective to what really matters—core values. We're bringing the core values to "front and centre stage" instead of who I am and what I do.

49:18

Think about that. Is it not worthy of a Bill Gates? Is it not worthy of a Bruce Black? Is it not worthy of an Isamu Masuda? And, is it not worthy of you and anybody you possibly know? It is worthy of all of us, no question about it. This is an opportunity, an ideal opportunity that is worthy of the best, so why wouldn't you find those people? Why would you not communicate to those people? Why would you just not go out after the best?

49:50

Everybody has a list of people that I am sure you have not yet challenged because you would not have the foggiest notion how to challenge it. You do not feel that you have a value to offer them, so what on earth would they come into this business for? You compare yourself to what you have been comparing yourself to, and you say they would never come into this business. This happens, especially those of us who have been at it for a while.

50:16

What if we just wipe the slate clean and say to ourselves—that's what I have been doing, but that's not what I want to be doing. You and I want to build a business that is worthy of the best of them. We want to be able to communicate to them in such a way that will attract them to at least review it, at least take a look at it. We want people to at least have the point of view that, if it is not for them, they could contribute to making this vision a reality by showing us who we should be talking to or guiding us in some way. These are people who are accomplished and they have no problem helping other people, if they are the kind of people we want to be in business with. That's not to say that everybody is that way.

51:00

So, it's about reframing your business. It's about looking at what it is that you want to build, not what you want to do . . . what you want to build, not what you want to be . . . what you want to create. We're talking abut freedom and the underlying emotion is spirit. "B" and "I" quadrant people are highly spiritual. They are so in touch with spirit and spirit is about freedom. Spirit is about growth, which is what spirit is all about. The opposite is fear. Fear is shrinkage, fear is small and fear is about holding on to what you have. If what you have is so good, you wouldn't be reading or studying this.

51:44

Let's go after what makes our spirit sing and soar! Let's go find those people who are waiting for this type of an opportunity to emerge. They don't know they are waiting, but when they see it, it will connect with their spirit because we are presenting it at the "B" and "I" level . . . not at the "E" and "S" level! Think of what the presentation looks like, the one we are delivering relative to what it could look like. Now let's put something of substance into it; let's add some meat and potatoes to this dialogue . . . so the right person will understand the value we are offering.

52:25

B Quadrant Business

This is a "B" quadrant business. A "B" quadrant business is a business of inviting people to help you in building something, creating something. It will create cash flow, it is part of the nature of this business. It is cash flow independent of you—independent of you and your qualities, independent of your intellect, independent of your nature. Do you know why?

52:51

Because you are attracting to this equation people who go way beyond your abilities, people who go way beyond your skill level, people who are far more capable and far more competent in building a business. How would you feel if you recruited somebody who is way better at this business than you are? Do you have to be the smartest? Do you want to be the smartest? Ask Ahuva who recruited Eli. He and his group in Israel have $400,000.00 in earnings his first year in the business.

53:27

How would you like to have a few of those kinds of people on your team? How are you going to talk to them? How are you going to attract them? They exist. They already exist in your sphere of influence. You have not seen them because you have blinders on. You think, "Who do I know that is hurting? Who do I know that needs this opportunity?" Who are all the "E" and "S" quadrant people I can find who need this business? Maybe you have talked to one or two "B" quadrant people and they shot you down because you came from an "E" and "S" quadrant mentality. So you convince yourself this is not for them. And you look for "E" and "S" quadrant people and then you can communicate in a way that they relate to.

54:16

We do that and then what happens is that we start defending ourselves. If you have been guilty of this, I understand. I really do. We do this because we have not been humble enough to understand the opportunity we have in our hands is so much bigger than who we are and could offer us all the things we want, once we figure out how to turn the tap on and get the thing flowing.

54:43

We are sitting there banging it with a hammer, doing all kinds of things, but not turning it on. And, of course, the "B" quadrant business will lead you to "I's." You will have all kinds of opportunities come as a result of building a business that is worth building. It is a business independent of you.

55:12
Vision

Let's go back to the vision. Let's think about what it is we are going to create. Before we can figure out what we need to do and who we are going to do it with, we have to ask ourselves, what is it that we are trying to create . . . not trying to do, but attempting to build, trying to create . . . and that will help us in the process of evaluating who we need to attract.

This is a perfect example; it will give you a very clear understanding of why you are incompetent in doing this, and why that is okay.

56:00

I do not know of too many businesses that you could build into huge businesses and not feel like most of us. Most of us have come from the *Poor Dad* mentality ("E" and "S"). Our family is in this category and so we have been taught, "haven't you learned yet?," "you want to make another mistake?" That is the kind of stuff that has been programmed into our mind for so long and so we are afraid of making a mistake and that is why we try to stay on top of things, keep our hands in it and stay in control of the situation. We avoid the unknown! But, where is the freedom? Where is the fun? It is in doing something you have not done before in a bigger and better way.

56:44

Most of us have had the most fun in our lives with other people involved, not alone. And so that means somehow, somewhere, we have to find a way to attract these people. All we need is an excuse to get us together. I just need an excuse to attract people, so now the question is "who do I want to attract?" That will determine what kind of excuse I need. Who do I want to attract?

57:10

Get a mental image of these people. Write down a few points or qualities of the people you want to attract. Now, on the other hand, what is the excuse I need to attract these people?

If that excuse is a reasonable one, and offers exceptional value to the world at large, then how does the world repay value? How is it designed? How is it set up to repay us? Economically, it is designed to pay us back with money—money and recognition. So, if I get a good enough excuse, a big enough excuse and attract the right people who can make that excuse become viable, then the business would have done something important enough that money and recognition and all of it come as a consequence.

57:55

If I am trying to assemble people for the sake of being somebody so that I could have the money and recognition, is that the right motive to create something? Is that the motive that will create something that is in line and in harmony with our five pillars of health philosophy? I think there is a cause bigger than money, but let's not forget the importance of money. It's relatively important but five pillars of health is the first cause that I have ever seen that has put it into perspective, its relative importance—it's at the bottom of the five pillars.

Mr. Masuda was bright enough to put money at the bottom, but it is only one of five . . . not the "be all and end all." I think the excuse that we have to assemble people is the best excuse I've seen on the planet yet.

58:40

It is a great excuse . . . this thing called Nikken . . . this thing called the five pillars of health.

Think of a dog house. Do you have an image of a dog house in your mind? Get that dog house in your mind! Now, you will need materials to build a dog house. You may or may not need other people to help, and you may need some money to buy the materials. You might need drawings or you may make it up as you go along. You've got a mental image of what it is you are trying to create, and now you can start to assemble the components, one thing at a time. It starts to come naturally. You will have an easy time figuring this one out.

59:30

Let's work on something more challenging. Close your eyes. I want you to imagine a 50 story tower in downtown Toronto, Gold in color. Let's say a 50 story building is your task. See that building in your mind—50 stories tall? It is huge. What do you need? Help?

1:00:01

Yes, you do need help. You will need materials, certainly a more complex list of materials. In fact, so complex you many not know what materials. You will need drawings; however, what may be sufficient as far as a carpenter drawing for your dog house will not be sufficient for this job. You are now going to need one of the top architectural firms in the city of Toronto. You will need money, certainly in a greater quantity and you are going to have to find some way to assemble it. You might need some help in just assembling the money.

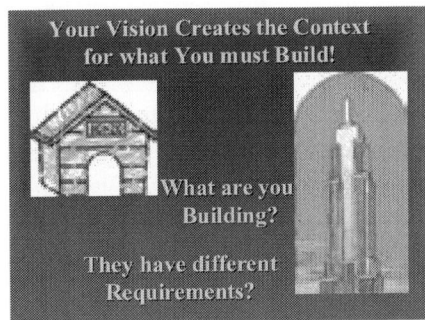
Your Vision Creates the Context for what You must Build!
What are you Building?
They have different Requirements?

1:00:34

Can you see the difference? Are you going to need people? Are there going to be contractors involved? Are there going to be people who are going to occupy the offices? In the case of the dog house, you probably know what the dog looks like, but in the case of the building you may not know who the people are who are going to occupy these offices, but you know that they are going to be there when it opens.

1:00:51

You may have some teams of people who are pre-selling office locations. But, you see what happens and how your mind begins to solve the problem once it has a clear, mental picture of what it is supposed to be doing.

So, I go back to the initial question. You join this business. You came to a presentation, or you went to a number of presentations. You attended a number of trainings and you heard, "If it is to be, it is up to me." What do you want to be? A Royal Diamond? Somebody who is trying to be a somebody? The person has this image of lifestyle and we say: "Build it!"

1:01:32

What is the first thing that you think? Where is the beginning? So, we get to achieve senior. The next step is to become Silver and everybody pumps you up when you're going to go Silver. The language is just driving you to do all the things that I am saying have absolutely no meaning whatsoever. Who cares about going Silver? Are you going to build a lifestyle going Silver?

1:02:01

It's comparable to thinking about building a foundation. But do we even know what size of foundation we are going to build or what the building is going to look like? Who is going to determine what the foundation is going to look like? Are you an expert or do you need some help figuring that out?

1:02:23

Do you see what I mean? If you don't picture the end result in your mind, how on earth are you going to interpret the training that is coming your way, when it has no relevance? It's like saying, "There. That is how you make that piece of glass fit." A piece of glass? What is the importance of that? I don't know. I just know how to make a piece of glass fit. There is no relative importance. Now, if I knew why that piece of glass had to fit that way because I had a building that was made of glass, then that would make some sense.

So, understand that you are hearing bits and pieces of information, absorbing bits and pieces of information and you try to interpret this without having a clear, mental image of what it is you are trying to create and why. What is the importance of building such a building?

1:03:13

Why do you want to build a Royal Diamond business? Well, if you are coming from the vibration of security and that's where most people are really coming from . . . if you are really honest with yourself, you don't need to build a Royal Diamond business. You don't need to do *any* of the things that the Royal Diamonds have been teaching you for the last five years and hence you don't. You just do *some* of the things. You arbitrarily pick, at random, some of the things you are going to do or you arbitrarily hear and your mind filters out all the rest. You only hear what you want to hear, to serve what you want to hear, based on the mental image of what it is you want to build or what you want to be. So, maybe all of this information has been good but maybe some of it has gone to waste because the context of the information was not first put into place. The container was not built to house this information . . . but you know where it belongs and how to put it together. So, if you want to build a Royal Diamond business, can you tell me what it looks like?

1:04:28

Building a Royal Diamond Business

We have a compensation plan that tells you exactly what it should look like. Notice that it says first level. Mr. Watanabe was very specific in defining our compensation plan. He did not say go and find somebody in the tenth level, and make them a superstar. He said first level qualified. He had a very specific reason for that and I was one of the first to challenge him on that reasoning way back when.

1:05:03

In 1993, I was invited to the Nikken Head Office to sit at their boardroom table and was told the marketing plan had changed from needing 10 Silvers to be Diamond and 16 Silvers to be a Royal Diamond. By the way, two months earlier I had qualified as a Diamond, so that was great news for me! Now you have to do it all over again, get 6 Golds or 6 Platinums or the three option. I was one of the first people who said to Mr. Watanabe, "Now, come on. For crying out loud! What is the probability that someone is going to get three first level Diamonds or three legs in general that are Diamond? It is the same probability, slim to none."

So, five plus years later, we were in Paris, France for the Convention and I approached Mr. Watanabe and asked him if he remembered our conversation which was not really a conversation because I was pretty heated, but that was that young blood in me—not understanding the way of the world . . . but I was really on top of this thing. He said he remembered, and I told him that I really appreciated the wisdom in the compensation plan and the way in which it was designed.

1:06:14

If it was not for that plan and if I had not built my business according to it, I would not have any personal freedom in my life today. I took it and ran with it. And what I found were first level competent people, people who were willing to develop competence. And if they weren't, I would abandon them. That was the rule that tied me together with somebody. Either you do it the way it's got to be done or we don't work together.

1:06:40

It remains that simple with me. Die on the vine or build something independent of me. It doesn't' matter to me. I've taken people up as high as Diamond and then they back off, which causes me to back off. I am not going to wait; I am going to find someone else to build.

Golden Rule

1:06:59

So, I've had one Golden rule that I've worked with in this business, and that is: first level qualified. If they don't exist, I am not going down ten generations. It's a first level person. If that person is somebody who is willing to do this and build a business worth building, and has a vision for that, and whose motives are correct—that is what is going to keep us working together. What causes me to actually work with somebody is their commitment to evolving, their commitment to growth to the next stage, the next level. If they are not committed to the next level, I have no interest in working in their business.

1:07:42

That's not my vision. I am not here for the sake of making a pay check. I am not here just to work. I am not in the "E" or "S" quadrant . . . you know, "if I do my time." I'm in the "B" quadrant—I want to build. I want to keep on working with people who want to build because that's when I am at my best. I am at my best when I am in my most creative mode. The reason why we are doing these programs is that I am at my best right now.

1:08:04

I am out there building . . . if not with a Diamond, with a new Platinum. I am in the building mode. That's when I create new tools, when I am in a building mode. Think about that, building mode.

If we understand that we want to build something significant, the more significant we identify our vision to be, the more likely we are going to need to attract people of higher competence. For instance, I might have settled for any old drawing for the dog house but I may require an architectural firm that is the best architectural firm in the city for the building and I will not compromise on that. Do you follow? What do you want to build? What is your image?

1:08:50

If you have come into this business like most, with the idea of a pyramid, where you start at the bottom and you work your way up to Silver, and so forth, and that idea has been supported in all of the training you have been to, all of the tapes you have listened to, do you think you are on the right track?

There's not one person in this company who is Royal Diamond who has ever set a goal to go Silver. Not one of them. So, now you may be thinking—wait a second, I am confused. Everyone has been hammering the point of going Silver. Mike DiMuccio has not. Check my work and you can see that I never ever told anyone to set a goal to go Silver.

1:09:39

I've always encouraged—go Gold, because Silver happens. Going Gold is an exercise in finding leaders; going Silver is an exercise in finding volume. You may get the volume but you will not get the leaders, so you get stuck at Silver. Do you understand that now? Now you know why I am saying—let's go beyond Gold, because you know what? Even Gold distributors are not satisfied. So, what do you want to build?

1:10:09

There has to be some relationship with what you want to create and how you want to live. Is there a place in Nikken that you could live the way you want to live, having created what you have to create? Remember, what you have to create has to offer value in society . . . if

The Science of the Nikken Business

it does not, then having built it will not give you the lifestyle you desire. So, where in the Nikken compensation plan could you live the way you really want to live?

1:10:47

Diamond? Some people might be thinking, "Hey if I can just make ends meet I will be happy. If I could build a business that I could make $3 or 4,000 dollars a month I will be happy." Well, this training is probably not the best training for you, because I am not here to teach you how to do that. I'm not concerned about earning $3—or $4,000 dollars a month.

1:11:15

I am here to change the world. And, it's going to take a heck of a lot more than $3—or $4,000 dollars a month to change the world. That is the scope of my vision . . . hence the size of my organization is in direct proportion. What is the size of your vision? You will attract according to the size of your vision. So, what about if you did this for something bigger than you? **If you really want to attract some really heavy weights into this business, think big . . . think bigger than that!**

1:11:52

Now, ask yourself, what does Nikken want you to do? Does Nikken want you to start on the bottom and work your way up? You know you could not do that even if you tried. Do you think you could work your way up to Good Vibrations International . . . to CEO, Mike DiMuccio? Do you think you could work your way up to my position? Could you pass the person above you and climb all the way up the ladder and take over my position? No, you could not. But the world you come from would suggest that's how you do it. So, you bring that interpretation into this world and it is not correct. You cannot work your way up to me.

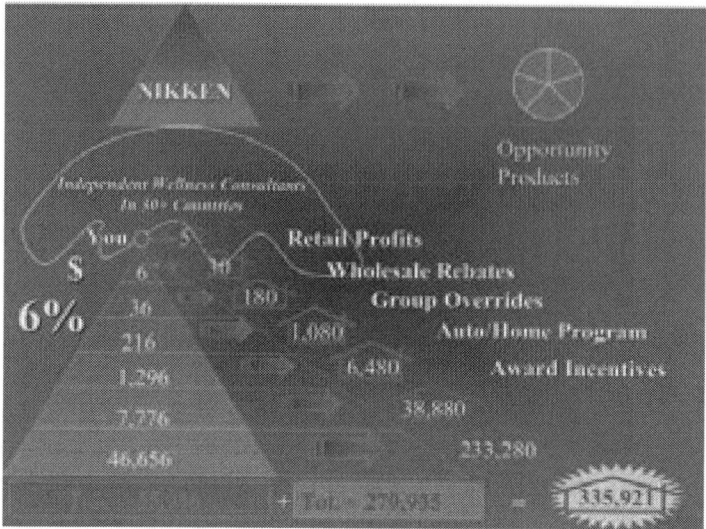

Diagram 15

1:12:37

In fact, Nikken does not want you to do that. What they want you to do is start from where you are and work your way down to create your own pyramid. In fact, they go even further to tell you that they hold you responsible, if you choose, to build the next 6 generations of your organization. It—Nikken—already has an organization.

1:13:03

They do not need you. They would like to have you, but they do not need you. They already have an organization and if is not you, it will be somebody else. But if you are going to be in Nikken, you might as well do what they ask you to do. And they are saying, "We would really appreciate it if you build the next 6 generations. We don't really care about 7, 8, 9, 10—leave that to somebody else. Your job is 6 generations. Look at the compensation plan. How many generations will Nikken pay you on? Six generations. If you worry about the 7th, whose responsibility is it? Not yours. Do you see what I mean?

---

146   The Science of the Nikken Business

1:13:37

So your responsibility, if you take on this mission. is to build the next 6 generations.

I am going to give you some statistics as we go along, to help you understand why the possibility exists to do such a thing, why the need is there to do such a thing and how you might be able to communicate that to people who would appreciate those numbers, and appreciate that vision. Then, what you start to realize is . . . well, if this is my mission, I need help, because I cannot build this by myself.

1:14:14

Now there are a number of ways to build an organization. You can start a company and have employees. Would you like to do that? Would you like to employ people? That is a way of building an organization. No! Why? There's a lot of money involved in that, and would that be a "B" quadrant thing? So, what about franchising? Would you like to franchise a whole bunch of people . . . start a franchise company with Nikken's products and franchise? You would sell franchises around the world. Would you would like that and have 50,000 people call you on the phone everyday? No! But it is an option, isn't it?

1:15:00

Is there perhaps a better way? Maybe we do not want to employ people or franchise people. So, how do we do it? How do we build an organization and get the help that we need to do it, but not have to be overburdened by the responsibility of having to house and employ and do all the stuff that is required to service all these people?

1:15:29

Well, Nikken gives us the opportunity to self employ these people. And to self employ these people means Nikken will service them. You just have to bring them to the table and Nikken will service them and all you have to concern yourself is the first generation.

1:15:41

Teach sufficient competence to that first generation to secure the next generation, so it will secure the next generation. That is why I focus on my first generation, because if they are not competent, who is going to build generation #2? And if they are not competent, who is going too build generation #3? And there are a lot more people in generation 2 and 3 than there are in generation 1, and I don't have time for that lifestyle.

1:16:12

So I would rather work on building first level competence than building downline incompetence.

Build 6

What happens if I build 6 competent first level people and they do the same, because that is what it means to be competent? Then they build 36 and on it goes. By the end of it of it we would have built 55,000 independent Wellness Consultants (refer to Diagram 15, Page 146). 55,000! Can you imagine trying to employ 55,000 people? Can you imagine trying to franchising 55,000 franchises around the world?

1:16:51

But with Nikken, you can self employ people and work with six and then help them build competence. Then, through the duplication process, the effect is the same 55,000 people working at something . . . building something and creating value in society. The result is always the same to you. 55,000 people in your organization working toward the end, and the end in mind is the five pillars of health. That's a little bit different than what you thought we were doing in this business, isn't it?

1:17:26

Instead of working from the bottom and working your way up, you're at the top, starting to work your way down. The top of what? Well, what do you want to build? Do you want to build a dog house or do you want to build a tower? It's up to you what you want to build. So do you want to build a Silver distributorship or an Ambassador distributorship? What do you want to build?

1:17:59

The size of your vision does not have to be who you are. It would be fair to say, when starting out in this business, each and every one of us is not yet competent at building a royal ambassadorship. That would be a fair statement, simply because you have not done it. Then, clearly to be a Royal Ambassador would mean you either become super competent or you surround yourself with competent people. So, if you are not competent, but you can surround yourself with competence and by virtue of doing that, actually learn something from these competents and become competent in the process, that would be an easier challenge.

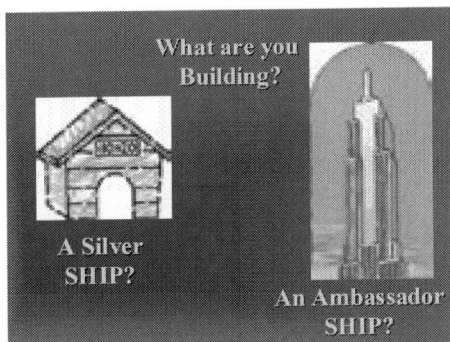
What are you Building? A Silver SHIP? An Ambassador SHIP?

1:18:46

Stop trying to becoming a Royal Diamond in mind, heart and soul, because you can't become one until you are one. You can't understand that until you become one. Would it not be easier for you to take out a challenge of just employing people?

Self employment—attracting into your business those people who could contribute to the realization of this worthy ideal, this worthy cause.

1:19:06

If you have done so, then you will have earned the recognition and all the perks and so forth of a Royal Ambassadorship. It takes the same thing to go Platinum as it takes to go Royal Ambassador, so **I don't know why anybody would not want to build a Royal Ambassadorship**

from day one. A Royal Ambassador is going to find six leaders; you might as well find six leaders. And instead of encouraging them to become Silver, which no one wants to be anyway, help them become something they want to become. Help them build something that they want to build. If you do that, they are going to be what they want to be; they are going to build what they want to build. And, chances are you are not going plateau at Platinum, you are going to go way beyond that. Some people may get stuck. Some may stop. Some of them may lose their vision, but that doesn't mean that you have to lose yours.

1:20:07

The only company that stops growing is the company whose leadership has lost its vision. So, what's your vision? What's the vision you want to have and then we will start to talk some statistics and so forth. We will start to put this together in terms of how I communicate to these people. Whether I'm standing in front of somebody, if I'm on the phone, it doesn't matter. What could I possibly say? And how would I say it? What kind of presentation would I want them to be exposed to so they could appreciate what it is we are doing, why we are doing it and trust they might get excited about being a part of it.
1:20:53

The Science of the Nikken Business

The Missing Link—Part 2

:15

Wе need to be very focused so we can move on. Let's say you are the CEO of a future company, a future organization. With every major corporation and every large business venture, there is a Board of Directors. What is the role of Directors? They advise the CEO. What if the CEO does not take the advice of the Board of Directors? What would the board usually do? They would go out and get another CEO, which is what I have been saying!

1:10

I am considered one of the Board of Directors with the people I am working with. And if they don't take my advice, then I simply replace that CEO with another CEO and start another business. You will have 6 generations of Boards of Directors. So, what happens if the Board makes good decisions, gives you good advice and guides you in the right way? They have a vested interest in your success because they make a percentage of your success. If you don't do well, they don't do well. So there is no hidden agenda. This very much parallels the corporate world but there are limitations to structure and the working world cannot expand exponentially without having a huge supply of capital.

1:56

If you want to attract business people

Your organization can expand exponentially without a huge supply of capital because everyone brings their own capital to the equation, almost like the stock market where everybody brings their capital to the party. This is a business of extraordinary proportion, but rarely do we talk about it in terms of a business. And, if you want to attract business people, you need to explain things to them in a way that they are going to appreciate and that's attractive to them. Rather than simply explaining how this business is different and having them say, "That may be so, but I am not interested in reeducating myself or starting all over again."

2:36

If you can show them how it is very similar, how it's unlimited in scope then they are going to be a lot more interested in seeing how it parallels rather than being so different. Use the language they are familiar with.

Let's start talking in terms of what it is that we are going to create. Let me give you an analogy, because a lot of our presentations at Wellness Previews get to a point where you're at the flip chart, it shows the compensation plan and there's debate as to whether or not there's any value in that piece of information at a presentation.

3:28
The McDonald's Model

We could probably define it very differently. The percentage breakdown—that is all remedial stuff. Let me give you an example. What business is McDonald's in? What would you think the unanimous answer is?

4:11

Hamburgers! Well, I can appreciate you thinking that because really what contact do you have with McDonald's? And the answer is: the restaurant and the commercials that are designed to encourage the people to come to their restaurant to eat. So, for the public at large, their contact with McDonald's is through their restaurant which is their retail outlet. Now, that is interesting because **McDonald's is not in the restaurant business!** In fact, somebody owns that restaurant, and it is not McDonald's. Now, there is somebody in the hamburger business: the owner of the franchise. This franchise

owner is in the hamburger business, and they are very interested in the public coming to their restaurant and eating hamburgers, because this **turnover creates for them, cash flow.** That is their business—the restaurant. We all understand that.

5:18

But if I ask people in general, what business McDonald's is in? They think it is the hamburger business. So, when I ask you—what business are you in? You may not even know how to answer this question. It poses an interesting question if you are you looking to attract the public. If you are looking to attract the public to eat at your restaurant, then you want to present certain information to the public about the value of eating at your restaurant.

5:53

And it's true, the value of eating at McDonald's is not the value of the finest hamburger in town; it is the predictability of the hamburger. You know what you are going to get before you go there and you know the timeframe and so what McDonald's sells is fast food or more specifically predictably fast food. They have the most predictable foods on the whole planet and hence that concept took off. What business are you in?

6:21

Don't answer that question yet. Hold that thought. Can you see how, even your concept, your perception of the business you are in is affecting your ability to recruit people, especially if you don't have a clear understanding of the business you are in?

6:41

You might then say, let's s talk about the McDonald's Corporation. Let's take the McDonald's Corporation which has a CEO and board of directors, a large infrastructure. That infrastructure has to manage and support a lot of activity. Now, what did McDonald's do to sell their franchise? They must have had some kind of presentation designed to sell franchises.

7:10

You might argue McDonald's is in the franchise business and you would not be far off, because you know they have a lot of McDonald's all around the world, don't they? Thousands of them—in countries all over the world. So, they sell franchises. But are they in the business of selling franchises to sell franchises? Are you in the business of recruiting people, to recruit people? That is an interesting question. Or, are they in the business of recruiting people to sell hamburgers? Are you in the business recruiting people to sell magnets? You may not be sure how to answer that question.

7:51

Let's explore another concept. Why then is McDonald's in the business of selling franchises to self employed people so they can sell hamburgers in a very predictable way?

The answer: because underneath the business is a piece of property that the franchise sits on. That franchise sits on a piece of property and out of that cash flow that is generated, they are able to finance the cost of the property. Who do you think the proprietor of that property is? McDonald's.

8:40

And so McDonald's has created this elaborate system if you will, perfecting the concept of a franchise to the point where it is so predictable that they could predict the cash flow in advance of a location, they could then locate that location on prime real estate and sell the concept of the franchise to somebody to run and operate as an independent businessman and they could do that all around the world so that they could acquire real estate. However, the underlying concept is: they are one of the largest land owners in the world.

9:15

So what business is McDonald's in? **Real estate**. Isn't *that* interesting? Is there an analogy here? Because if you don't **understand the business of the business,** you may be selling the wrong thing to

154   The Science of the Nikken Business

the wrong people and not accomplishing what it is you have in mind to accomplish. You might be selling hamburgers to the public, thinking one day you are going to be a large land owner.

9:42

You think that owner would be a fool if that's what they were doing? The more hamburgers they sold, chances are they were going to be a big land owner? No, because that was not the way it was designed. So, what is the business that you have? What is this Nikken thing that you have your hands on? If you don't understand the business of the business, you may not understand how it is possible for you to become a huge land owner in the metaphor.

10:13

Let's look at this. Does Nikken have a public face? Does it? Where there's a place people from all walks of life can come, they can dress any way they want, any time, and they can come and learn about or get fed . . . instead of hamburgers . . . wellness? We have something called a **Wellness Preview.** That is our **public image, our public face.** Now, instead of it sitting on one location it could be a hotel, a room anywhere . . . it could be private, not necessarily a large public gathering but a personal gathering in someone's home, or even a one-on-one.

10:59

Nonetheless, there is a public face, the public presentation that delivers the idea of wellness technologies to the public for the purpose of serving the public what? Wellness! Now, is that the business you are in?

Many have been taught, if you want to build a huge successful Royal Diamond business, you have to bring people to Wellness Previews. Time and time again. And you think . . . these prospects are going to get it. Wow, they are going to be so excited about this. And then they're not. You may conclude, the speaker wasn't' any good.

Ahhh! Have you ever been to a McDonald's restaurant?

11:54

So, does it matter who is serving you the hamburger? It shouldn't, right? So if this was designed properly, this public presentation or preview, then it wouldn't really matter who was delivering the presentation. But it should be a good presentation. It should provide enough information for someone to be able to say: I can appreciate the value of what's going on here. I like what I see! How do I become a consumer?

12:17

That would be our Wellness Preview. And, if I was looking to sell somebody on the idea of owning a franchise, a MacDonald's restaurant, do you think I am going to use the same presentation to sell the hamburgers, to sell them the franchise? No, I probably would not.

Do you think that the Wellness Preview is a sufficient presentation to recruit business builders in the B quadrant? That is why Mike DiMuccio created a presentation years back; it was the original business presentation on slides which eventually became the Wellness Preview reconfigured . . . but in very basic, general terms. And, as a result of that, he created another presentation called **"It is About Time"** with Marty Jeffery. You may remember that presentation

13:11

That presentation was similar to MacDonald's selling the franchise. It was not the franchise selling the public hamburgers. It was the corporation selling the idea of owning a franchise. It was a totally different presentation and many people thought we should replace our Wellness Preview with that presentation. Two different presentations; two different outcomes.

13:40

Then we evolved to another presentation called "**Trading Time for Money.**" That presentation from the point of view of this organization selling franchising is a presentation that helps you understand this. It goes one step further than we've ever gone before in terms of explaining the business of the business. It speaks to why would we sponsor a whole bunch of people, what's the point of that? Why?

14:20

There is an underlying current. There has to be a reason for us to do what we do, and that reason has to go beyond us. It is a business. McDonald's is comprised of a CEO, many shareholders and so forth. The land is owned by a whole bunch of people, not one person, so it does not serve one person. Nor will your business.

14:47

The creation that you are about to create will serve many! What is the value of what you are creating? What is the underlying value of what you are creating? What is the underlying value of what Nikken is creating? Why has Nikken created the opportunity to sell franchises . . . each franchise cable of dealing with the public with wellness technology? Nikken does not deal with the public. So why has Nikken created the multiplicity of franchises through this network concept? Put another way, what is Nikken's goal? Have you ever heard Nikken state their goal? Do you know what it is?

15:23

Nikken's Goal: Worldwide Wellness

Worldwide wellness through the five pillars of health. **Worldwide! That is their stated mission,** so they have created this elaborate game called Nikken and network marketing and magnets and so forth. It really is a game; it is a facade. I am saying this to stress a point. But, this game Nikken has created has been created with a cause in mind: that the creation of and successful evolution of this game will cause an underlying thing to happen. Worldwide Wellness!

16:12

What have you noticed about the people whose lives have been touched by Nikken? What have you noticed about those who have climbed the ranks?

The higher up they go . . . they get better, they get healthier, they get more balanced, and they become more and more involved in each of the five pillars of health.

16:35

This is Nikken's idea of worldwide wellness! That is what I like about five pillars of health. Nikken has created a concept that they can create worldwide wellness, one person at a time, one family at a time that spreads out internationally. This is a brilliant concept, it is absolutely brilliant. But it would not happen if it wasn't altogether.

17:17

McDonald's would not be the largest land owner if it was not for the whole concept, irrespective of what the public sees. It is the whole concept that makes this work, so if what you really want is wellness, balance and all the prosperity that goes along with that and get the full impact of what Nikken is, then you have to position yourself properly.

17:43

You have to become the McDonald's corporation; you have to be somebody who starts to sell franchises. And each of those franchises needs to be capable of putting presentations together that service the general masses, because without the franchise actually serving the public, the franchise has no reason to exist. In our case, our franchise is an individual. How do you measure success in this business? It is measured by how many presentations are going on any given night. That is how you would measure success.

18:20

Think of this. Would McDonald's sell more hamburgers having one restaurant in the city of Toronto, one big restaurant, downtown Toronto, or would they sell more hamburgers having a whole bunch of restaurants, smaller restaurants spread out twenty minutes apart? They would sell more hamburgers having a bunch of more restaurants. Right?

18:45

Would you make more of a contribution to wellness if you had one big presentation and you were the one who made that presentation happen? Remember, in the "S Quadrant"—I am in control . . . only I can do it, as good as I can do it. Bring everybody. Everybody come to my presentation and I measure my success by the size of my presentation, irrespective of how many people of my organization are there.

19:09

That actually happens to people in Nikken. That is an "S Quadrant" person's thinking; their mentality in this business. They measure the success by the size of the Wellness Preview that they do, instead of by the number of Wellness Previews that are happening in their organization by others. I would rather have 10 small Wellness Previews going on, because that would mean there are 10 people out there presenting instead of one person doing it all.

19:38

Which business would you rather have? **Would you rather own a McDonald's restaurant or would you rather own McDonald's?** That is a very different concept, isn't it? **Now what is your business about? It is about franchising around the world, creating presentations all over the place . . . small, large, any kind, presentations that deliver an impact to the public. All together these presentations create an underlying current—they help balance the five pillars of health.**

20:21

That's your business! That's why you need to recruit, but each person that is recruited needs to develop their ability to present to the public. That's why they need to do this. Do you now understand why we encourage people to present? Why it's important to go to Gold training? Nikken encourages you to do the Wellness Preview, that's why.

You measure your success by the number of presentations that are happening on any given night, or any given week, anywhere in the world.

20:58

Now here is a vision for you. Imagine having a thousand independent consultants out of all the ones you end up recruiting over the next ten years. You have a thousand who are capable of putting on a presentation for 50 or 60 people, once a week. That means in your organization, every week, 50,000 people are exposed to this concept. Do you think you might get some consumers? Do you think you might get some people to see this as a business?

21:32

Now, if I wanted to recruit somebody to join me in this business, a "B" quadrant person, not an "E" person or an "S" person, if I wanted to recruit and "E" or "S" person, I just would take them to a Wellness Preview and say, "Hey, you think you can do better?"

"Sure! Heck, yeah! That person sucks. I can certainly do better." So that would be an easy way to recruit one of these people, you just take them to a Wellness Preview. But if I wanted to recruit a "B" person, that would not do. It would not do, because it is not in context.

22:07

The "B" quadrant person wants to understand the business of the business. So I would explain to them the business of the business. I would explain the concept of franchising through a specific presentation, and then I would bring them to see the franchise in operation. I would take them to see the customers that come to one of our presentations. So, when they walk into a Wellness Preview, instead of saying, "Do you want me to join the ranks of these people?" . . . you want them to walk in and say, "Whoa! Look at all the people here. This is fabulous . . . this must be a great place. Look at all the people who are here. Did you hear those stories? Man I heard that story. This must be an incredible product that makes this an incredible business." Darn right. I want to be a franchise owner. I want to have 100 of these franchises all over the place.

23:01

That's what they would see if they would be presented the vision first, then followed up by the products . . . and that's how you presented it to them. Which, by the way, is exactly what I did when Marty Jeffery came to town. He flew to Toronto with Lauren Collins. We sat down at the table and I presented a little bit about **my vision, and this vision was all about worldwide wellness.** And if you ask him what was the one thing Mike talked about at the beginning, he would tell you I talked about Nikken's vision, not mine. My vision is Nikken's vision.

23:37

Who do you work with? Who is your board of directors? Who do you take your instructions from? Ultimately, who pays you? And why would they, if you weren't doing what they needed you to do and are asking you to do. So if Nikken were to say, "If you want to be part of this thing and be part of our team, here is our vision, here is our mission." What would you be doing going off on another mission? You expect to get paid going off on another mission when their vision is clear—world wide wellness. Think about it. We are all part of Nikken's organization; we are all here to serve Nikken in the realization of Nikken's vision. Within the context of Nikken's vision which is worldwide wellness, there are many opportunities for us to experience all the fruits of our labor and all the joys of life because their world vision is so big, that clearly, there is enough room in it for all of us.

24:35

So why would you create another vision? Why would there be a vision separate from Nikken's vision. Why wouldn't they be one and the same? Why wouldn't it be your responsibility to help generate the next 6 generations of Nikken's business? There are going to be generations after that, but you are here to help Nikken expand the next six generations, the next, six generations. What does that say about the generations before you? Who cares? They are not yours. The only thing you can gain from Mike DiMuccio or Dave Johnson, Reid Nelson or Bob Colee . . . the only thing you could possibly gain from us is that we are on your board of directors. We can help you make decisions that are in the best interest of your business. We can help you communicate to some of these people that you attract into your business from the point of view of a board of director, from someone who understands the business of the business.

25:43

People want me to get on the phone with their prospects and talk about the products. Why would you waste my time and your time talking about the products? Send them to a Wellness Preview or give them a back roll. The products speak for themselves. I am here to talk about the business. That is how to best use my time. Put me in front of someone who needs to understand the business of the business and let me go.

So, these people who come before you and who are going to help you build the next generation—they are your responsibility, the next generation. What comes after this?

Let's get back to Marty flying to Toronto. I presented the vision, then I showed him how Nikken was set up, because he had done franchising before. I explained to him the benefits as I saw them . . . of our franchise system, the independent network franchise.

27:09

The value of your network

So, if there is one—you—and you work for you, yourself and you, the value of your network is one. Think about a fax machine. What good would a fax machine be if you are the only one who has one? But the second that there were two, the value of the fax machine became four, and the second that there were three, the value became nine, and with four the value became sixteen and so on, and so forth. So, the larger your network is, the more valuable it becomes, considerably more by the value squared, and this is the rule of business not a rule of network marketing. Exactly what business are you in?

Robert Kiyosaki says:

"Rich people build networks,
poor people look for work."

3COM / Palm Pilot guru Law says,

"The value of your network
is equal to
the number of your people
in your network, squared."

27:50

The network business. A network of people focused and committed to an end in mind: worldwide wellness. Now, if your focus is to be somebody, and you have a network of people trying to be somebody, what is the use of this network? What would the value of this network be? Self-serving people looking to be somebody and to measure their importance by how other people see them, instead of serving people, and measuring their importance by the number of people they are serving, by what they have created.

28:29

Are you clear on what you are building? By the way, after the presentation, I took Marty and gave him a back roll which, by the way, is explained in the **YOU³ System.** Then I took him to a Wellness Preview because it was at that Wellness Preview he was going to get the validation he needed; he was not there to get informed. I already gave him the information. He went to the preview to see whether the information I gave him held up in a real situation. And the real situation was all of these people who we had no control over—they were going to talk and explain what they thought about the products.

29:06

At the preview, one fellow had a button on that said—Ask Me About Magnets. So Marty said, "What about magnets?" Marty was interviewing people, while he was at that presentation. Would your business prospect do that if they were coming to a Wellness Preview to be informed? No. Marty was there to be validated . . . to find out if these people were for real. He was looking into their eyes and asking them to tell him their story.

29:33

So, he saw the presentation, commented that it was too wordy . . . too many words on the slides and that we could modify that. He is thinking like a business builder who is going to build a business. He was not there to be impressed with new information. He was there to see whether the information he had heard was substantiated. Do you do this way when you are recruiting? Why would you do it this way?

30:05

Let's review. What is it that we are building? There is a company called Nikken that has invited us to join them in their already existing organization. This organization stands 27 countries and climbing. Soon it will be in 200 countries with or without your decision, with or without your participation and here you are here somewhere in the equation. And the only value that you can bring to Nikken is to extend the organization. Because with all what Nikken has done, they have created a success story into themselves. Nikken is a very highly respected company. Whenever anyone looks at the company Nikken, the business of

The Science of the Nikken Business

Nikken, there is nothing but ultimate respect for a company that has been able to do what they have done and continue to do.

30:56

Their track record is impressive and so is the way they are structured. It's like McDonald's. People look at the structure of McDonald's and say, "That is brilliant." Not too many people know it, but it is brilliant. In Nikken, when people learn the business of the business, they may say—these guys are brilliant. And, it too is a brilliant concept, but exactly what is **Nikken's mission?** What are they doing in business? **Five pillars of health worldwide.** And what have they created to make this a possibility? **The opportunity.** And what have they created to substantiate the opportunity? The products. This is the order of the value that Nikken offers.

31.40

So this is the **value that Nikken brings.** They have given us a vision. *They support that vision by creating a franchise-like opportunity where we can work independent of each other but in an inter-connected way . . . building a network. They validated it by creating a technology and continue to evolve that technology so that what we offer the world is current and valuable, which substantiates the opportunity and that substantiates the vision.*

32:17

It's comparable to what I have just said: **we have a product because we need the franchise to work. But we need many franchises so that we can create the underlying current. We need a product to make the opportunity work, but we need the opportunity to make the vision work.**

So when anybody asks you, why did they do it this way? Why would they choose network marketing? Why would they not go the traditional way? Ask them this: Why would anybody go with what you consider traditional? What has that proven? Turn the table on them and ask them to prove to you what they think is better because you have not seen results like Nikken's—anywhere. We're talking about Nikken. They already have an organization and you are just a small cog in their big huge picture.

33:11

So what value are you going to be to Nikken so that Nikken will pay you what you now earn in a year, on a monthly basis? What could you add as far as value? If that is what Nikken is adding to the world as far as value, then how are you going to contribute to this?

What Nikken said is simple: don't sell product—that is not the focus. That is the consequence, that is the back bone of our business, but that is not the business. Though you want to sell product, you want to affect the world, build a whole bunch of franchises, you want to sell "hamburgers"—referring back to the McDonald's analogy. But, there are only so many hamburgers you can sell at one location. We already know exactly how many that is, but if you want to be effective, you want to alter hunger in the population of the planet, then we are going need a whole bunch more than just one restaurant, so **learn the business of the business.**

34:02

That is what Nikken wants you to do. They want you to **learn the business of the business,** and the sooner you get to this point, the better. If you have to fumble around the products a little while until you figure it out, whatever! The sooner you get to the point where you realize what Nikken is asking you to do, the better . . . and it is written in their own compensation plan. Do you know what the compensation plan is? It's an incentive. In essence they're saying: if you create this, this is what we will do as far as paying and recognizing you. It is compensation, an incentive.

34:34

They are telling you, this is what we want you to do, and this is what we are going to do in return. Now, I have seen all kinds of ridiculous compensation plan interpretations (some with seven legs!!) and I can't figure out why anybody would want to rewrite history, when Nikken's plan is sufficient. I've yet to see many people actually maximize the business plan that Nikken offers, why do you need seven legs? One for reserve? Then, what are tap roots all about? Aren't they the reserve?

35:15

If you have Platinum, backed by Platinum, backed by Platinum . . . isn't this your reserve for each leg? Why would you need another leg? What about, if you just build what Nikken asks you to build? Let's look at the possibility of you doing just what Nikken asks you to do. Let's look at simply doing what they've suggested we do.

35:38

What would happen if we actually did exactly what Nikken suggests: five, six, good posture, why not three? You can do three or you can do six, so let's examine three. You sponsor three, who sponsor three, who sponsor three. That is nine and that is 27 and then I (me) becomes 81, quickly calculate . . . 3 8's or 24, 3 and then 3 again, 729, one, two, three four, five, six generations—there you are, there is your organization. What is the size of this organization total?

36:14

About 1,000 people. Now six. **So, six, who sponsor six because that's what you are teaching . . . do as I do,** do as Nikken would ask us to do. That's 36 who sponsor 6, 216 who sponsor 6, 1296, who sponsor six. What is it? **55,000+ plus people now.** It's important to consider: how much more effort did you invest? If you have been listening carefully, how much more effort did you invest? Did you put in 200% more effort, with two times the work? How many times the results—55? So then, that's 55,000—correct? Fifty five times the results would be 5,550% return. Now tell me something. If somebody said, "Give me $3 and I will give you a $1,000 back in two weeks," or they said, "Give me six bucks and I will give you $55,000 back in two weeks," which would you give them?

37:51

If you put a little more effort up front, in the long run it will be a lot more in return and that is why I have always encouraged people to build six not three. Yes, you could do it with three, but why would you do with three when you could do with six. A little more effort up-front will pay a great deal more on the back end.

38:15

This is where we are going to learn some important stuff. These are important numbers. This is what you are going to present to people; we are going to formalize this presentation. But if I just did that, found six competent people who are visionary and who want to build a business . . . not secure a job or start a small enterprise . . . people who have a big vision, to see the big picture, and I was capable of leveraging these people to get them to see the big picture, to validate to them the big picture, that you only need six people. Not 600, not 60 . . . because if you find the right 6 people who want to build the business, they are going to want to do what has to get done. They are going to say to you, "OK, describe to me exactly what we are building. What are the tools that we need? $1,500.? $2,000.? $5,000.?" Whatever?

39:11

They are not going to say, "Well, can you buy a pair of mags? Can you start off with that?" If you are getting that, you already know you have the wrong person. And so how do you convert from that to something positive? Maybe say, "When you are really ready to do this, to build a business—call me."

39:31

You are here to build a business. You are not here to baby sit people who want to pretend they are building a business because they have put their name on an application form. You are an independent Wellness Consultant. Have you been to Silver training yet? We wear these badges as if that's who we are. Remember, that's the world we came from. It should be what you have built lately, that's what should matter. A lot of people live in the past . . . you know the type . . . once upon a time I was a pro. They live in the past and their whole future is about the past.

40:12

I would not want to be a person in that position. I want to leverage from my past to build the future, instead of living in the past. These are people who are stuck on being somebody. The other day I heard somebody say, "I would rather have been somebody, than never be somebody." And I thought, there is a person who has a lot of hope for a better future? What about, "I would rather be somebody who knows there is going to be a future than somebody living in the past."

Now 6 people—if we did that, it is 55,000 people. *Now*, do you think auto ship a good idea? So, for those of you who have been bartering with the idea, should I get on auto ship or should I get on auto ship? Maybe I will get on auto ship when it is worth it! Let's duplicate that thought and process shall we?

41:05

So, when 46,000 people have a down-line the size of yours, they will probably think its worth it too, but by then where will you be? So, why don't we start with the right habits and build what we are looking to build.

Why don't we build what we want to build? Let's take a look a this! **100 points auto ship.** You are the CEO remember. Make a decision on behalf of you and your business. What is that decision going to produce if that's the business you are building? Well 55,000 x 100 points is $5,500,000 dollars in volume and what do you get paid? Six percent.

42:02

Notice that I don't talk 5% and the rebate you get from this person and that person? Please! That is like majoring in the minors. Who really cares about what you earn on the discount and the percentage of this and the percentage of that? And, how much do I make on my seniors? Are you really going to get excited about that? How many seniors do you figure are going to stick around long enough for you to make a few dollars? So that is the part of the marketing plan that I don't particularly care about. That's not what we are building. A person is not coming into the business so that they can be a senior, a direct seller under you for the rest of their life.

42:36

So, who cares now? What we are building? We're building a business that comprises of creating an organization, an organization that has, as its underlying purpose for its existence, a desire to spread worldwide wellness.

Is there a need? Is there a good time to do this? You should read Kiyosaki's and Pilzner's books. Between each, they will explain why now is the place. Now is the time and place, and this is it. This is your justification if you need an excuse. Here it is. You need a new vehicle, and here it is. Between these two books, we have a whole new business. Between these two books (Kiyosaki & Pilzner) we have a new concept going, and we could have a new name, Independent Wellness Consultant.

43:39

Six percent—that is the big picture. Six percent! $5.5 million in volume. That adds up to $330,000 dollars per month in income! Do you think you might be able to do some of the things you enjoy doing? Do you think maybe with this kind of a business you might have some investment opportunities open to you? Did you know that it explains in the book (*Rich Dad, Poor Dad*), in order to invest in the business opportunities that the rich invest in, you have to already be rich? Otherwise what you are buying is off the rack. You are buying the retail product—small potatoes. You are buying mutual funds—small potatoes. Now, the people who put the mutual funds together, big potatoes. The IPO's—big potatoes. They buy it after the fact and it is a retail product that is available to the masses. To be able to invest where the rich invest, you already have to be rich. You have to have a million dollars in net worth plus $200,000 US per year income to qualify legally under the law in the US to qualify for these types of investment opportunities.

44:49

Ever wonder why the rich get richer? They are the ones who create the laws. *Magna Carta*—read the book. When they took it over the Crown to make law, it was the rich who decided the laws. And that was it. What changed the world? So, here we are, unaware of what is really going on, expecting to be big in a world that we do not even understand . . . a world we are playing in. That is what this program is intended to do . . . to help you understand and appreciate what you have and to see it with a whole new set of eyes.

45:24

It's available so that you can go out with confidence and be able to articulate it in a way that's intelligent and will attract those kinds of people who will understand and appreciate what you are presenting, instead of complaining about 6%? Why not 7? Knowledge is ever-present. Keep learning.

45.54

What if your business was a bit more visionary? What if your business looked a lot more like the McDonald's business looked? What if your business had all components functioning properly? What if it had a presentation that was functioning properly where you really learn to appreciate and value somebody who is a consumer? Have you ever lost any distributors? OK, so let's change that. What if we just re-qualify them? What if we did not lose a distributor, but what we gained is an understanding that they are not going to build a business; therefore, all they really are is a wholesale consumer? Then we have not lost anything, what we just gained is an entirely different audience.

46:44
What we have just gained is an entirely different audience

What we have just gained is somebody who has already been through the process and appreciates the value of wellness and we probably kicked them out of the door on the way out because they were not building a business. You probably ticked them off, that's why they left. Can you hear it? "Come on to the meetings! You are not coming to the meetings! Buy the demo pack!" Instead of doing that, why don't you re-qualify them in your mind? Why not just call them something they are, a glorified consumer. Maybe they signed up just to get you off their back. Or, they just signed up so that they could get some products wholesale. So, what? Do you have a problem with that? Do you know any business that does not like customers? Do you know of any business in the world that treats their customers with such disrespect like ours? Think about it!

47:35

What if we just re-qualify them in our mind? What if Nikken, in a few months, or a few years from now, even thinks about it like we are thinking about it . . . putting systems in place where it would actually shift these people from independent Wellness Consultants out of our genealogy report on one side, into a new genealogy report called, "Preferred Clients?" You might be questioning whether you understand me correctly. You're telling me that if I build this pyramid, that I am automatically building a second pyramid? You probably have lot of people in your business who are not business builders but who joined your business.

48:11

So, if you keep on treating them like a business builder and they're not, you're going to tick them off and they will leave. But if you re-qualify them as somebody who at least took the time to learn about this, they are now what Paul Zane Pilzner refers to as a "wellness consumer." These are consumers who try a product and have a positive wellness product experience. Sound like any of the people you know?

48:45

These people typically become voracious consumers of more wellness products and services if you don't tick them off and push them away. Just think about it. Think about all those people who you have discounted in your mind because they're not business builders . . . they are not coming to the Wellness Previews, they are not doing the things they are supposed to do. Most of us just eliminate them from our lives . . . people that, at one point in time, we had high hopes for, we took the time to involve them, to communicate to them. How would you feel, **instead of losing these people, you would gain a whole new division of your business?**

49:35

Now your business has **a preferred client division,** and it has a **business builder division.** You know what? You never know which side they are on until they're around for a while anyway. So, give them the time they need. Give them a month, give them two months. By that time you should pretty well know which side of the fence they are on and in your mind you re-qualify them. And then, instead of badgering them with business building concepts, you might invite them to some wellness concepts. What's that?

50:08

Let's focus on sleep. We are going to talk about sleep because it is an epidemic and most people don't know why they are not sleeping well. Most people don't know they are not sleeping well, so we devised a **presentation called sleep.** It is one of the many, many Wellness Preview presentations that we are doing as well as Wellness Consultants. Why? What do we do? We educate the population; we are independent Consultants. That is the business at the public level.

50:45

Imagine if we changed our Preview formats as we've come to know them and, instead, we had presentations designed to feature the product—just the product. And, further, instead of just **designing these**

previews around the product, they were designed around issues: for instance **sleep, water, energy, nutrition.** What if we designed presentations that were informative and educational so that we really took on the mantra that a Wellness Consultant could be a public servant, an education distributor, intellectual distributor and these presentations were very easily done as efficiently as the flip chart presentation that we have now? It could be on slides. It could be on a computer, a PowerPoint presentation off a disk. We could have hand outs and everything, so that anybody who came to a presentation they would get some value, they really would get some information.

51:48

What if they did that? What if we did that at our public events? One night could be sleep, next week it might be on nutrition, the following week we could talk about water. Eventually, in a city the size of Toronto, on any given night you could go to a water or sleep or nutrition workshop and so forth and you would have **public education Wellness Previews designed to inform the public** about products and technology that can address very real issues in their lives, and that would be the focus of the presentation.

Golden Rule

If you are a business builder, you need to be hosting Wellness Previews.

52:32

What if you made it duplicatable so that anybody could do that presentation, so that anybody could learn to do a flip chart presentation? Now, does everybody have to do one? No, not everyone has to, but your business builders should. Otherwise, you will have re-qualify them too.

What does a Board of Directors do when their CEO doesn't follow the business plan? They replace him or her. One of my Golden Rules is: **if you are a business builder (that is a Silver Distributor) and you are not hosting Wellness Previews, I won't work with you.**

53:09

That's **one of my Golden rules.** That is how I know whether or not I am ever going to have anything to do with you. I have over 21 first level Silvers, 11 of them inactive. Do you have 11 active? Have you even sponsored 11 people? I may have lost more than many people have built? Why? Because instinctively I learned early in this business, intuitionally, maybe I was operating in the "B" quadrant as an unconscious competent . . . but I would dismiss someone when they would not pick up the ball. At the Silver level, one of the things that I was taught was that you had to pick up the ball. If you refuse to, you've only got two chances with me. That is **another Golden rule, two strikes and you are out.** I will find somebody else because I do not want to waste my life, not one moment of my life, on people who talk the talk, but don't substantiate the claim.

54:14

How about you? How would the CEO of a multimillion dollar enterprise behave? Would you expect any less of them? Why would you expect less of yourself? **You are building a multimillion enterprise, start acting like you are.** You will begin to attract those people who will turn the business into a reality. Now is there a place for those people, there sure is. I have no problem with somebody being involved in wellness. I have no problem with somebody learning about what is new. I have no problem keeping them informed, but my level of expectation in them as far as building the business, is very different.

54:59

Now, hindsight is always perfect. The truth is that I have lost more than 60 people because I did not know this. Way back when, I did not have the vision for what I was sharing. But had I known that in 1992, today I would have 60 preferred clients, probably more. Imagine 60 preferred clients, 10 business builders. Now that may not seem like much, but if you make some product sales every now and then for 60 people you are keeping in contact with, multiply that down the line. What if I had been taught and taught from the beginning, find 6 business builders, and re-qualify those who aren't going to build the business into preferred clients . . . say 10 of them. So, build 6. Just find 6 business builders and service 10 clients. Find 6 business builders and service 10 clients. That is your business plan and that is what we are going to set up in motion. What would happen at the end of this? If there are 55,000 business builders, how many preferred clients are there? 550,000! You say you want to make a difference, a difference that you can measure?

56:17

How many of these 550,000 are you personally responsible for? Ten. Now, let's say one of these 10 people buys a sleep system in one year. That would be amortized over the year, the equivalent of 100 points per month, correct? What if you had one on auto ship, what if one referred you to somebody because they had great product experience . . . you kept in touch with them? What if out of these 10 people the average volume that was generated by these 10 people was 100 points per month, $100 dollars a month, just by keeping in touch with 10 preferred clients.

56:57

Let me qualify what I really mean by this. For all intents and purposes, these are people you have no intention of making money on. You will extend your price to them. Why? Well, because these are 10 customers who are going to buy from me for life. Go ahead and do the numbers now. If I had 10 people I extended my prices to that I did not make a cent on, who would those 10 be? Who will those 10 people be? Who could I offer that to? Would it be anybody? Or if I could only do 10, if I could only offer 10 people this special service, this special privilege, would I be talking to them a little differently? Would it be people I was particularly close to? If I really felt it was a privilege that I thought I was extending to them, how would I make them feel, if I believed it was a privilege for them to be able to purchase at my purchasing power?

The Science of the Nikken Business

58:01

Then all I need is 10 people, and they probably would be people from my own family. I would not go outside the circle of my own family. How about you? Doesn't Nikken come out with new products every once in a while? If you started with one product today, how many weeks would it take you if you did one product per week to communicate to your inner circle of your family and friends each of these products? How many weeks would it take you?

58:28

Instead of dumping all of the product on them at once, why not a little bit at a time . . . just like Nikken did to us as they evolved their business throughout the world . . . introducing us to one product at a time. Just one product at a time. So, what about having a **Wellness Preview at your home** every month, with your immediate influence? Something to the effect, **"Guess what? Your Wellness Consultant has something new—as always, it's at my price, come and check this out and bring a friend!"** Just ten people. So, multiply that by 550 thousand times @ 100 points and that is $55 million in volume at 6%. And remember, you are not making a single penny off these 10 people. But what you are making up for is the volume that is generated by other people in your organization following suit. **55 million x 6% is $3.3 million dollars in income per month in addition to your little bit of $330,000 a year.**

59:34

Tell me something. Do you know any business person in North America who would look at that and say, "That's peanuts! *Do you mean to tell me that I don't employ anybody . . . these people operate on four continents in multiple cities and, in multiplexes of cities they operate independently. This company is willing to provide service to support each and every one of these preferred clients, each and every one of these independently Wellness Consultants directly? This company will service each of these people on an individual basis . . . I don't have to? All I have to worry about is finding 6 business builders who understand this vision and service 10 people I would anyway because I believe these products are valuable?"*

In so doing, in the next three to five years, I am going to generate an organization that is going to be producing **three to five million dollars a month in business in income.**

1:00:29
You think there might be a few business people you overlooked out there that could be impressed with such a presentation? How about it? What if it would take 10 years to develop this? I assure you that once we get this right, it will not take 10 years. Evidence of that right now is in Germany. Here is an organization of people that has been built in about five years. They learned a lot from what we've done, but they also learned not to make the mistakes we made. They simply learned and built an incredible business that is generating extraordinary volume, in such a short period of time.

1:01:16
I know that this is representative of what is going to happen. I believe and I have always believed that a 6-figure income per month was not only possible but should be commonplace. I always believed 7-figure per month income was very real in this business. Once we understand how to do this business the way this business ought to be done . . . instead of building this business like Joe's hamburgers . . . once we start to apply the McDonald's hamburger concept to this, then we're going to have a real business.

1:01:46
We are going to have a business that people are going to flock to, to understand and see, because this produces incredible, incredible results. Do you know if you took this concept further, if you can afford to give these people your products at your cost, based on what is happening here, **because you cannot afford to give them away. Hear me out. Do you know any world organization that can build**

an expanding organization of products that they can afford to give away for free?

1:02:17

Do you know what I have just said would turn every head and affect every corporate infrastructure on the entire planet if they knew what I just said? Do you know of any? Think about it at some point in time . . . you might be able to afford to give your products out for free. That means as your organization gets to a certain point, you can give them away for free, that means people in your downline can afford to give them for free. As this organization continues to expand, there will be a growing organization of people who can give their products away for free. **Do you know of any countries in the world that could use some of these products and cannot afford them?**

1:02:53

Who knows, this might even evolve to that. It certainly could and nobody would lose any money. **Volume is volume; you get 6%** on the volume. Think about that, that's the kind of business we are talking about. It is something that could never be done in any other business. It could never be done. That's what is so exciting about what we are doing. It is not only incredible, it offers each person something of extraordinary value, and it **could change the world, just in the way we do business. Not just through** our business products . . . but **the way we do business is a life changing experience.**

1:03:35

That is why you should be excited. That is the kind of presentation you should be talking about presenting at this level. So, in time, you are going to start to see business briefings unfold. I refer to them as **business briefings** not **Wellness Previews** because a Wellness Preview is what it is and a business briefing is different. You may have already started to see some of these presentations. **Special presentations** where the focus is on things that are relevant, issues that are relevant, water, sleep and so forth. If, in fact, the first edition is already available . . .

some of you may already have received your CD's available through Team Tools.

1:04:12

There is also a new brochure available. It's called, **"Investing in Your Business."** It explains why you should be investing in your business and what you should be investing in. It gives you the low down . . . what should your initial order be . . . the importance of your initial order . . . and gives you examples, good, better, and best.

1:04:36

Do you think that the CEO or a person who buys a McDonald's franchise gets to choose what color? No. **They are buying a ready-made business because it works.** One of the first things that I do when I launch a new distributorship is that I put one of these things together because I do not want the down-line thinking. **We have to move quickly and we don't have time to think, so let's do the thinking now. Figure it out in advance. If they do what they need to do, they follow our structure, our business plan, they will succeed. If they don't, re-qualify them.**

1:05:08

What tools do you need? We've put together tools for your education, tools for your information, and then there are specials that Team Tools puts together as ready-made packages. Why should this be a difficult process? Either you are here to build a business or you are not. If you are here to build a business, there should be a business plan, and it should be predicated on what we know to be successful. If you are not here to build a business, then do whatever you want to.

1:05:44

We have no problem filling in this pyramid; I assure you, the retail customer pyramid will be filled quicker than the business builder pyramid. But now you have a reason to do so. Now you understand the value of doing so. I have been trying to stress this point for ever. **As soon as I say** the word retail to anybody at Nikken or anybody in leadership—the Diamonds . . . they tell me not to say that . . . don't say that too loud. Don't talk about that. We have to teach these people how to recruit; we've got to recruit, recruit. I certainly understand your point of view . . . let's teach these people how to build a franchise, but let's not tell them how to operate it. That's ridiculous.

1:06:26

Think about it. It's such a simple concept and a lot of people stick their heads in the sand because it is foreign to network marketing, it is foreign to what we have been taught and many of us have grown up in that environment and are resistant to change. But you know, familiarity breeds contempt. **What you are familiar with often causes you to ignore what is not obvious to you. But is obvious to others**? I think this is brilliant and this is business. This is **the best business plan** I have seen since I have been in network marketing. It is one that **will produce the most valuable results** for everyone involved, including those who have come through, but have not gone on with us in the business building capacity. We just re-qualify them in our mind as wellness clients and we re-invite them, we re-invite them to learn about more about this. (See diagram—Page 303)

1:07:21

By the way, did you know you could take somebody to the web site and purchase products at your price which means they pay taxes on your price, they don't pay tax on the retail? Somebody had foresight at Nikken and started listening to this concept and implemented that strategy on the internet. Go to the web site, get an upgrade to 100 thing so you can purchases products through your web.

1:07:57

I'm working on something. Can you imagine if Team Tools came out with a form that you could have at these presentations and instead of a person signing up as a distributor, they can sign up as a preferred client. And what they would receive was a periodical—information that informed them and educated them about wellness issues. For example, there is a brilliant one put out by Kathleen Crowler. So here is a service that they could purchase for $15, $20, whatever it is. For $19.95 they could sign up as a preferred client and not only do they get this periodical, but they also get a card, a magnet that they stick on the refrigerator. It could have your name, their name, preferred client status, your ID# and your 4 digit pin # that you were assigned as a standard pin # for somebody who is buying products at a 5%, 10%, 15%, 20% discount off of your web site.

1:08:55

So now they have the information and they can just log on and go straight through to your web site. Some are not going to do that by themselves, but once in a while you can keep them informed about something. Now they are your preferred clients and they did not have to buy into becoming a wholesale distributor. I love what Beverley Ford said. She wondered if we realize how many people we've sold a $100 pair of mag steps to because we sell them a sales kit, and then we sell them mag steps. So instead of buying a $50 pair of mag steps, or two mag steps, we sell them sales kit so that they buy the mag steps wholesale. Why not just sell them the mag steps and give them the wholesale price? It's twice the volume—you double your volume overnight. In our mind we think, maybe these people will convert. Ever the optimist. The obvious is so obvious, but not obvious to us. Why? Why build your business on chance or luck? Why perpetuate the myth that there is such a thing as **LUCK**—**L**abor, **U**nder, **C**orrect, **K**nowledge.

1:10:08

We invented the word luck to describe the effects of unknown causes. Why not just become competent and create a business of choice, rather than hope and pray that somebody might decide to join you, they might do something, they might sponsor somebody if that day comes . . . and, if that day does come we can deal with it. In the meantime, why not deal with what it is reality.

1:10:52

I am sure there are many things I have not covered as yet. But we only have so much time at our disposal through this program. I believe we've got around two 90 minute tapes. That is probably, roughly, as good as it needs to be.

1:11:12

This is a presentation that you can begin to present in private and as you begin to learn new things and start to apply some of these things, the results of which are going to give you big, big, returns. This concept is one I want you to embrace . . . this "think like the owner of a business" that you really respect and cherish and value preferred clients. That is the business I want to build, if Nikken wants to build it or not, I am going to build it. And if they don't put the support in, I will put the support system in. I will not wait for them and so if you see what I see in terms of value, you will start thinking about and building it as well . . . and the mechanism will come, it will follow.

1:11:52

That is the business of the business and I hope this has helped to shift your mind set a little bit as to the reason why and what we are doing. We started at the top and worked our way down; most importantly, we have to extend ourselves. How do I invite somebody, to be a part of this? Perhaps now you will understand why we needed to cover all of this, because now you have an understanding of the size and the magnitude of what we have done. In the month you earned $3.3 million or $3.5 million dollars, what did you personally do?

1:12:36

You have been working with your 6 leaders, to help them in the building of their business. That's what you have been doing which, by the way, I have learned—**if I teach this first level to be competent and I help the second generation become competent, and I help the third generation become competent . . .** meaning I am working with my first level to build two more generations of competence. So, I am teaching the first level. It does not end with you.

1:13:12

Let's make sure we get the second one together. Let's make sure we get the third one together. What if I taught the second generation to teach 3 levels down, and the third generation to teach 3 levels down . . . **by insuring three generations of competence, I guarantee 6 generations of competence.** So really where is my business? This is where I am working (top 2 generations only), there are way too many people 6 levels down for one person, but if I work at building competence and help them understand what that means, by building those tap roots one after the other, three legs, that is 6 x 3 = 18 people. Could you manage that? Working through 18 people?

1:14:01

I get requests constantly. However, I operate according to principle not according to requests. **I am not looking to service everybody's request.** *I am looking to build a business that can service everybody's request . . .* big difference. Now, *that is a mind* set.

Now, getting back to the main point. By the way, the main point was in that month—$3.5 **million. I am helping 10, these 18 people and I am servicing 10 people. Is that too much to ask from somebody who is making $3.5 million dollars a month?**

1:14:44

Honestly, we have people at the top of the ladder who think they should kick back and do nothing for their rest of Nikken life. They have lost complete touch with why they joined Nikken in the first place and how they earn what they earn. We are not here to retire. That is not the reason we came into this business. This business never dies. These businesses die when that person dies, this one never dies, if you build this right, this one will go on for your next generation, and the next generation and their generations and so forth. You are not here to retire.

We are here to build a business. That is why you are here. So, I don't know what you have been "sold" up until now, but I hope we helped to set you straight and that it might help you in a big way.

1:15:32

Getting back to getting people to listen and join you in your business. Understand that you have a big "tower" to build and you need help. So, you might say, "Bruce, I've come across something really big. It's so huge. I know it is over my head." And, Bruce is probably thinking—yeah, it is way over your head. But then you say, "Bruce I think it's got the opportunity to help millions of people." Now, if that mattered to him, is that the kind of person you want . . . where something like that would matter to him? Yes!

1:26:05

This thing has the potential of helping millions of people; it has already proven itself in countries around the world. I could really use your help. I know you like to help people/ I've seen it the way you are with me and others and I really respect and admire that about you. For that reason I would like you to help . . . if nothing more than to just review this and lead me in the direction you think I should be going. But I would rather you did it with me.

1:16:40

You could approach anybody with that . . . anybody who you saw as bigger and better and bolder than you. In your mind, you can perceive others who are more capable, more financially savvy, but if that person did not care about helping people, would you find out quickly? Yes! And is that somebody you want? Probably not. They might review it and say, "Hey I appreciate it and this sounds like a good business, but it is not for me." And you might think—OK, they saw it and I guess it did not go anywhere. Think about it for a moment. You may want to ask the person, "I came to you because I am asking for help. I realize it might not be for you and you articulated that it is not for you, but would you help me? Tell me who you think I should be talking too."

1:17:34

Could you say that? Could you rightfully and respectfully request that they help you? And if they said they agreed they would help you, and you stated it up front that it may not be for them but they might know somebody . . . might that work? If you came to them with the vision that I just presented to you, do you think that they are going to think it's small potatoes or peanuts? If you got them on the phone with some of the board of directors that you have, and brought them to a presentation so that they could "kick the tires" and look at it and be sure it's for real . . . do you think there are going to look at this in a small way?

1:18:01

You are here because you need help. You need help from up-line and you need help to create what it is you have in mind to create, if what you think you have in mind to create needs help or warrants help. If your vision is not big enough, why not surround yourself with a bunch of incompetent people who whine and complain so that you can baby-sit, then you could feel important. If that is what your idea of helping people on this planet is all about, well I guess you saw *something,* but it certainly wasn't what I think Mr. Masuda had in mind. So, what is your idea of helping people? What is your idea of building a business and helping people? I hope it has changed and now you realize, more than ever, how much you need help, and why it is OK to ask for it.

1:18:58

The Plan That Gets Big Results—Part 1

:21

This is specifically geared to Silvers and above. So, if you're not Silver, this will still be good training for you. The reason why it's specifically for Silvers and above is because I've made some assumptions that en route to Silver, you may have gotten "beaten" up emotionally. You had some excitement . . . you had some achievements . . . you at least had some. So, you've had a little ego bruising, but you've learned some. Now you have got a better appreciation for the business having gone through that explosive learning curve that takes place going from zero to hero in your process of going Silver.

1:03

For those who are not Silver, what I'm going to share will give you some structure. I think you are going to get a really good level of understanding of how to apply these concepts to your business. But, I'm not going to be talking to you where you are at in your understanding of the business, I'm going to be focusing my talk on people who have been around this business for a while.

So, let's say you have been promoted; you are at least Silvers and you have been working the business for a while. **Now, you really want to "get your teeth" into this business and really get it hopping. Are you at that point?**

1:37

I've covered a lot of things on the previous two videos. One was called **"What I've Learned."** It's excellent! If you haven't, got it you must. It will definitely add some light to what I am going to share with you today.

2:02

There is a set of videos called **"The Missing Link."** These are what I consider **to be the future of the business model for our business**

"The Missing Link." It's very key information. I personally am excited about The Missing Link," because for me, it's been a missing link.

I've been at this business for just over a decade and I think that I've made a study of this business, in my building of the business. I've really focused on creating **an awareness of the business and modifying it and innovating it . . .** not because there is something wrong with it, but because there isn't, **but it can always be improved.** I think that is human nature—to improve upon our circumstance and to improve upon our environment. And, since I've chosen Nikken to be my career, my home, I want to make home improvements. When was the last time you redecorated your home? Probably for most, it's been awhile . . . maybe even 10 years!

3:18

For now, we're going to talk about a couple of concepts. One that I specifically want to focus on is how to turn **the rhythm of the business** (which has been discussed at many levels in many different environments)—how to **turn those ideas into application . . .** how **to take a business approach, a business model and apply it to your network marketing business.** I've actually covered this material previously in a very abbreviated version because I didn't have the time at my leisure to talk more about it then, but now I want to give it the dedication and commitment it deserves.

4:02

I've just come back from Europe and also had a great trip to Australia where I had a lot of time to really elaborate on this subject. So, I felt I needed to cover the same ground (albeit an abbreviated version) and make it available to everyone.

4:28

I've been doing this business on purpose, pretty much the whole time that I have been at this business. My first month in Nikken was an explosive month. I was not alone nor would I suggest anybody build their business alone. Bo Tanas was one of the people building the business with me in that first month and I say with me because we were building it together side by side. Even though Bo is technically in my down-line, that is not how it was when we first got started.

4:59

In our mind, we really didn't have up-line or down-line. He was just as new in this as I was and there was very little that I could teach him and visa versa. We were both brand spanking new so we were virtually working side by side. **The key ingredient** to getting a good start in the business is getting a good pre-start, **pre-launch** before you actually go into launch mode. We are going to talk about that, but before I do, let me digress for a moment. I want to talk about a month where Nikken had a "two for one" sale on the sleep system.

5:40

Did you see an explosive month in your business? Actually, it was the biggest in the company's history. I believe I was told they had **sold the equivalent of four year's worth of sleep systems in one month.** Pretty neat. My check for that month was $303,000 . . . not a bad little month. I really would like to do that again—so would you I'm sure! But rather than just be impressed by our results, I think it is worth looking at **what caused those results** because it's going to play on what we talk about and getting a launch going in this business.

6:28

Since you have already launched your business, this is not so much about you re-launching it but it's about—what do you do, now that you have found somebody or a group of people who really want to make something of this as a business. **How can you get involved in launching their business with some predictability and what can you do repeatedly so that you can hold my skill as an expert, as a master launcher of businesses.**

6:59

That is really what I see myself as. *I see myself as somebody who plays a role in helping others launch their business. Yes, they are part of mine and they are part of Nikken's, but my role in this is not only attracting them but in launching them* and giving them the best start that they can have.

Again, I'm presuming you have already launched your business. You can't do that again, but you can learn from that and you can now apply that skill and hone that skill to make it better and better for the next person you sponsor, with the hope that maybe you might break some of your own records, which always remains a personal challenge for me! To do it I do it better and better the next time.

7:36

In that "two for one" month, Nikken had generated phenomenal sales. I believe that some of what caused that growth was the **alignment of people's belief systems.** I'll bet that you really believe in the products at this point in time. Seeing as you are Silver and have been exposed to Nikken for several months, I'm pretty sure your belief in the products is unshakable and that you really realize the value that these products can bring to people. So, **your belief system about the products is right up there at 100%.**

8:23

If I asked you to do something contrary to your beliefs, I would probably be met with some resistance. There might be some second guessing, there might be some doubt, there might be some reservation. And, rather than applying yourself 100%, you might apply yourself 10 or 20%, or you might kind of test it. You might see whether this really works or not. You might not jump into it, and my guess is that for most people who get started in this business, their belief system about the business is very small. First, they may have had no experience in this type of business. I'm talking about the business of network marketing. Furthermore, they might actually be in the negative (10 or 20 points) on the point scale, because they have been exposed to it in some way previously. Maybe in the past or in various ways they have been exposed to it and it has not measured up to their level of what they thought it should be or what a business should be.

9:17

So, in fact, they may be starting in the basement rather than on the ground floor. One of the very first things we need to do in building our business and I want to clarify what I mean by **building the business. There** is a very **big difference in building a business and helping people. These are two very different things.** Helping people with the products is something you can do and you can do it one at a time, and you can do it very effectively. You can have a blast doing it. But building a business is not about doing that, **it is about building an organization that helps people. Building a business is about everybody doing a little bit that adds up to a lot, rather than you doing a lot.**

10:01

Do you understand the difference? A lot of people get confused because at the very beginning of the business most gravitate to the products. Your beliefs are locked into the products at the very beginning and so your tendency is to talk about the products and to go **looking for people who you can help with the products. That is not building the business . . . that is simply doing Nikken.** You will hear that term used frequently. A person will say, "I'm doing the business." Yes, that is "doing" the business, but it is not **building the business.** So, you want to be very clear on what that is especially when you're at the point where you are launching somebody brand new.

10:42

Let's go back to the story of Nikken's "two for one" sleep system sale. I believe what happened was many of us who really believe in these products and know that, although all the products are beneficial, there is one product that I personally like and I'm sure you will agree it is the product that influences people more than any other product, is the sleep system. So, when Nikken did the special on the sleep system, were they working with or against your belief system? Absolutely with

your belief system. You already knew the product was a good product and you already believed that whatever the price was, that the product was a good product for the price it is, but when they cut the price two for one double the value—that really rang a bell in your mind because of the outstanding value. It was an outstanding value and you got to take advantage of it. You had to let people know about it. You had to get out there and inform people. All of a sudden, it broke down all the barriers about talking to people . . . all those **barriers came down. Why? Because you are talking to people about something you really believe in, you emphatically believe in.**
11:35

12:03

It magnified your belief because now you knew, not only was it an invaluable product, but it was an exceptional value and you **went way out of your comfort zone** and way out of your way to tell people about it. And, because of your enthusiasm and because you saw an opportunity to make the most of the situation yourself, all of a sudden there were **more people to talk to in a short period of time.** Here is what also happened . . . according to Nikken's recruiting statistics, they also recruited more people in that month than any other month. Isn't that an interesting correlation?

12:36

Now **what's building the business? Recruiting people. Recruiting people into your organization, so that they can start their own independent wellness consulting business**—that's building the business, by building your organization. What's interesting is that the by-product of your enthusiasm, the by product of your excitement which was totally in alignment with your belief system was the fact that you became excited and when you became excited, you excited others. It's that kind of thing that happens . . . **people want to be around people who are excited** . . . people want to be around people who are going some place . . . people want to be around people who have got passion in their life . . . and the result of that was: people just want to be part of this, whatever "this" is.

13:22

These people did not have any comprehension of what this business was all about. They probably just got excited and so we had this incredible month, an absolutely incredible month. It was amusing to me that the very next month I was in conversation with some of the Royal Diamonds and they wanted to do a recruiting promotion. I found that quite humorous because the biggest month's volume in the history of the company came not with a recruiting promotion but with a product promotion. What does that tell you about learning from your mistakes? We always learn and continue to learn from our mistakes. So, the bottom line is working with our belief system, this is something I called **cause-oriented marketing**.

14:08

Let me give you an example and paint a **picture** for you. We are going to use this in our launch strategy because when I look at **the most successful launches** I've ever had, at the root of it there was something, **there was a cause.** There was something that we bought into as a team, as a collective, that just really got us out of our comfort zones, that pushed us beyond our own personal desires, our own personal rewards. So, let's talk about cause-oriented marketing for a while.

Focus Beyond the Board

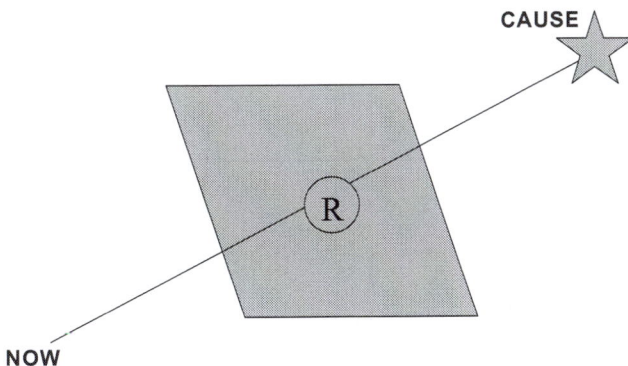

Diagram 11

14:46

Let's say that is a board. Have you ever done the board-breaking exercise? It's like a karate exercise. You take a one inch board and snap it, you break it with your hand your hand goes right through the board. The key to breaking the board is looking beyond the board. Brian Biro's book "Beyond Success" explains it perfectly. That is exactly what he refers to in his book and how I interpret that. If I want "this" to happen,. my focus must be "ahead" of it, my mind must be focusing on what I should be thinking. I've got to be thinking out of the box, beyond the goal.

15:41

So, if I turn my attention to the board, what happens in the process of attempting to break the board? It's called eye—hand coordination. Well, in the law of physics or the universal laws, **you create what you think about,** what you think about most. Your most dominant thoughts are manifested into reality. When you take your focus off your vision . . . you lose sight of what you want and start to think about all those things you don't want. The **key to achievement is to stay focused beyond the achievement** and in the marketing world I call this cause-oriented marketing.

16:20

Let me explain. What is the cause that we can focus our attention on? It's going to be "that cause" that gets us **to perform in a certain way and do certain things. The result of which is . . . we penetrate . . . we break the board.** That's the consequence, not the cause, not the motive.

Without exaggeration, I've used this example a thousand times before. Whenever I talk about breaking **Silvers, I mention that "Silver should never be the objective," it should be the consequence.**

17:10

The objective should never be Silver, it should be the consequence if you want to assure yourself of breaking more Silvers. There are a lot of people who set their goal to go Silver. In fact, they are erroneously taught to set their goal that way, and I would like to give you a new way of thinking about this. Go beyond Silver. Nobody wants to get into this business to go Silver. I can assure you, nobody signs up to go Silver . . . they don't even know what that means. They don't even know what the experience means until they've gone through the experience. It's just a thought . . . it's just a word. In fact, that word "Silver" does not even cause a picture to enter your mind. What do you picture when you say the word Silver?

17:46

Silver! When I think of Silver, I think of fashion jewelry or something like that. Silver, for most people, does not mean what it means to us having gone through the experience of reaching Silver. And, yet we place that expectation on people without really realizing that they don't know what the heck we are talking about. And, there is no way this new person can follow instructions about something they don't believe and they can't possibly believe, because they don't know what we are talking about.

18:10

So *if we do not work with their belief system and if we work against their belief system, we create this friction or this resistance that we may not even be conscious of. And, the results are that people attempt to do the business and they do the work—whatever that means—and they do the business—whatever that means—and they get results, but those results are never consistent with what we are desiring*, rarely consistent.

18:39

So, how do we apply this in a way that produces monumental results, we will come back to in a moment. Let me give you some statistics, some interesting information. I really believe in the value of this information! There are a lot of people who think that the key to success in this business is to just go out and talk to a lot of people.

19:20

I'm sure you know that **you can say the wrong thing to a lot of people and get absolutely nowhere. Let's agree there's a better way.** Yes, there is an important component in talking to a lot of people because that is the business we are in communications, but **if you don't know what to communicate**—or how to communicating it, what you are conveying may not produce the results you are looking for.

19:37

There is a lot of truth to what you are being taught, but there are also some things that are being overlooked, things that sometimes are valuable little gem stones.

Let me give you an example. There's a group that I'm much more familiar with than some of the others of course. I referred to Marty Jeffery's story previously and I may refer to it again but I had another opportunity to experience the launch procedure first hand that I want to share with you.

20:02

However, this time it was unique because the couple I was working with was not personally sponsored by me. So, I did not have the same kind of rapport that I had with someone I personally sponsored. Secondly, they live in Australia as opposed to a short flight away where I might possibly get to a few times in a month. So, it was a long distance group that I was working with and these people, as people go, were not the epitome of success when it came to business. They were great in what they did. One was a massage therapist, one was a consultant a personal consultant as far as life experiences and the like. They were not business people as we consider business people . . . a la Marty Jeffery.

21:00

So it was a real opportunity for me to validate myself . . . maybe for the world . . . to see if this process really can produce consistent results.

This process **being building a game plan and following the game plan to the best of our ability and producing results . . . results that anybody can be proud** of. By the way, they had a pre-launch (and I will talk about what that all means) and they went into a 90 day launch procedure.

21:30

Their 90 day launch procedure was September, October, and November in 2000. So, they launched in September 2000. Their volume starts in October, because technically you could not buy anything in September all they could do was register people by handing in application forms in the month of September . . . but it was part of their three month activity, whether they can buy products or not. So, in September their volume was zero because they could not order anything on the first day of September. They were Silver as a consequence of the people who signed in and purchased products.

22:25

Now, it's interesting. In October they could only buy one product (the demo pack); they could not buy anything else. This couple was really limited, unlike us. They were really limited in what they could actually do. Take note, there's something interesting to be learned from this. Maybe giving people too much to do or giving people too much to think about is not what we want. In fact, **maybe what we should do is not tell new people in the business everything. Maybe** we should tell people only what they really need to know and **maybe *we* should be the ones who know.**

22:25

That, in itself, is a paradigm. I believe in training but I believe in giving people what they need to know, when they need to know it and not before so you can keep them focused on doing the little bit that they can do and that they understand. We will touch on that as well later. So, on their first day they went Silver. By the end of the first month (October), they had 62,037 points. They did 60K and they broke a couple of Silvers.

23:25

It's important to note they had done their 60K by the 11th or 12th of October based on all the momentum that built up. People were allowed to order a sleep system, so that's the only thing that changed . . . was people were now allowed to order individual sleep systems. We're allowed to do that here. So, guess what they ordered? Sleep systems. Plus, they had sponsored more people. The momentum was building and by the end of November (remember September was zero, October was 62,037 points, November 208,526 points), which was their third month, their combined two month volume was 278,564 points. They had 193 distributors only having personally sponsored 18. Remember that number . . . they had 12 Silvers in their team, 6 of which who were front line. They completed two successful "21 Clubs" and of course two Paragon Awards. Their first month commission check for October was $10,587.00. Their commission check for November was $28,600.00 and that was not their best month.

24:40

That just gives you an idea of what launching somebody can do if it is done in a calculated and orchestrated way and you've got willing participants. I admit, I certainly was as willing as they were but they did not have the benefit of knowing what I knew, but they were willing to do what they were being told to do. That is not the only time I've seen that happen. I've experienced this a couple of times and that is not to dismiss the "grunt" work (that's what we call the work that has to get done—**you've got to do back rolls, you've got to do meetings, you've got to get out there and talk to people).** All that is true and all that happened but I was involved with that launch strategy for ten days and that increased my income $20,000 per month.

25:31

So, I'm talking about **applying yourself in a very specific way.** By following through on these instructions—now, does that sound like a business to you? If I opened up a McDonald's, or if *I called McDonald's and said I'd like to start a McDonald's restaurant, do you think they might give me some statistics? Do you think they might be able to tell me,*

"Here is what you do. Here is what you can expect based on our market survey, our demographics. Here is the kind of income you are going to be generating." Do you know by now, I bet McDonald's are within 5% of their predictions, they are probably so phenomenally accurate.

26:17

So many of the things you already know—it just has to get done. It's about getting it done in a certain way. There is a book called **"The Science of Getting Rich."** You can order it through LifeSuccess Productions, Bob Proctor's organization (www.antonioraimondo.lifesuccessconsultants. com). In that book, a little green book, the message is loud and clear . . . it's not what you do . . . a lot of people are "doing" Nikken . . . **it's the way you do what you do, that's the difference.**

26:44

There are a lot of Nikken Wellness Consultants but there are only a handful of Royal Diamonds. The point of the matter is **the people who excel in the business, they are all doing Nikken, but they are doing Nikken in a "certain way."** It is my advice to you to figure out what that "way" is . . . perfect it. Or, maybe don't perfect it, but get better at it. Keep educating yourself so that you can get better at it, so that you can **become a master at launching and sponsoring and breaking Silvers.**

27:18

You might even find yourself breaking Gold in a month. I'm sure you know of people who have done that. Platinum will be the next challenge breaking platinum in a month. It's possible . . . you apply the principles exactly the same way . . . exact same principles . . . only the numbers are just a little bigger at the beginning.

So, **how does that relate to cause-oriented marketing?**

27:48

In Australia, I had the benefit of focusing all these people to one cause. What was the cause? **Launch Australia!** Now, that is an easy thought, everybody can understand that. Launch in a new country; an opportunity for us to put a proven commodity to market. If I had been the first owner of a McDonald's in Australia, knowing the history of McDonald's, do you think I would have had any doubt my investment was sound? No! So, it's really easy to sell the launch of a new country by contrast to maybe starting in a market that has been around for ten or twelve years. But, I've got news for you. Guess what the market penetration of Nikken in Australia was before? Before Nikken started in Australia, they maybe had a few customers with a market penetration of 0%.

28:47

We're the envy of the world when it comes to marketing the biggest consumer-oriented market in the world, the North American population. What is our market penetration in North America? That means if you added up every single human being who ever put their name on a Nikken application form or an order form of any sort, what would be our market penetration? It's approaching 1%. So, is Australia any more a ground floor opportunity than North America? It's an important point, because this is what a business person would look at . . . not a network marketing person. If you have been in a networking industry, this is what you would be taught. This is the paradigm you have been operating under and what you think is true.

30:05

You may be thinking, "Yeah, but this guy has been around for ten years!" You may even go out and try to get your next fix and your next fix is to sign up with a brand new network marketing company that nobody knows about. Guess what? Nobody knows about us even as much as people know. We're virtually unknown. And, you would be hard-pressed to find anybody who has heard of Nikken, let alone what Nikken does. And, most have not heard about magnetic energy, they don't even know what that it is because they've never tried it, if they've even heard about it.

30:43

You would be pretty hard-pressed to find a population of people who really know about what it is we do. That population is infinitely small, and even at that percentage . . . how many really, really know what we do? How many people sign up just to buy the products wholesale? About 80 or more percent of this population, probably even more than that. And, are those people actually in the business, doing the business? How many of them really know? I'm sure you're getting the point.

31:16

The truth of the matter is: where does the "ground floor" need to be for this to be as golden an opportunity here in North America as opposed to anywhere in the world? Anywhere! So what makes us so excited about launching Australia? Because **we think it's new!** We hook into some idea . . . remember, we believe **we operate according to our beliefs** . . . and because we think it's new, we act like it's new. What do you do when you have a brand new shining car in the parking lot? Have you noticed that the older the car gets, the fact that it's dirty doesn't bother you.

31:53

But when it is brand new, it's got to stay clean every day! **It's just perception it's just our own mind playing tricks** on us. It's just perception. You know for anyone who has never had a car before, I'm sure they would be pretty excited about your dirty Mercedes or your dirty anything. Take your dirty car and put it in Africa and see how excited they get.

32:29

I'm quite serious. We have a distorted perspective and **the key to success in business is to remain objective.** That is the key to success in business . . . in this or in any other business. The key is to remain objective and not subjective. Don't allow yourself to be influenced by your own thinking. Allow yourself to be influenced by those around you only to gain perspective. That's when your thinking actually has value. You can fool yourself into believing anything. So, I went to the outside world and I started looking at whether these statistics mean anything. What I concluded was what I'm sharing with you.

33:10

Nikken is just as ripe for the picking in North America as ever before and **we have an advantage in North America** that they don't have anywhere else. First of all, we all speak **one language.** That helps, it really does. 400 million people who speak the same language makes a big difference when it comes to marketing. You know the biggest challenge they have in Europe is trying to figure out what the person next to them is talking about (because of language) . . . and you don't have to go very far to not know what the person next to you is talking about. So, we have a very big commodity and that is a population who all speak the same language and who are experiencing the **same cultural effects,** the **same mental effects,** the same emotional effects, and the same paradigms. We are all aging. We are all at that point in time where we're **recognizing the importance and the relevance of wellness.**

34:04

The point I want to make is that perspective is so important, objectivity is so important and aligning your belief systems with what I am talking about is going to be so important for you be able to get out of your comfort zone, to get out of the box and really attack this thing with the kind of passion that it warrants. I was in a conversation with a fellow in Australia and by the end of it he said, "Boy, there is going to be quite a few long nights." I said, "Well, you can have 90 days of long nights or you can have the rest of your life of long days . . . you decide." It doesn't matter what the excuse is, you should only be **interested in results—that is objectivity—results-oriented activities. That's objective!**

35:19

What I've learned very distinctly is—*I can't get people to do what I want them to do unless I get them to do what they want to do, and if it happens to be in alignment, then I will get what I want them to do but keep them focused on doing what they want to do.*

I know for sure that nobody is coming into the business to become a Silver. I know that for sure. So, why would I sell them on going Silver? Why would I talk to them about going Silver? It has no relevance, no importance, no significance . . . it's not going to get them to have those long nights or miss bowling nights so they can come to a Wellness Preview! It's just not going to get them out of their box. It's got to be in alignment with what they really, really get excited about, so the **first thing I need to know is what they are excited about?** What would get them out of the box?

There are a couple of great questions we need to ask.

36:14

What could your Nikken business provide you and your family that no other business or career could?

That's a vision statement exercise: **What could your Nikken business provide you and your family that no other business or career could?** What a great question. Wouldn't that help somebody really help put Nikken in the right perspective in terms of their priorities? We could find out what this business could give them that no other business could give them, that no other career could give them. What is important to them? What are their beliefs? What are their values? You've got to **align your cause with values.**

36:47

If I want to get anybody to do anything, especially if it's going to be something that's going to take work (they're probably already working). So you've got to make sure that you are clear on what it is what you are doing with people. You know Nikken is one of those situations where the results are delayed . . . it's that exponential growth curve, it kind of kicks in and all of a sudden you wonder where it was all along. With the couple in Australia, it was very clear as to what their core values were. Just look at their occupations one was a massage therapist, a person who is physically helping people through their stress and emotions and so forth. The other person was dealing with people on an emotional, psychological level. It was obvious these were caring people who really wanted to help people. Clearly, that is what they are motivated by.

2 **What could your Nikken business provide society that no other business or career could?**

38:02

Asking a person this question is about having the person dig down and discover what they see in Nikken and whether Nikken's cause is a worthy cause to them. Is it worthy of their life; is it a worthy ideal and is it worth them taking the time and making the effort, going the extra mile and doing all the things that big results require. Is Nikken really something worth doing? You've got to ask those questions, because if you don't have those conversations with people, you are making assumptions that they are excited about this for your reasons and you can never tap into the cause that is going to really get them go out of the gate in a frenzy.

38:55

I want to know what makes them tick. I want to know where their values are, I want to know if they have related them to this business . . . to the creation, to what we are about to do.

39:08

If they haven't, then this will just be a "doing" exercise and they already have a ton of things to do. They've got to take the shopping out of the car, get the dirty clothes to the cleaners, pick up the kids from school. They already have so many things to do in a day! We do not want this to be another one of those things. We want this to be "front and centre stage," priority number one when it comes to activity and result-oriented activity. It's got to take a lot of focus.

So we've talked about cause! Let's go back to the situation in Australia. Their **cause** was pretty clear. They wanted to **help people** and they wanted to help people in a big way. So, what they were given and what we were presenting was the idea that they could make a huge impact in Australia.

39:54

These two could be responsible for creating the wave that puts Nikken on the map in Australia having understood and appreciated the value—what Nikken and the Nikken technology can offer people. That is a pretty big vision; it's a pretty big cause. Now, one of two things is going to happen. They might shrink because the vision is so big and overwhelming that it frightens them into inactivity . . . and as a sponsor or somebody who is about to invest their time and energy—I want to know what they are made of.

40:26

If they shrink, that just reinforces that I will operate with them with much less of a priority. They are going to fall low in my priority with people I'm going to work with. Or, they might rise to the occasion if it excites them. If you start to see a twinkle in their eyes, you know Nikken business inspires these people and now I've got something I can work with. If they are not inspired, there is nothing there. ·

41:00

So, it was important to figure out where they were coming from and then to tie them into the company, into the business, into the vision and what we are about to do. Here is another scenario to contrast this one and it just shows you how different situations can be. Again, it's easy to relate this to launching a country.

41:20

Back in 1994, two years after we had launched Canada, I had the pleasure and privilege of sponsoring a guy by the name of Marty Jeffery. What an experience this has been for me the entire time, and still continues to be. But, in that opening sequence of events, implicitly understanding what I'm about to share with you is critical. I say implicitly, because I was not nearly as conscious of it as I am today. But, implicitly, I knew that we needed a cause to attract these people into our business and I don't know if I got that from Marty or Marty got that from me. It doesn't matter. The bottom line is: from the very moment we started **promoting Nikken in Brandon, Manitoba, we talked about setting a world record.**

42:05

We talked to the Brandon people about setting a world record right there in Brandon, Manitoba. As Marty would say, "the geographic centre of trade in the world, the economic centre of trade in North America!"

But think about what we were doing for this group of people in Brandon, Manitoba. Do they exist in Brandon, Manitoba? Yes. Does much news come out of Brandon, Manitoba? No, it doesn't. So here is an opportunity for these people, who otherwise live a pretty routine life, to do something different, something extraordinary that could be the talk of the town. Maybe it was for a week, maybe it was a month . . . who cares! They were in it for the party.

42:55

They wanted to get involved with something that could excite them and inspire them. We were able to inspire them to a cause and the cause was based on their beliefs about being nationalistic, or as they would say, "Brandonistic." Whatever it was, they were excited about being members of Brandon and we were reinforcing that idea into their mind before it was the real thing. We were pumping it into their head and we were saying, "This is what we are going to do." And what we were basically stating is: with or without your involvement, we were

206   The Science of the Nikken Business

going to put Nikken on the map in Brandon, Manitoba. We are going to set a world record right here with your involvement. You can be one of those people. How do you think that would make them feel?

43:33

This is what happened. I remember anytime anybody ordered products or signed up a new person, whether they followed the system or not, they felt like, somehow, they were contributing to that little cause . . . they were somehow contributing to putting Brandon on the map!

43:54

It was **the cause, I think, that was the underlying thing that really motivated people**. The thing that holds them together is that cause and you might say that it could not have mattered as much as making money. And yes, all of that stuff plays a role. But I've seen this business done without a cause and I've seen this business done with a cause and the difference is huge in terms of results in a short period of time. The difference is huge, so you want to tap into it. This idea means when you sponsor somebody new, you need to figure out **what is the cause, what is going to get these people out of the box?** What are their core values that we tie back to the business. Have we put them in the driver seat of the business that is making those values and projecting those values out into the world? Is their business going to have value? Is it going to make a difference in the lives of other people?

44:47

If that matters to them, then what about a cause that will bring other members into their group? We were able to recruit people to this cause. A lot of marketing today has really taken on this flavor where they are asking you to buy into a cause. For instance a lot of charitable organizations are solely based on this concept that you donate your time or you donate your money or you donate your products or you buy tickets to the circus for this cause. That is called cause-oriented marketing and it is big business.

45:28

I suggest you start thinking about your cause. I'm not giving you answers. I'm going to give you questions so that you can start asking yourself questions. What is the cause? What is your cause? A lot of you have been in this business for a while. What **has taken you so long to get to Royal Diamond** is what I'd like to know! I can tell you what it is **you have not tapped into a cause bigger than yourself. You are being limited by yourself.** This business is worthy of every ounce of effort you have because many, many thousands of people can benefit from you getting out of your comfort zone. And guess who is the first person who is going to benefit you guessed it YOU.

46:19

I love what Bob Proctor said:

> "You are either going up or you are coming down.
> Because there "ain't" anything in between."

And if you are not going up, you are on your way down. So get going, get on it, start to get hooked into this thing. Why is Nikken getting so important to the world? Why? Who else is offering total wellness? Tell me who?

46:48

Tell me what *other organization on this planet is offering total health?* Who does not want total health? Who doesn't need total health? You may argue that their methods are a little **strange; who cares! The results are what matters are we getting results?**

47:06

With your help the results will be a lot better than without your help, but either way we are getting it. So make your decision about what your cause is. Start thinking in terms of factors like cause; that is what gets people locked into doing stuff, into getting outside of their comfort zone. It is a cause that is where the passion comes from. You will not stay passionate about making money even when you are making it. Do you honestly think Bo waits for the envelope to arrive from Nikken with baited breath to see how much his check is? Honestly, do you think he even looks at his check? Not any more. Honestly you'll want to get to the point where you won't even look at your check. So the bottom line is—even this idea of making money fades.

48:19

I think Nikken's vision of the 5 pillars of health is the real thing. I think that

Vision

Nikken's vision is going to outlive all of us. Magnets may be over in 20 years. They might have invented something else; magnets may become redundant. But one thing that will never be redundant is the vision of Nikken. The 5 pillars of health is not something that becomes redundant, so it is something you can tie into, something you can plug into, something that you can articulate, something that you can get people to buy into!

48:52

Why now? That is so important in creating an explosion. Why now? Why not next month? Why now? Part of creating an explosion has to do with core values. When do they want what they say they want? **And why would you delay getting what you want?** If it's inevitable that you are going to get it, then why would you delay it? I think another thing that you have to **create in your cause is the sense of urgency.** If you can't create a sense of urgency, you cannot align people to do what you need them to do as a collective.

The Science of the Nikken Business   209

49:36

Here is an interesting thing—the experience with Marty's launch, back in Brandon. The record was 189,000 points. We had set a goal at the beginning of the month to do 200,000 points to help Marty to become a Platinum consultant in the process. That was our goal. That was our business objective and I will show you how we drafted it out. Nobody had done 200,000 points. 189,000 was what Reid Nelson did when he launched his business way back in 1989. Who were we to think that in a little tiny town of Brandon, Manitoba—population of 45,000 people that we had a chance to take down that record.

50:22

I mean think about it. But, you know everything begins with what—it's got to be a Vision. That **vision has be something that gets everybody excited.** I was excited about breaking Reid's record because I knew I could do it. Given the right chance! Given the right person! Given the right combination of things! And Marty, whose ego fortunately enough, was healthy. If he has got to do something, he wants to do it in a certain way. That's Marty. Marty has always been good at what he does. He likes to be one of the best in what he does. Then why the heck would he not want to be the best at this? So it was for him an appealing subject and so **the two of us became inspired.** Inspiration is where it all begins; the impossible begins by inspiration!

51:12

We still have to get people to buy into this idea. They are not going to buy into Marty Jeffery doing $200,000 in business and breaking the record. Who cares about Marty Jeffery? They are not going to buy into Marty Jeffery going Platinum in one month. They are not going to buy into that either. Marty Jeffery going Platinum in one month is not the cause. It had to be something where they could feel they were actually contributing to it—the cause had to be outside of him. The cause had to be a part of everyone, a cause that brings everybody together. The cause was to put Nikken on the map in Brandon, Manitoba—to raise the flag.

The Science of the Nikken Business

51:48

Here we are ten and a half years later in Canada, and you've got a brand new person. You know that this new person has a shot at doing something big. You certainly believe it. Maybe they are giving you the indicator that they believe it, now what? How are you going to bring those guns to bear so that when you **put a business plan together that it has certain activities, activities that have to get done in a certain time frame.** A business plan that is going to mean taking up a certain responsibility—that they are going to do it. They are going to get out of their comfort zone, and so are you, because **you are inspired and not only that, but you inspire others.**

52:26

I don't care what day it is, what month it is or what year it is. Nikken is going to be important in North America a hundred years from now. I can start from zero a hundred years from now and build this thing to Royal Diamond. People are doing it right in this room. Why couldn't anybody do it? Well, anybody can. Why? The reason is because Nikken came up with another product called CardioStrides. Do you know what percentage of the North American population have CardioStrides?

52:58

Every time Nikken comes out with something new it's like starting all over again. Think about it. It is getting a whole wave of involvement, a whole wave of education, a whole wave of product into the market all over again. It is like we have not done anything! The only thing that people might recognize is the name Nikken, and still they don't recognize the name Nikken. How many of you recognize the name Sony? What percentage of the population recognizes the name Sony? So you see how far we have to go before we even register on the Richter scale here in North America? That is why Nikken is such a phenomenal opportunity and why anybody can do it. Why the timing is perfect today, why it was perfect yesterday, and why it will be perfect tomorrow. But why would anybody want to do the Nikken business today—that's the key. It goes back to this—you have got to figure that out—you want to ask yourself that question?

54:11

You want to ask yourself—*when I'm launching somebody new why should it get done today?* And you know, *it may have nothing more to do with the fact that you want it done today.* Let me tell you a secret. Let me tell you with whom I have worked. I have a lot of people who love to spend time with me, talking on the phone, picking my brain. I only want to work with those people who want to work with me NOW—who are in **NOW mode.**

54:50

Do you know what now means? It means we are going at it now. I'm not doing this next month. I'm not doing this two months from now. That does not exist to me. All that exists is **now.** In fact, that is just not a statement, it's the truth. All that exists is now; tomorrow is just an idea in your mind. Yesterday is past—it no longer exists. The only thing that actually exists in reality is this very moment; it just went. This moment—it just went. This moment—it just went. Just now—that is all there is. So why would you want to think about spending time and energy in the future when all there is, is **now.** Now is the only time you can make anything happen anyway—and by the time that happens—the future happens, it's actually the present, it's now. So even then it's going to be now—so why not make it now.

55:39

Think about it. It's the truth. I want to get you thinking about this concept. This idea is something you've got to take some time to think about. You have to think about somebody you are about to work with. Put that person in your mind and start asking yourself these questions. Have I had that conversation? Do I know where they are coming from? Have I made the relationship between them, the business they are about to build and the value that it is going to create, and what they hold in value? What do they want from this business? What can this business do for them that no other business can? If they don't make this a priority, they never will.

The Science of the Nikken Business

56:16

There are all kinds of people doing Nikken, **but who is getting the lifestyle that Nikken promises?** It is not people who are "doing Nikken," **it is the people who are building the business.** And there is that distinction again. Now we want to talk about building the business. Before we leave this "cause" concept, let me take you back to the story of the biggest month we had in Nikken. For me it was a validation to the cause theory, having seen that explosive growth and so forth because of working with people's belief systems, working in alignment with their belief systems, getting them to do what they already believe is relevant.

57:01

I was sitting with Kendall Cho, Nikken's former CEO. Were you around when Nikken came out with the billion-dollar challenge? Do you remember what that incentive was? The incentive was geared toward recruiting seniors and the Paragon Award. The incentive was about recruiting seniors and a recognition program. It was a reward program for recruitment. It was a recruitment incentive. That incentive idea fell flat on its face, and I can tell you exactly why. Because you don't recruit for the sake of recruiting.

57:39

There is something very interesting about Nikken people. Even though we may have a great desire to build the business and a great desire to make money, we don't recruit for the sake of recruiting. You would not have been attracted to Nikken. You would not even be reading or watching this program if there was not something at a **very deep level in you that wanted to help people.** You would have been in some other network marketing company. There are a lot of "flash in the pan" network marketing companies that do a great job in recruiting greed-oriented people. But Nikken does a terrible job at recruiting greed-oriented people; they don't last very long in our business. They've come and gone because **being in this business actually means you've got to care about people** and that's the beautiful thing about our business.

58:28

As a result, **we attract very caring-oriented people.** You want to know that what you do is heartfelt, that what you do matters. Even if it means "Mag-boying" somebody, and seeing the result that happens should provide you with gratification. Whether you get the pay check or not, there is a tremendous sense of satisfaction from knowing that you are doing the right thing. I know that is true about you because I have been at this long enough to know what makes people tick in this business. It is true about this group of people—people who really are inspired to be in this business and build the business.

59:12

You are inspired to build this because something inside of you says this is the right thing to do, not just for me but, in general. So when Kendall Cho said "What do you think it is?" I said, "I think it's the biggest mistake you've ever made." You want to do a billion dollars? Here is what I would do if I was looking to do a billion dollars. I would forget the billion dollars. Who cares that you want to do a billion dollars. Congratulations Nikken—you earned a billion dollars. What the heck does that mean to me anyway?

1:00:00

I'm not interested. Nikken doing a billion dollars is not why I'm here. I'm here because I want to make a difference; I want to make a big difference. What can you give me where the consequence is a billion dollars. What can I do that is in alignment with my belief system, the result of which will produce a billion dollars? It is the consequence, not the cause. Doing a billion dollars is not a cause. Do you see that? Do you believe that? Here is what I would do. I would do a "United Way" style thermometer and I would post it in the Nikken magazine every month so each of us could see how in some small way we have contributed to the overall picture—the big picture.

1:00:49

I got the thermometer idea from you people. I was walking by Paul Peccianti's office one day and I happened to notice a thermometer and

The Science of the Nikken Business

it was goals that Nikken had set for Silver training. I thought, that is brilliant. How come we don't know about that? This story inspires me. I'll tell you something—everybody ought to know what they are inspired about. I was really inspired by the fact that they were tracking Silver training goals. I was inspired that Nikken was setting goals in the same vision that Mr. Masuda had from the very time that I was first involved in this business.

1:01:23

Mr. Masuda set goals for Silver training. He called up and found out from California what the numbers were for Silver training, not what the sales volumes were. Because Mr. Masuda inherently knew that **we, as human beings, were** more important than selling sleep systems. Silver training **goals was his measure for success.** So I asked Paul, "Why don't you put the thermometer in the magazine. I think it would help us become more conscientious about getting people to Silver training." If I knew it was that important to you, then that is inspiring to me. More people would be involved in it, and personally seeing the thermometer move, making that notch go up a little higher on the scale even though I'm just one of many distributors—well, I would be proud that I had something to do with it going higher. That approach is **cause-oriented marketing; it means that even though I'm not the issue, I'm contributing to the issue that I believe so wholeheartedly in.**

1:02:17

I said to Mr. Masuda, "You want to do a billion dollars this year? This is how I'd do it." What one product do I know? Now you've got to keep in mind, when this happened it was . . . what one product do I know that has maximum impact on Nikken's vision statement which is the 5 pillars of health? **What one product has maximum impact on each of the 5 pillars immediately—the sleep system!** That is a very practical tangible way to affect somebody's 5 pillars of health. So why don't we set a goal as a company to introduce Nikken's 5 pillars of health through our most impactful product, our premiere product—the sleep system. Let it affect the lives of one million families in North America.

1:03:11

Let's make it our goal for this year. Quickly, what is a million times a thousand? It's a billion. One million times 1,000 points wholesale is about one billion dollars.

Thermometer

Let's make a difference in the lives of 1 million people in North America.

Meter can show the number of sleep systems sold.

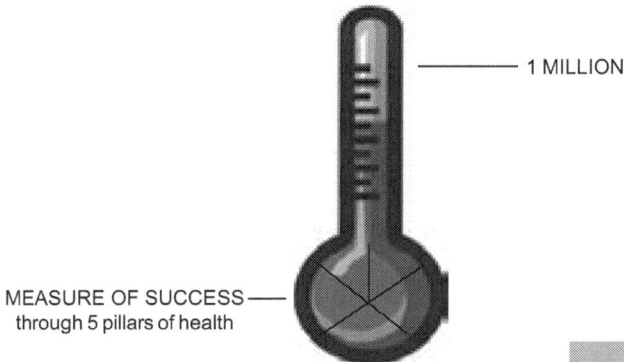

1 MILLION

MEASURE OF SUCCESS
through 5 pillars of health

Diagram 12

There you are—Nikken does a billion dollars. Doing what? Aligning itself with what's true to us. I did not get excited about the billion dollar challenge. Who could care less about a billion dollar challenge? **But I do get excited about making the difference in the lives of a million people** *especially if I knew that I could contribute to that number.*

1:03:45

Do you follow? And the same affect is true, we still do a billion dollars—only this time we actually do it because it means something to us. And every month you watch the thermometer. And, if you had sold a sleep system and you are watching the thermometer, you know that you were one of the people in that month who made the thermometer go up. Would that inspire you to do more or less? More! And this thing would start to go. What happened in the Jerry Lewis Telethon? They set a goal and you see this thing—and you wonder, they're never going to make it, and in the last 5 minutes of the show—vroom! It's like, what the heck happened?

1:04:34

Did you remember that? Do you remember how it accelerated, and accelerated, and accelerated because, guess what, even people who gave once, gave again. They see it getting closer . . . come on, we've got to get it there! I'm not in this thing to lose! I want it to go and that is what happens when you get people who are focused on something consistent with their belief system.

1:04:59

If you like this idea, I want you to do me a personal favor. If I've done anything that helped you in your business career at all, here is how you can repay me. Let Nikken know you want this, because I want this. And we will put the 5 pillars of health right at the bottom of it and we would watch it grow. And we can do that for Silver training. Offer a free Silver training for every sleep system. There are so many things that can be done when you start thinking about the cause that brought us all together in the first place.

1:05:40

The cause is Nikken. That is what makes it possible for each of us to have our own personal objectives. As long as we align ourselves to making sure that Nikken stays on the map and continues to prosper and grow, we have guaranteed ourselves our jobs. We have guaranteed ourselves our future, not for us but for our family and generations to come. As long as we do what is in Nikken's best interest, we are doing what is in our best interest. Right? Right!

1:06:07

Now, here is one really quick point about our launch strategy. *When you've got somebody you are recruiting into the business who is making money, you've got to associate your launch strategy with the kind of money they are making* because, guess what? They only get excited about making a fraction of what they are making. You can't blow the picture either by talking to them about making ten times what they are making because they don't BELIEVE it. They do not have the belief system which supports that.

1:06:45

In fact, the one way to guarantee that you blow somebody out of the water is to overpromise and under-deliver. So now what you need to be aware of is where are they at? Where are they at, what kind of money are they making and to set a goal that is tangible, practical, and achievable in a specific period of time because even if we get close to that goal, guess what that is going to do to them? It's going to cause them to get more serious, more involved in the business and really become a student of the business.

1:07:16

For the first 90 days of somebody's career in Nikken, they are a passenger. *If you are doing this right for the first 90 days of their business career in Nikken, they are a passenger in this launch of yours.* They are a participant in this launch, even though it's their business you are launching—they really are a passenger. If you want them to get really involved with the business and start becoming a student and taking others through the **process, you've got to get some success happening quickly.**

1:07:50

The first 90 days in this business are critical. I have had some great discussions with a fellow out in Australia, the managing director of Nikken in Australia, Chris Rochester, whose background was over a decade of working with people from Amway and developing strategy and stuff. This is a company that has been around some 30 plus years, 37, 38 years, and still going. Why? You think that they think they are old? They can't afford to think that they are old. Can General Motors afford to think that they are old? No! They are brand spanking new, every day, because it's with a new pair of eyes, a new vision, and new ideas that they are moving forward. Everybody is brand spanking new. What about you? Can you afford to think that you are old? Because when the mind goes everything else goes with it.

1:08:48

The other thing I want to point out is the security of someone's income is also very important. In the early days of your business, if you only managed to push that ball up to a point where you are a Silver, you are going to see huge ups and down in your income. You know they say the average income is, well, average is the best of the worst and the worst of the best. These huge spikes mean that it is not very secure. It's hard to get excited about going out there when your income is going up and down like a yo-yo. Gold still goes up and down like a yo-yo but not quite as much.

1:0926

Platinum as well. It does in all ranks, but some have a little bit more padding than others. So you want to get somebody's income up as quickly as possible. There is a good book out there written by a good friend of mine Dave Rolf. It's called "Vested Interest." You've got to get somebody to have interest, a vested interest. If all of a sudden there is money sitting there.

1:10:01

Maybe $5,000 wasn't a lot for Linda at the time, but you know it's there and you kind of wonder how the heck it got there. Maybe I should figure this out and if there is already $5,000 and I could get another $5,000 . . . and I haven't done much to get the first $5,000. Maybe if I actually apply myself, that $5,000 could turn into something interesting. Many of you would just like the first $5,000. It's all relative, it's all relative. Marty Jeffery came into this business and he was earning 3 to 4 times what I was earning as a Platinum, a good successful Platinum. I had to do something pretty significant to get this guy's attention. When I set goals, I set goals based on where he was coming from *even though I personally had not done what I was trying to do with him.*

1:10:47

How many of you feel limited by your own personal success story? **You cannot measure the potential of somebody else** and you are not repeating the past. Unless you are repeating the past you can't take what you've done and parlay it to something you've not done, based on experience. That is what evolution is all about. Evolution says I've gone this far, what can I learn from what I have done? Let me launch somebody new, only this time I have the hindsight of experience. I might be able to help them along. Don't you want that for your kids? Doesn't every one of us want our children to get further than we did? Frankly, if we base their future on what we've done, there is not much hope for humanity.

1:11:34

We want more for them. We base our expectations for them on our experiences . . . that we can give them what we've got. **Based on our experience maybe we can get them along a little further.** Based on our economic position, we are a lot better off today than we have ever been as a nation. The average income of the population in the world is going up not down. We are all moving forward, some faster than others. The **bottom line** is you've got *to get them to a place where they can identify and relate.* So when you set goals for someone in their first 90 days, set their goals in proportion to where they have come from.

1:12:12

If you stretch it too far, the elastic will break. But, if you don't stretch it enough, there is no tension in the elastic, you are not going to get emotion. Do you follow that analogy? Now I would like to show you how to do the extreme, because I figure if I can show you how to do the extreme, you can manage anything in between. Is that fair? I'm going to show you what I would do, given that I have the right willing participant, to **create a Platinum distributor in 90 days.**

1:12:53
The goal is to create a Platinum in 90 days.

How would you like to be able to at least try to create a Platinum in 90 days—at least experiment with it? What if it's not a big success? What if you try it and it does not work, or the person you are working with bails out on you. If the plan fails, you go back to the drawing board and you ask yourself,—What did I miss, did I miss anything? Do we have this figured out and so forth? Did we set the strategy up right? If I did miss, possibly I did not have the right person. They set the goal but they did not really make a committed decision. Is that my fault? No. I'm going to find the next person to try the plan on. And I will repeat the process, and on and on it goes.

1:13:34

You win some and you lose some. It does not matter, as long as you are truly in the game, you are going to hit some. Did you know that in major league baseball, players are paid millions of dollars a season to miss two out of three balls! Think about that for a moment. They are hitting one out of three and they are treated like heroes. That means they are missing two out of three and they still get paid millions of dollars. Think about that. Not even Christ tried that. He had 12 and he lost one. I mean even He is not perfect in that way. So give yourself a break when the plan doesn't work out this time. What was the question to ask them—what income level are they currently at? When someone is making two to three thousand dollars a month, then set a goal of three to five thousand dollars a month, maybe as much as five to ten thousand dollars a month. That is the kind of target I would set and focus on for the next 90 days.

1:14:43

Here is why. **If the goal is not big enough or attractive enough and if we can't tie all of the plan's parts together, if the package is not airtight, then they are going to find ways to escape.** They are going to find ways not to do it because initially they are not going to believe that they can achieve Platinum in 90 days. You are not going to inspire them, and if they are not inspired, then no matter how clear the climb is and no matter how precise it is, no matter who they are, we have to get ready to work with them. But remember, if they are not inspired, nothing happens. They have got to be inspired, so you have got to find out what inspires them. You may ask—where do people get inspired? I am not talking about **being hyped because that is dangerous too.** You can guarantee they are not going to execute the plan if you are telling them things they don't believe are achievable. You guarantee yourself they are not going to work the plan because they are going to be lying to themselves and they will be lying to you too.

1:15:42

Remember, the goal is we want to break—**Platinum in 90 days.** I told you there is a sequence of actions. First there is a **pre-launch** and then there is **a launch** which can be broken down to month one, month two and month three.

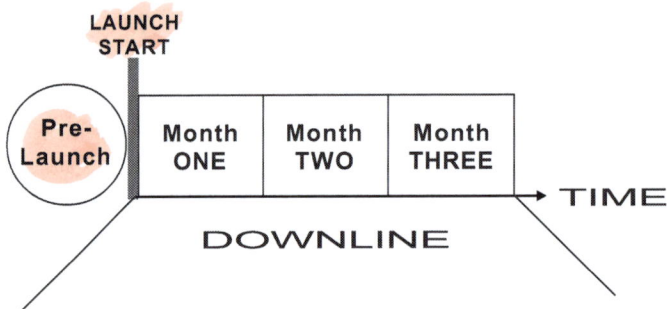

Let's imagine this is your down-line. We have time going across horizontally but we see ourselves building our down-line vertically, so this is what I am going to ask you to do. Imagine this is time but if you reverse (horizontally), it is the growth of your down-line.

1:16:20

The race starts at the beginning of month one—so we have to define the launch. It is really easy for us to say here is the launch date or here is the launch window when it is Nikken setting the dates for us. We are launching Australia and here is the date. Here is another date when we will be launching Switzerland. It's easy when somebody tells you the launch date but what you have to get into the habit of doing is creating your own launch dates. You are your company's CEO. You can't expect Nikken to tell you when your launch dates are. You've got to decide.

1:17:05

How many of us have **a launch every 90 days?** How many of you have a launch every 90 days? You might be saying to yourself—this business is every 90 days? 90 days was also what Amway discovered. Before they discovered the 90-day cycle the business was sporadic and it was not highly "duplicatable." There were a lot of people not succeeding before they discovered the 90-day cycle. What they discovered, and by the way it is apparent in all businesses, every quarter, every 90 days is when they create reports and measure profits. There is **something about 90 days that matters** to every form of business.

1:17:59

I believe there is a psychological effect to it. People can hunker down for 90 days, they can see 90 days out. Don't ask them to think 6 months. It is too much for them. Today more than ever, it is getting harder to get people to think long term. Today things happen so fast. Our time is so compressed that to think in terms of 90 days is a stretch. Do you know what you are doing 90 days from now? Do you have plans? The fact is most people aren't thinking far enough ahead. Do you know what you are doing tomorrow? Most people know two things—what they are doing tomorrow and what they are doing on the weekend. They dread tomorrow and they live for the weekend. But ask them what they are doing the following weekend—they don't know. They have not planned that far ahead.

1:18:55

When you build a 90-day launch plan, it takes a significant effort. When you build a **90-day plan, it keeps you focused.** What people are afraid to do is to set goals. Why? Because people are afraid they are not going to hit those goals. Well, if you think setting goals is so that you won't miss the goal, then you have missed the point. Achieving goals is not why you set goals, goals are there. I have heard it said, for two primary reasons—**goals are set to stretch you** to cause you to do something you have not done before, to get you out of your comfort zone, to achieve new heights. Otherwise you are dead. Remember, you either going up or coming down. So, if you are not setting new goals to do something you haven't already done, it might be nothing more than you resetting your goal that you didn't quite make during the last 90 days. Remember, because you did not hit the goal in the first 90 days, **you don't change your goal, you change your strategy.** Let me repeat that—you don't change your goal you change your strategy.

1:19:51

How else are you going to figure out how to set the goal? Ask yourself—will you get there by abandoning the idea of getting there? Or will you get there by working at it, working at it until you figure out those course corrections. Do you know airplanes are off course 95% of the time? That is correct. They are off course 95% of the time. Correcting to get back on course. We are human beings. We are self correcting, we make decisions, we act on them and we get results. Let me give you an example—don't touch that! It burns! Some of us have to learn it twice—some of us don't learn very well. The bottom line is we learn from our mistakes, that is how we have been designed. So go out and make some mistakes—try it a few times. If you do it long enough you are going to be a master at it. And the world is going to be paying you millions of dollars because you worked it through.

1:20:44

Let's return to planning. There is a **pre-launch,** month one, month two and month three, and then there is a launch date. What is my goal for the launch date? I want to have all engines "go" on that launch date. Think of the analogy of launching a rocket or of launching an airplane. In this pre-launch phase what is it that I'm trying to do? I'm trying to **get** things lined up. I am trying to get a sufficient number of people on my front line all at the same mental place.

That is the key—they've got to *all get to the line with a certain idea in mind, a certain cause, a certain idea, a certain "here is what we are doing." Can you imagine trying to win a Super Bowl or win any team game if your players were not playing the same game or if they weren't playing at the same time or if they were not trying to coordinate to get a goal.*

1:21:42

They have to **work together toward an end in mind.** We are all on the same team, and the common goal is the cause—the cause must be acutely relevant. Because you may have an idea of going Platinum, but that doesn't mean anything to anybody else. You may have an idea of making a billion dollars, but that doesn't mean anything to anybody else. You have got to find that idea or concept that has deep meaning to all of the people. The cause must be there for everyone on the team to strive for so that in 90 day's time or thereabouts, we are all sitting around holding the winners' cup.

1:22:10

It takes a **team effort when you are launching the business in a big way.** The *pre-launch is all about selling a certain number of people on an idea*—of winning, of crossing the finish line. When you are selling people on the idea of getting into Nikken, do you think about that? Hopefully you are not selling them on the idea of arriving at this finish line without having defined to them what **this cause** means. You may just be selling them the idea of getting to the line. Nobody is saying let's go. You are just getting them to say—I'm in. Now what do you want them to do? If the plan is not clear very soon you will be saying—I have to rescue this person and I have to save that person over there. Think about it. Is that building a business? You can have fun doing the rescues and it's great to do them, but don't confuse these activities with building the business. Don't think that by rescuing this person and saving that person that you are building the business.

1:23:17

There is nothing wrong with helping others. I love doing it too—every once in a while I need to remind myself. But I don't confuse myself when it comes to **doing the business. I need to be clear on what has to happen. I've got to find somebody to work with; somebody in a specific place based on my strategy for my next achievement, for my next rank promotion**—a promotion of somebody in my down-line. I'm working with drawings. I'm seeing the thing because you know what, all architects start with drawings. And you are exactly that—an architect.

1:23:51

You are an architect of the business. You want to help people win by planning for them to win. Let's assume that the "star" below is your next super star.

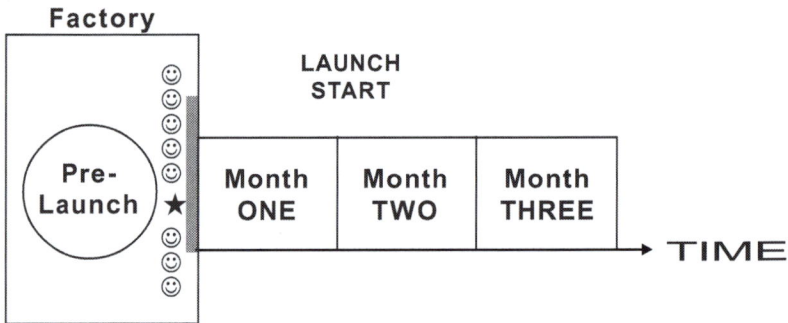

You have got to work with them in a pre-launch capacity to accumulate a certain number of people who are all in the same space in time and mind, more or less, and are all ready to go. So whatever has to happen in this—let's call it a factory—this factory creates people who are ready to go.

1:24:29

Creating people who are ready to go is what this factory creates. We are going to define that this factory creates people who are ready to go. Think of the pre-launch as a factory. It produces people who are ready to go. What do you need to **produce** in the next 30 days, 60 days, 90 days? **People who are ready to go!**

1:25:00

So we have to duplicate that factory, we have to recreate that factory. Remember what the factory is. **It is a number of activities and events designed to communicate information in a certain way that causes somebody to get to a certain place in their belief and in their conviction and in their commitment to do something.** That is what that factory is. We often refer to that as the process, and I will get a little more specific about the process. A lot of people are circumventing the process, mistakenly thinking they have taken someone through it, when they have only taken them partially through it. Remember all of them have got to be at the same place at the same time, mentally, emotionally ready, so you have got to get them through the process. That also means that this process needs an ending point. We need to plan an activity that can bring them all together so that we can get them on the same page at the same time.

1:26:06

I call that **a lock-in,** some kind of a lock-in event. An event that not only affects them on an intellectual level, but **something that affects them on an emotional level.** If I can get people locked in on an emotional level at the same time—a group of them and they have a set plan where they know what to do—they have been given simple instructions, all they have to do is tap into it, not create it because I've created it. They just have to tap into it, then they are going to **have events, activities, and things they can participate in from which they will be able to produce their ready people.** So here comes the next generation. So from this batch of people comes another generation of people, then we repeat this process again.

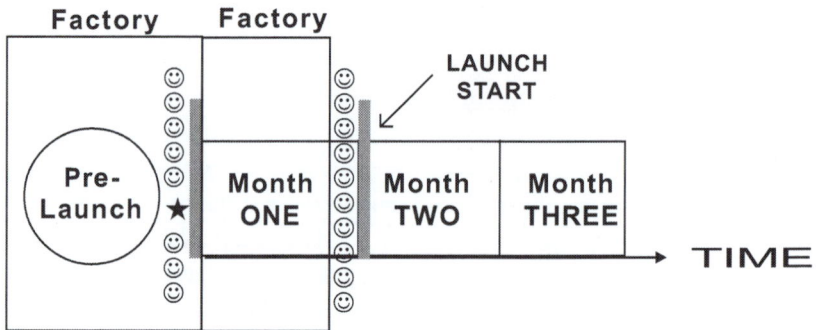

From that batch of people comes another batch of people and we do it again. From that batch of people comes another batch of people. If we've done it well and we've done it right, then something is definitely going to happen. We have pretty much guaranteed our results, positive results.

1:27:19

Now all we have to do is figure out what this factory is, figure how many people we need to put in the factory to get the people that we need "ready" out of the factory. We just have to repeat this process and take into consideration certain things that we have learned historically. There is what could be called a natural law in this business called **the rule of thirds.** I have not been able to get around it. I've tried and I've tried. There is something about this business, probably all businesses that indicates that the rule of thirds simply is. The rule means *one third of the people will pretty much do what you would expect they would do, the other two thirds won't,* and that is okay. If we know the rule going in to the process, then we can build our factory with a little bit of redundancy. We build the factory and we take into consideration the rule of thirds, so we know what the results are. Recall that our goal is Platinum.

1:28:25

Here is the key to this concept. If Platinum is the objective, where should we set our sights? This is critical. What you are going to communicate will be a function of your vision. If I want to ensure

Platinum I have to ensure six Silvers. Why 6 Silvers as opposed to 3 Golds? Simple mechanics—3 Golds means that I have to break 9 second-generation Silvers and they are one more level removed from me. I have less control over that which is further away from me and to create a Platinum distributor would require 9 second-generation Silvers as opposed to 6 Silvers.

1:29:29

Some of you may think that breaking 3 Golds would build a stronger business but I assume you are going to build a strong business one way or the other. But in 90 days, what we are looking to do is to build something with enough momentum, enough excitement and build enough wingspan so that our airplane gets off the ground. In our case, 6 Silvers is the logical choice. Now if I want to ensure 6 people go Silver, I need a good plan because financially there is no reason why anybody goes into this business to become Silver. Economically speaking, on average, most people in Canada earn more than what the average Silver earns.

1:30:12

Going back to our inspiring people, **what is going to inspire somebody to make them want to earn half of what they are making into something close or to what they are making in a 90-day window?** We are always thinking 90 days. What is going to inspire them? *If I want to inspire somebody—the Gold level is more likely to be inspiring to the majority of people rather than Silver or Platinum.*

1:30:42

Platinum might be too big of an idea for most people to buy into at such an early stage. Silver might be too small of an idea, but Gold is something well within reach. So if I want to go **Platinum in 90 days what do I have to sell?** Remember, I've got to get these six people to be at a certain place in their mind at the same time to launch their business, inspired by all the things we've talked about including money.

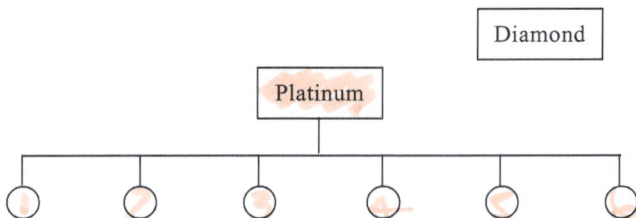

1:31:10

So **I set my vision on Diamond**—I build that plan. If I'm working with you, I'm not going to necessarily tell you all this. But today I am working with you and I have done it before. I do have the experience so this is what I'm going to design. I'm going to talk about **selling 6 people on the idea of building a business.** First, we are going to talk about what we are doing, **why are we doing this and why this business is worth building.** Then I'm going to sell those 6 people on what they want. I'm going to sell them what they want. I will sell them on their values, *their cause* and then we are going to bring it down into something more finite and immediate—that 90 day thing we call the business plan—the business launch strategy. So I'm going to *help them visualize and understand that they will be the proud owner of a brand new Gold distributorship*—a Gold independent Wellness Consulting business in the next 90 days, on its way to achieving the objective we set from the beginning.

Your Vision Creates the Context for what You must Build!

What are you Building?

They have different Requirements?

1:32:20

Now we are bringing in something a little bit more tangible, something they can see. I'm going to introduce them to some of the Golds so that they can see they are real—it really happens. They are real

---

The Science of the Nikken Business

people. And there are Platinums and there are even Diamonds. Yes that is where we are going. We are finally meeting a few people who are in the business. I'm going to validate all of that too. Meeting successful Nikken distributors is validation, and validation is part of the process of getting their heads in a certain place and time so all of them, at the same time, are ready to go. Think about this for a moment. If I'm selling somebody the idea of going Gold in a certain period of time then what **must I be thinking in advance?**

1:32:57

I must be thinking they are Silvers. So already you can see how I have to contemplate not the people I'm bringing in, but the people they are bringing in.

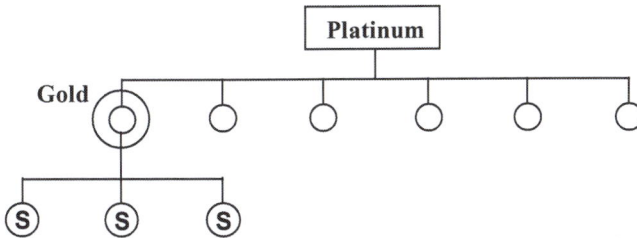

Many of you are just thinking about the people you are bringing in, or for that matter, just the one person you brought in. Many of you are seeing not "that" person, but the person "that" person is bringing in. Before anybody exists, you must be thinking in advance, planning ahead. If you are not thinking in advance then where are you planning to be? Have you heard the expression "If you build it—they will come." First you have to build the place for them to come to. You expect them to come, don't you?

1:33:42

Have you heard the story, I think it's a Biblical story, about the guy in the desert? Where is the rain? Where is the rain God? God replies, "Where are the trenches? If you expected rain you would have been digging trenches?" Think about that. You have got be preparing in your mind and in your business plan which means you've got to know where you are going to be if this new person is going to exist 36 to 90 days from now.

1:34:12

Your new person is going to need a Wellness Preview to get in the business, aren't they? So you've got to **plan a Wellness Preview.** At that point in time when should you plan it? **"Now"**! If you do the work now, then all you have to do is done at once. Then everybody knows where they are supposed to be now. When Bo and I first got started on this concept, the first thing we did was put a calendar together and we were working double time.

1:34:47

During the day it was Tuesdays, Thursdays, Fridays—business briefings. Tuesday nights, Thursday nights—Wellness Previews and Saturday training that was double time. Instead of doing one Wellness Preview, we were doing two. Instead of doing one business briefing, *we were doing three every week to expose more and more generations of people in the shortest span of time. That is how we created such a huge explosion. It is the same thing, only doing more of it in a compressed time. That is the strategy—that is the difference between doing the business and building it.*

1:35:15

There is strategy involved in building it, because then that means you are an architect . . . rather than just going whichever way it goes, whichever way it leads you. When we build the calendar for a month and it was only a month, we had that whole calendar and everybody on that team had that calendar. Every Wellness Preview on that calendar was there so that as people came in, they took the calendar and as people signed up, they took the calendar. Why? I wanted them to know where they had to go next. They didn't have to know where they were going to be two years from now, but they had to know where they were

232   The Science of the Nikken Business

© 2005, Good Vibrations International + Success8

going to go next week. I got everyone in line to do something at the same time. It's taking all these different ideas and moving them in another direction. Here is the interesting thing—we really didn't have a good idea just yet!

1:36:01
We only did that for one month. I remember in the second or third week of the month Bruce Black and I thinking that we were approaching the end of the calendar, we realized we had to get another calendar and we hadn't thought through the next month. All of a sudden we had to whip up a calendar for next month to keep people focused on next month—so that they felt we were moving in a direction.

1:36:26
Well, what I've learned is that if you want **to do some phenomenal things quickly, you have got to think** not one week, not even one month, but **two or three months down the road,** because that is what you are building toward. Keep in mind that I am telling you this because you have been in the trenches and you have been at this business for a time.

1:36:49
You are now looking for how you can sink your teeth into this, how you can take somebody really good and have them do better than what you have done. Creating phenomenal results is not about somebody watching a video of a brand new senior distributor. What you do need to know is if you expect to go Platinum, create Golds. And once they've created Silvers, believe me, they will have an interest of learning how to do it too.

1:37:25
So now I'm thinking this through, but if I'm thinking this through, what does it take to break Silver? At some point in time we have to ask ourselves that because this factory has to create Silvers too. Well then, I have to look at this person and this person, and also this person getting into the business. I have to look at a strategy that will create

a Silver distributor in a certain period of time. What about 5,000 point packages times 4? That will do it.

1:37:53

Some of you may be wondering: "Well I never did that." I am not asking you what you did. I'm asking you what could you do? What would you do? What would you want to do? When Marty and I were first working together in Brandon, Manitoba, part of the Wellness Preview included "How Do You Go Silver?" The answer was to find four other, actually at that time, find three other people with 5,000 points. 5,000 points and you are Silver—we used to say that right in our Wellness Preview. Did everybody do it? No, but did some? Yes, every one of the frontline did.

1:38:23

We created four Silvers that first month, one of which was Gold. For a Gold who broke a Gold they had to make 220,000 points or 219,000—and that meant an $18,000 pay check for Marty, $9,000 for Lauren. For Collin who was a Gold and the 77 new distributors in the organization, it meant an average purchase of $3,000 per distributor.

1:38:49

So if you aim, aim high. But if you aim low, you've got to set standards. That is one way of doing it. There are many ways you can do it. One way is 4 X 4 at 1700 points—a 'demo pak' and a 'career pak.' There is clearly more people involved here and that takes more time and time is our enemy. We don't have time. We've set a specific goal and we've got to do it with a certain amount of time, so we are going to need to raise the bar a little bit.

1:39:22

Don't be afraid to do that. This is a business and if you are selling the business properly, they are not buying products, they are investing in a business. They are not getting in to fail, they are getting in to succeed. If you are giving them the impression that you are not going to succeed, then you are probably doubting yourself. So if you have any doubts about your ability to succeed, plug into somebody who does not have a lack of confidence.

1:39:47

Now I've got to think about these people getting in the business because when these people buy their products, these people become Silver, and when those people become Silver, these people become Gold. And when those people become Gold, this person becomes Diamond. What happens if only one third of this happens? As long as you get what you have to get and this starts to breakdown as it gets away from you, you will still hit your target.

1:40:21

The fallback position is you will hit your target as long as your vision is strong. The fallback position is this is going to happen. What if I was setting a goal for somebody to go Silver? Getting them to go Silver was my goal for them because they were part of my business strategy for somebody going Gold. I wouldn't be telling them that, but it would be my goal for them. What would I be talking to them about? What would I be focusing on? What would I be working toward? Helping them go Gold in 90 days. Do you think they are going to go Silver at least in that time frame?

1:40:52

They will probably go Silver sooner, probably the first month. In fact if I've done this correctly, they will go Silver just by personally sponsoring the people who are going to play the game. On their first day they would become Silver or if it was not on their first day it would be their launch day, and that is how it should be. Why are you recruiting this team anyway? To get into Nikken?

1:41:26

Is that why you were recruiting them? You win. Let's pop open a bottle of champagne. We are done, now what? Or are you recruiting them to accomplish something? Think about it. Think about being a coach in baseball or a coach in hockey. Are you bringing these people to your team just to play hockey or are you recruiting these people because you have got on to a pennant race or you've got a Stanley Cup you are trying to win?

1:41:57

People recruit people not for the sake of recruiting people but to accomplish something. Why are you sponsoring people? Is it only for you to sponsor people, or is it for you to get ahead or is it because you need their help? Let me ask you something. If we set a goal to help Nikken get a million homes on this sleep system, do you think you might need some help? Isn't this a goal that would automatically inspire you to recruit people because now you know you need help?

1:42:34

I have a reason to recruit. Nikken has a reason to recruit distributors because they need people to do the work. I have a reason to recruit. If I said of that million I am going to be responsible for $20,000. How am I going to do $20,000? I need help, don't I? Now I have a reason to recruit. Do you see how this cause-oriented stuff works? *If you want people to recruit, give them a reason to recruit.* They will do it automatically. Don't just tell them to recruit because they won't do it just for the sake of recruiting.

1:43:18

If you want people to do the work, you've got to give them a reason to do the work—a reason that is beyond the work itself. Any questions so far about where we are going? Do you understand structurally what has to happen? What we are going to do is we are going to look at what has to happen to create Silver, because what has to happen to create Silver . . . has to happen to create Gold—has to happen to create Platinum. It is really just duplication, all accomplished in 90 days.

1:43:48

But I'm going to add one other thing that most people don't take into consideration—the human element. The fact that you can control, you

---

can control what you are going to do, or you can help control the person you are working with. You can have that kind of relationship where you are like a dog with a bone, you are on them to get the job done and that's your job. If you really want to be the best sponsor you can be, you need to be in their face and you get them working. You need to get them on that track and you make sure they get the job done because if they are not there, if they fall short, then all of the planning does not matter. You are not going to hit your goal.

1:44:25

So your job is to make sure they get where they going, and then it is working through the rest. You create such momentum that things just somehow fall into place and even though there is a human element, it's still going to give you great results. I did this with another fellow and it was a disaster. In his pre-launch, in his two weeks where he was supposed to get things together, he got called away on other business trying to get his other business work finished.

1:44:43

So we pushed back the launch date. But we had a launch date, we even put all this on paper. We knew what we were doing, we had all the events lined up, all the special guest speaker events, everything . . . and it just kept messing up. And then something else happened and he didn't hit his target and we pushed it back a little more. But you know, after a while you can't push it back any further once you get to 120 days.

1:45:21

Anyway it got to the point where we knew Platinum was out of the question. It all just got pushed back to the point where we couldn't make things happen, but Gold was still in the running. All that didn't even happen, because by the rule of thirds he still made $11,000.00 in his first month and next month did 60K. That was still more money than he had made in his previous profession and it took him years to get to that level in his profession. Let me ask you, would you have distributors complaining if even though your business plan failed miserably but you had still created enough activity that there were still results that were tangible?

1:46:12

The pre-launch is nothing more but we are going to do this over and over and over again. We are going to give them more time to do it, so the real pressure is on you and the person you are launching to get it done in two weeks. So you **pre-launch in two weeks.** Don't push it by trying to go to three of four weeks. You'll lose the opportunity to get all the people at the same place at the same time, and remember that is **the key—getting them at the same place the same time.**

1:46:50

If you've got one way ahead of the others, that person is going to start placing demands on your time and you are going to be pulled in one direction over another and you are going to leave the recruiting behind—and the next thing you know you've got a one-legged wonder. You've got one super star—that is all you've got, because you did not do the work up front (pre-launch). Get the width up front, and so I really depend on the fact that people don't know what they are doing for the first couple of weeks, so I can do what I need to get done. If I can get enough people who don't know what they are doing they are not going to do anything without me, and then I can get them all on the same page at the same time. It is actually an advantage for you; in a nice way you want to take advantage of their ignorance.

1:47:27

Here is the deal. Let's look at the process. I want to take somebody who is a qualified prospect. **One thing** you have to do is to **qualify the people** (see diagram, page 241). You are going to invite them to the party. There is a *difference between a product or a retail prospect and a business prospect.* The **first thing** we do we **create a list**, we create a list of names, then we categorize that list so that we can identify who the business people are versus people we want to help. The reality is that we are going get to those people we want to help. I recommend you watch "The Missing Link" video. It will explain what you need to do. Another video to watch is the "What I've Learned" video. It will explain what I do with all the people who I don't want in my business but who are people I know and people who can benefit from the products.

1:48:29

What do I do with all these people? Let me ask you a question. Have you gone through the prospect list for the business? Come on, be honest. I have another question for you. How many of you have at least a hundred people you know for sure who are not on the product—the sleep system? At least a hundred people you know for sure who are not sleeping on the sleep system?

1:48:51

Every one of us knows a hundred people who are not on the sleep system and just because they may not be a business prospect and just because they may not have said yes to us about the business, doesn't mean they should not be on the sleep system—our premier product, the thing that really makes the heart and soul of Nikken sing. So why can't we invite them to a special meeting in our home or to wherever, with no holds barred. I would tell them right up front, "Look, I really believe in this, I believe in wellness, I believe in the experience, I believe in the process, I believe in these products. I want to give you a massage, I want you to see for yourself, you can leave your wallet at home if you have to, I want you to know what I know. At the very least I want you to evaluate these products." I guarantee you this, you will be selling sleep systems.

1:49:43

We put together a special presentation called **the sleep presentation** just for that reason, because I know you know at least a hundred people, no matter how long you have been in this business who do not own a Nikken system and should. Now I can tell you one thing—if you make a point **in the next two weeks of exposing those 100 people to the sleep system, something is going to happen.**

You might actually even recruit some, not because you intended to but because of your sheer enthusiasm, excitement and the challenge of doing it is going to make something happen. You are going to **inspire people**—that's how it works. Now qualified business prospects—we have to create interest. There are all kinds of trainings out there. I'm not going to get into how we create interest, that should be pretty standard. All of you know how to do that, you are all Silvers. That means you've got at least somebody interested, an **interested prospect** meaning they want to know more.

1:50:42

If I'm creating interest about the business, clearly it is the opportunity I'm attracting them to. I've got something I think can make a difference in the lives of others. Mr. Bruce Black, I've come across something that I believe can make a difference in the lives of millions of people. I know you like to help people. I've seen the way you are with me and with other people around you and I believe somebody in your position can greatly influence the possibility that this company that I have been introduced to recently is making a difference. I don't know if it is for you but if it is not, then the very least you can do is to introduce me to people I need to be talking to. Can I show you what I am talking about?

1:51:23

That is the cause. That's how you can get people interested. **Sell them the cause,** because if they are not interested in helping people, then all the money in the world is not going to make them do anything. That is what it takes to make this business go, somebody has to get hooked into the cause. Now that I have gotten them interested in it, they will want to know what this business is all about. I have to introduce them to the business. I have to introduce them to the products and I'm going to use any means I can—whether it's a video tape, an audio tape, an up-line, a presentation, a one-on-one, a presentation in a coffee shop, a presentation called the business briefing, business preview, executive lunch, I don't care what you call it—the presentation focuses on the business.

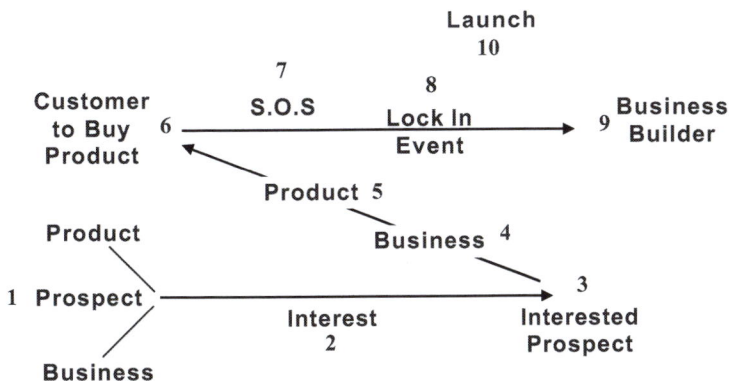

```
                              Launch
                                10
              7
   Customer            S.O.S         8                Business
   to Buy    6 ─────────────  Lock In  ──────────▶  9  Builder
   Product                    Event
                 ◀
                    Product 5
   Product                 Business  4
                                                       3
 1 Prospect ───────────────────────────────▶
                       Interest           Interested
                          2                Prospect
   Business
```

1:52:07

Then I'm going to expose them to the products. I'm going to give them back-rolls. I'm going to give them product demonstrations. I'm going to do everything I can to bring them to a Wellness Preview, anything I can to **show them that these products make a difference.** After that I'm going to ask them to buy the products. How many of you ask them to join? You are asking them the wrong question. Why don't you ask them to buy the products because then joining is implied.

1:52:45

Do you want paper distributors? Do you want products on distributors? You want to ask people to buy the products? What you are going to get is a customer, you just don't know yet if they are going to be a business builder. You know at least they are going to be a client, maybe a consultant.

1:53:04

The next thing I have got to do, the big thing, is to get them from a customer to a consultant, because it is over here where we get ready to launch. This is the big step in the process and a lot of people don't really appreciate how important this step is. I've got to convert a client into a business builder, which means we've got to get into some real heart and soul discussions. We've really got to talk about the structure of Nikken. What are the ranks? What is it that we are looking to build in terms of the compensation plan? If you have not had this discussion yet with some of the people that you are working with, then this is probably the reason why you are not as successful as you want to be.

1:53:53

This is a very important step in the process. I call it the strategy session, some people call it the S.O.S., the Strategy Orientation Session. Some people call it basic training. I don't think it's training. Training is on the job. I think this is a "let's get together and decide on what it is that we are doing here together". Can we get to a mutual objective? What is the reason you are doing the business and what is the big picture? If I am going to show you how to build this business, if I am going to work with you and try to get you into the compensation plan, there has got to be a good reason.

1:54:24

You've got to be inspired. This is a strategy session. It might be a one-on-one, it might be with a group of people. What comes next is crucial. After or before the strategy session something has to happen that brings people collectively together at that moment of truth and I call this the lock-in event. There needs to be some kind of a lock-in event that locks them in emotionally to the business. A *Wellness Preview locks them emotionally to the products*, so a lock-in event locks them in emotionally to the business.
1:55:14

The Science of the Nikken Business

The Plan That Gets Big Results—Part 2

:11
The Plan that Gets Big Results

Let me describe a lock-in event to you. Many of you already know what a lock-in event is. I want you to go back in your mind to where there was an experience, you had *something happen that caused you to make the decision to act differently as a distributor or Wellness Consultant*. In other words, you may have been doing the business or you may have been new to the products, but something happened.

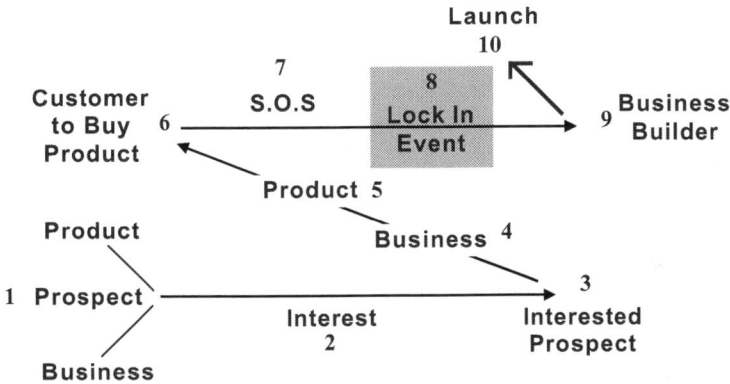

:49
You're some place where there was a group of people with you. It was a Nikken event of some sort, and it was *at that event that something crystallized* and you were not the same person afterward. When you came out of that event with some passion, some conviction, you wanted something to happen, you wanted to make something happen, you wanted to get busy. Does everybody know where they were? What that event was? A Team Diamond, an EXPO, a Team Diamond luncheon, a Silver training. Most likely there was an event.

1:25

There was an event that painted a picture. It was a big event, not a small event. Usually these events are a little bit larger than the average business briefing or Wellness Preview. It was a special event. It is *a* special event—a special Nikken event and you were able to touch and feel and see and realize the magnitude of the business that included the amazing product stories. But something happened to you that hadn't happened before. *You mentally and emotionally locked in to the business, you wanted to get busy.* Until then, you weren't sure . . . you kind of kept "dilly dallying!"

2:04

You get a very special kind of feeling. That moment happens to everybody, and it is the big events. Most of you said the Team Diamond events were when it happened. The Team Diamond events are the biggest events we've had. That lock-in event was the single thing that was a catalyst for you. Well, if it **was a catalyst** for you, do you think it might be for others? And, **if you know it is, wouldn't you plan it?** If we have two weeks to pre-launch and there is no event, then what do you do? You create one. If there is no event within those two weeks you must create one.

2:35

Now, is that the only way to create such an event? Let me tell you what I've learned. How do you ask people to get on an airplane? I call it the **big pill theory** *the more inconvenient you make this for people, the more likely they are going to take it seriously.* It's really true, I call it the big pill theory. For example, if I came into your office with a little tiny pill and said, "You know, this is really good for you. You should try this—take this when it is convenient." Or, I came into your office with a pill the size of a horse pill and I said, "Take this now, swallow it. Come on, take it right now." Is that going to get you up, to get your attention?

3:16

The **"big pill theory."** In other words, the more inconvenient, the bigger it is, the *bolder you are and the more serious they take you.* Do you want to be taken seriously? I'll tell you something. If you are going to get a whole bunch of people on the same page at the same time, you've got to be taken seriously and so I would create a lock-in event now. In the case of this person that we launched that was a dismal disaster but was a good lock-in event, what we did was a video teleconferencing. We went to a local place that had video teleconferencing and we beamed in all the big guns in Nikken to talk to these people we had organized to be in that room. It could have been a conference call before we had the Team Diamond event. How the heck did we do it?

3:58

We had conference calls. And they were very good. It was exciting to hear other people's voices. It's interesting because not everybody is on a conference call on a daily basis. They are talking to people from all over the place; you do what you have to do to make it happen. Keep in mind what I am talking about here is a very specific application. We are talking about launching somebody in a big way. It doesn't happen every minute. I call this **a pack call—a power of ABC, kick off call.** I love these calls. They are my very favorite calls. They are my favorite because I'm not chit chatting with people; I know there are people on the other end of the phone who are interested in building a business.

5:00

I love doing pack calls and what we will do is get two, three, four "A's"—put a bunch of "A's" on the phone and you, who is launching that new person, will be the host. "We would like to welcome everybody on behalf of so and so. We are just launching the business. You are all here to learn about whether this is a business worth building. We've lined up this call with Mike DiMuccio. Stay tuned. Sit back and relax. If you have any questions at the end of the call, we would be happy to answer them."

5:29

The first speaker comes from Barbados, Mike DiMuccio, a Royal Diamond distributor, and on the call goes. It's amazing. Many of you have used a pack call. Does it work? Yes it does! It is such a *great way to put the pressure on my new distributor* because if they know I have organized this call with all these top guns, the pressure is on them to get people on that call. Believe me it makes them work more diligently and I love putting pressure on the newest person in the business because I want to know now if they are serious or wasting my time, because if they don't get serious now, do you think they are going to get serious later?

6:07

If they are going to make excuses now, they are going to make excuses forever and I would be a fool to be sitting around listening to excuses all day. So, I want to know right now. I want to know what you are made of right now. Let's do it. Usually **when I launch somebody, I put a call out ten days later.** I have a call in ten days and who I have got on the call are Platinums or above. I can practically hear the prospect saying, "I guess we've really got to get busy." So, you can create a lock-in. When is there a Silver training going **on? Now is when it becomes important for you to know what is going on.** I*s there a Silver training going on anywhere in North America* in the next couple of weeks? Is there a special event of any sort going on anywhere in North America in the next couple of weeks?

6:51

Let me tell you about a lock-in event that I had for the group that I had to launch in Australia. It was in San Jose, California. Could I expect people to get on a plane from Australia to fly to California to spend 4 hours with me? Yes, because I knew what I was going to teach them, and I knew it would be good and I knew if they were serious, they would have a business to show for it 90 days later. The wise ones were those who got on the plane and flew to San Jose, California.

7:33

The majority of them today are Silvers or above. Some of them are Platinums. So, the truth of the matter *is raise your level of expectation—the big pill theory. Remember, the more inconvenient it is, the more serious they* will take you . . . *but that lock-in event could be any event—any event anywhere, any big event.*

Question: In that two week period prior to the launch, how does your new star or front line person find those 4, 5, 10 new people . . . do they need to go 21 wide? Answer: Well? I don't know where the number 21 comes from. I guess it goes back to 7. The marketing plan says 6, so I have always worked with 18 because that is the real number. Maybe it's the spares you need on the Nikken Highway?

8:16

That is what tap-rooting is for. **Tap rooting is to secure your business**—*tap rooting is the spare guys,* the length? Of the 7th leg—I don't care how many legs you have to sponsor to get 6 rock-solid legs. Do what you have to do to get 6 rock-solid legs.

8:40

Tap root your downline 3 generations deep and you've got yourself a lifelong income. Now where do these people come from? Let us nail this process down first and we will put some numbers to it. Can you see how you got to where you got to? You may not have had a lock-in event, but two or three weeks after you got into the business it may have been two to three months, but it did take that lock-in event. There was an audio cassette that I did called "Silver Is A Blast." I interviewed 30 people. I invited all the new Silvers who have become Silver in the last two months on a phone call and I interviewed them because I wanted to distill out what happened. You're Silver. What happened?

9:30

Some of them were brand new in the business but some of them have been in the business for as much as 8 months, and so I asked them how long did it take to go Silver. Some may have argued 8 months, but I asked more poignant questions because I know the truth is not that at all, doesn't take 8 months to go **Silver it has to happen in one calendar month,** those are the rules. So now we look at it and what matters was there was a decision-making event—**every one of them made a decision.** There was a moment that happened, something inspired that moment, there was a catalyst and it was inevitably everything they just described, so there was special event a lock-in event.

10:18

Therefore, if I want people to make a decision, a big decision and I need them to make it all at the same time, what do I need to have happen? I need them all to be at a lock-in event or get them involved in a lock-in event, the same lock-in event preferably all at the same time so that those who are prepared to make a decision make it those and those who are not, well, they get lost.

10:38

I only pay any attention to people who are in the process, who are interested **now.** If they get interested later, we talk about it later. **Now** is all I'm interested in. So, if I've got enough people in this process that is when this lock-in happens. The numbers that I need to turn on just happen. We've got people who are ready to launch all at the same time now. For some of you, this process might be a week or two. Usually, it's about two weeks; generally, speaking **it's between 10 days or two weeks where people get serious.** Then the really serious thing happens. When they get serious, when you start asking some serious questions, when you start talking about some serious things, you start getting serious. And, if you already **have a launch date in mind,** how serious would you be at the beginning?

11:28

You would be pretty serious at the beginning. Right? When I started talking to Marty's prospects, we were serious. We had a plan—this is what we are doing and this is what we are going to do. I was giving them the impression that a decision had already been made, what we were going to do, what we were going to create, the results were already going to happen. The only variable was whether they were a part of the results or not. We left them with that impression—the **fear of loss is an incredible motivator.** We had made a decision to present it that way. This group from Australia and Marty and I, and there are up-line people involved as well, who are my cousins in Italy. I sat down in front of their group of people on the first night I ever presented and I said, "Claudio, how the heck did you get here?" He tells the story of how he was first introduced to Nikken, and then how I got involved in the situation. I then told them how I got there, and I told my story. He presented his vision and I presented my vision and guess what comes next? Your vision—why are you here.

12:36

Why are you here? Here is *why you have been invited. We have decided that this is what we are going to do* and we would like you to be the first to know about it. We are inviting you to be part of this, and if I have done my job well tonight you will understand why it would be worth your time, and then I will begin my presentation. See, *I have already told them we are doing this with or without their participation*. With or without their involvement, this is what we are doing. I let them know that right at the very beginning when I start talking. T*he decision has been made, the results are clear.*

13:11

We know what we are doing. We know what we are building. We have every reason to believe it is going to happen. If I've done my job right, so will they have every reason to believe it's going to happen, and all that remains then is to decide if they are going to be part of it. Some say yes. How about that? Or say no. But, some say yes. You don't get paid if you are the yes people, you get paid to hear the no's. We did the calculation the other day. Remember, what every no has represented to me in income? $71,000 a "NO." How many of you would like to get a few "NO's" under your belt? $71,000.00 per 'NO.'

13:58

You don't get paid to get the yeses; *you get paid to hear the no's.* What is harder to get is that it is hard to listen to the no's. So are we all clear on this? We all understand the importance of this interview and what was determined? That there was a decision, the decision was prompted by a lock-in event . . . and the person who took the least amount of time, took 4 days to break Silver.

14:25

Four days from the decision. No matter how long you have been in the business—a decision is critical! The person who took the longest, took 6 weeks. So anywhere from 4 days to 6 weeks meaning they have done the pre-launch and the launch in the following month. Bang, they were Silver. So, within *anywhere from 4 days to 6 weeks I know I can break a Silver if I have a battle plan* . . . if I know what events to bring them to . . . if I **map those events** on a calendar, so I know exactly where they are happening, what hotel what time and so forth.

14:58

Then I know that person is going to go Silver if they have got somebody like me working with them, keeping them on track. But I **need that lock-in event** to get them where I need them to be in their head. So that lock-in event is critical to this process for launching people. So how important is the next event? How important is the next big event? How important is it to have these events? Frequently, if you are **building a 90-day plan,** and if you are, then you will be launching people every 90 days. Are you launching people every 90 days now?

15:30

See yourself launching them every month. Now you see how important is it to have a lock-in event every month. You see, there is a reason why we do the thing called the ***rhythm of the business.*** Because your business needs those things and if it has been inconvenient for some of you to participate or create those events, well guess what?

You get paid if it is inconvenient. I think it's a little bit more inconvenient to punch the clock 9 to 5 every day than to put on a event once in a while. What do you think? Those lock-in events are critical. There is your process.

16:14

The number of people I need to end up as Business Builders, determines the number of people I need to end up as customers, interested prospects and prospects. How much time and how many events? We work backwards, so let's go back to this battle plan. **I want 6.** I want 6 whose engines are going to fire up all at the same time. Well if I want to guarantee that 6 are going to fire up at the same time, then what does the **rule of thirds** tell me? That **I need 18** to attend. I need 18 people to claim that they are going to do something about it, to be sure that 6 are going to do it.

16:53

I'm telling you, this is not rocket science. Your numbers may vary. You know Marty Jeffery had 12 of 13 people say yes, 6 of which went Silver in the first two months. Well, does that happen to everybody? No. It didn't happen to me. I had 35 people say yes, 3 of which went Silver in 3 months. My numbers were terrible but I'm still here. And, I did the right thing; I compensated for my ignorance. I sponsored a lot more people than I really needed, or did I? I don't care how many it takes for you, but it all boils down to the same thing—one third! Six people who all want to be key means I've got to bring 18 people to that point in time.

17:42

So what do I have to do in those first two weeks to get 18 people to the point of being a customer, so that I end up with 6 as business builders? Well, if I *apply the rule of thirds*, then I'm padding it. I'm building so much redundancy to it that I'm pretty much guaranteed. What is 18 times 3? It's 54. So I need to get 54 people interested (interested prospects) in going Silver.

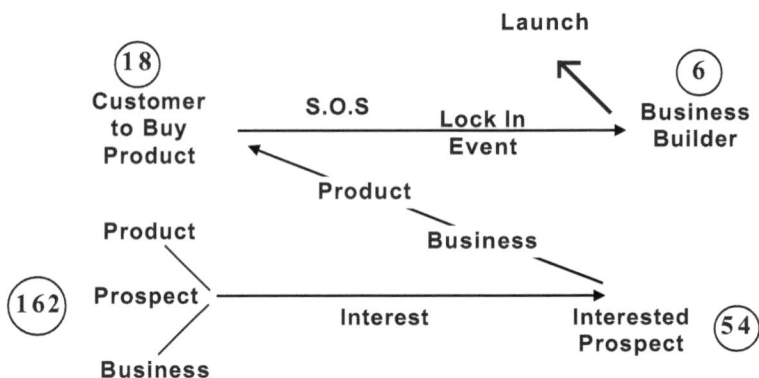

By the way, statistically, **we know it is 30 to 50 people guaranteed.** You ask yourself that question—what happened to you? You listened to those interviews that I did on that tape—30 to 50 people, exposed, created interest the results of which were enough people who landed on the tarmac, purchased products . . . somebody went Silver. But that didn't guarantee somebody going Gold. That is what I am talking about, I'm talking about going beyond Silver.

18:41

You've got to have a plan for those people who come in, not just the people you sponsor, but the people they sponsor and the people they sponsor. So—54 interested people . . . you have to start with 162 as prospects. 162. Okay, 162. Now—this list is 108 names. Why? Because the plan you are operating on is 4 by 4.

19:10

The plan below is for going Gold; the plan above is for going **Platinum.** If I am planning to **break Gold in 90 days, my number will be as such.**

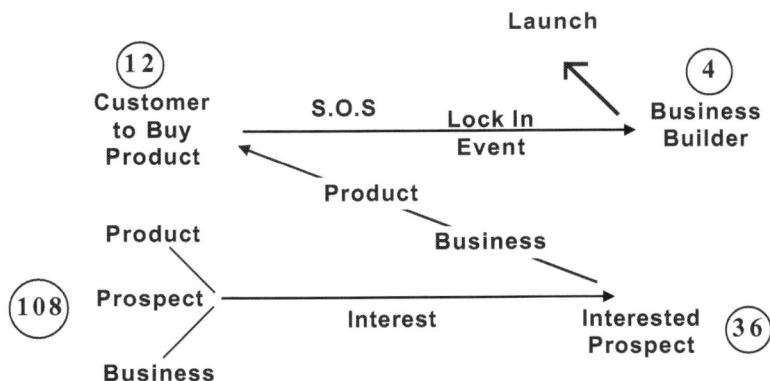

Launch

(12) Customer to Buy Product — S.O.S — Lock In Event → (4) Business Builder

Product ←

(108) Prospect — Product / Business — Interest → Interested Prospect (36)

Business

Notice what did not change. What did not change was the percentage. **The process did not change,** it's always the same. What has to happen has to happen. If you make this 2 day process into a one week process, this 10 day process turns it into a 2 month process and instead of taking "X" number of people, you are taking your time. It is what I call a "onesy and twosy," but I don't call that doing the business. People say I'm doing the business . . . I'm taking people to the Wellness Previews . . . I'm going to Silver training. Yes, but how many people and in what time frame? **There is a difference between doing the business and having a strategy for the business**—a huge difference. That is true about any business.

20:22

Can you imagine any company in the world operating without goals? Would your company succeed without goals? You might be the very first one but I wouldn't be betting on it. This is about putting some meat and potatoes together. This is something to get serious about. This is about taking this on as a profession. This is about doing the very best you can for the people you are bring in to the business because you care enough about them and you want their success. Now, are they going to do this—100% guaranteed? Absolutely not. No, some of them may amaze you, some of them may disappoint you, but the bottom line is: *are you committed to their success? Are you committed to their success?*

21:05

Do you want others to succeed as badly as you want yourself to succeed? **The onus is on you to get good at this.** They are new. They don't know what they are doing. The onus is on you. And, if I've done this well and I've planned this well, I know exactly how it will turn out. Let me give you an example. Let's take some numbers. One hundred and sixty-two people in two week's time. Let us divide by 2 that is 81. That means **81 people in one week's time.** Divide that into 3 **business meetings.** That means I've got to contact 81 people.

21:47

Pre-qualify 81 people such that one-third of 81—**27 people are going to get filtered into 3 business briefings**—Monday, Tuesday Wednesday. Divide the 27 by 3—that means **9 people to a meeting.** So if I had 9 people in my cousin's first meeting and I had 8 people in my second meeting, and so on. You are losing the numbers, so you make up what you don't get done. So there is the example. Nine people in three meetings. Can you handle it?

22:26

Work this plan as if your life depended on it. And it does! Your life as Royal Diamond is going to be dependent on it. So there is an example. Now, if you are doing Silver or Gold, just pull the numbers back—three people, five people per meeting—3 meetings, three business briefings Tuesday, Wednesday, Thursday. Thursday night you take them to a Wellness Preview, everybody all at the same time. This way you are leveraging your time.

22:56

We come together to the Wellness Preview. First of all, we find who is interested because they came to the Wellness Preview. Secondly, they get what they are suppose to get and your percentage goes up. The number of people who go to the Wellness Preview as a second step as opposed to a first step, they are going to become customers—80% of them. What are your numbers? Of the people you've taken to a business briefing followed by a Wellness Preview, what are your numbers of people who purchase products?

23:24

My estimate is a lot better than 50% and it is probably closer to 80%. At this point you've got customers. We don't know if those customers are customers or business builders. We assume because they sign their name as Wellness Consultants on the application form by mistake, we assume that means they are in.

23:53

At this point all you have is someone who has bought some products. I don't even know what level of commitment they've made. Maybe they don't even know what they heck they are doing there. Maybe this is their first exposure.

24:06

Have we spoken to them about the cause? Do we know what they are doing here? Do *you know what they are doing here?* Have you *talked about what you are doing together?* Has that happened yet? Do *they know what the compensation plan is? Do they know how they get paid?* What it entails? Do they know the work that is involved? Do they have any idea what you have in mind for the next 90 days? No, they don't know anything. Very well, let's get them in front of people who have made it happen. Let's find out who is in, because that's when it's going to really come together. That's when you really know and then if you've done the numbers right there is enough of them together. By the way, the Golden number—the Golden number statistically . . . we've proven that if you **get 4 people running at the same time, you're going Silver that month.**

24:50

You get 4 people in somebody's group running at the same time—they're Silver that month. The key is minimum number. It's called critical mass—you've got to have that many, you want Platinum to happen, it's a little bit more. There is the process (see pages 252 and 253). There is the time-frame (2 weeks to pre-launch). So you are compressing your time and effort. Does this take focus? Does this take making Nikken a priority? Would you make Nikken a priority if you were going Platinum the next 90 days? If you believed you are going Platinum the next 90 days, would you make Nikken a priority? Would you expect people to make it a priority? *So act like it, expect it. The big pill*—get them on an airplane. Why not? They are going Platinum in the next 90 days, so they will be able to afford it.

25:50

We have just **learned how to find these people (6 frontline people)** and how to line them up. Now they're in the starting blocks, **they have to know what comes next.** There has to be a calendar of activities. What is a calendar—we book these dates (to show them the product and the business)—now when do you want to do this? Do you want to ask every one of those six individuals what date is convenient for them? What is convenient for you? What is convenient for you? What is convenient for you? Who has time to be convenient? **Success and convenience are not on the same page. Success is never convenient.**

26:35

What I say is, "Here is the calendar, here are the events. This is our meeting. This is our business briefing. This is our Wellness Preview, and this is our lock-in event. We are not going to share the stage with other people. This is ours. **Some of you will have to learn to create your own meetings instead of being dependent on other people's meetings.**

26:59

Leaders create meetings, *followers attend other people's meetings*. Leadership bonus is about leadership. You want to learn about that. Get good at it. Start doing your own meetings. I do all of my people's meetings when I'm getting them started. Usually when I go to a place to get somebody started, there are no meetings anyway to plug them into. There certainly weren't any meetings in Australia, there certainly weren't any in Italy. I remember when I launched Guido. When we launched him locally, we did our own meetings from day one.

27:44

We started in his living room and then went to the Doctor's House. You want to build, that is the key. Do you want your brand of Nikken operating in this city? When I went to New York to launch somebody out there, there was lots of things happening. But I was interested in what was happening out there in **my** business. So I had to start something. If you are opening a restaurant in New York, are there not other restaurants in New York? But there isn't another *"your"* restaurant in New York. Do you see what I mean? **You've got to take ownership, you've got to help people become the leaders themselves**. It starts with you.

28:25

Going back now, if the process takes two weeks to get them to the starting blocks and we **map out a calendar** *of business briefings, followed by Wellness Previews, followed by strategy sessions.* What we did in our first month we did because we were working double time. There were about 5 of us. How many of us were really committed to this? 5 or 6 of us and we all operated on the same calendar. We were a team; we were running side by side. We were all in the starting blocks at the same time. My pre-launch was simply about assembling a team of people.

29:02

Your pre-launch is about assembling a team of people. It's not about having a dominion of people. It's about working with people, side by side. In other words, five of us. Five of us is sure better than one of us. Five of us who had prior knowledge of business briefings on Tuesday. I think we had some with luncheons and some without luncheons. We had a business briefing Tuesday night, we had a Wellness Preview. On Thursday's we had a business briefing, Thursday nights we had a Wellness Preview, Friday we had a executive lunch. Saturday we had a business training to get people organized on the same page. The following week we did exactly the same thing.

29:40

But now the new people had the calendar. They knew where they could bring their people and so that spins into the next. Let me read you something: **launching a business requires a focused action plan.** The recruiting process is simply taking prospects from one event to the **next event.** The **next event.** The most important event is what event—the next event.

30:09

Increasing in importance and **building in belief** until a decision is made, then repeating these steps for their prospects. Knowing exactly what and where the next event is gives everyone a clear understanding of the next activity to promote. Having this direction will become critical in staying focused and organized as your team begins to build momentum.

30:37

The leaders are those who create calendars and work toward filling those calendars with people. If your events are properly organized, then your machines work properly—"A" goes to "B", "B" goes to "C" and "C" goes to "D" and we start again. "A" goes to "B," "B" goes to "C," "C" goes to "D" and that's all there is to it. Repetition, repetition, repetition, *repetition—this week you have 4, next week you have 8, next week you have 16, next week you have 30, next week you have 60.*

31:09

That is how the business goes. How **important is it to organize your events and your calendar—both personal and business?** Or, do you make up your mind whether you are going to go to an event if you have something coming? Are you working your business in a **reactive** mode *or a* **proactive mode**? Are you ensuring you have somebody for the next event or are you waiting for somebody to come along to go to the next event? How are you operating? How do you think I operate? **I make a decision and then I act on it.**

31:42

That is the **difference** between **doing the business and building it. Building it is like being in construction.** *You are building it. Can you imagine if people didn't have deadlines, or if they didn't have objectives and goals? Would anybody ever move into new home? What kind of a home would it be anyway?* So now we **have a deadline**, we know when we are to assemble these people. We've made a decision it's going to happen in this two-week period—that period is our **pre-launch.** Bang! We've got these people, they're all locked-in, they're ready to go and they're excited. 18 of the people show up, 6 of the people get going, the other 18 they fill spaces in the chairs. They come with one or two people sometimes—the other 18—but the 6, they are there. They are there and you see it in their eyes, you'll see it in their focus. You'll know if somebody is interested, you don't have to be dragging them. If they are interested then they are dragging you, they're calling you, they're busy doing the things.

32:42

The next thing that happens is we have to repeat the process. We have to have a calendar that sees far enough ahead, not only for your people, but for their people and for their people! We make sure we have a lock-in event scheduled. We scan this calendar and we do this all at once. We do this in 90 days. I want all of you in the next 48 hours to build a 90-day schedule. On it you'll include St. Louis because that is in the next 90 days and on it you'll include the Team Diamond event in July.

33:48

There's going to be an event (Purpose, Profit, PINS) that is very important because it's going to convert the vision. Here's what you going to get. You are going to take the cause and turn it into a plan.

How important is that for your new people? How many of you want to have some business builders at that event? You let Nikken's event build their vision, hook them in, lock them in. You let Linda's event **get them focused on an action plan** so that when you all come home on the airplane together you'll be thoroughly exhausted, but you are going to know what you have to do and you are going to do it.

34:24

If you are **doing this process properly, you'll be breaking Silvers on purpose.** You'll be breaking them where you need them because you'll be planning people. You'll be planning to have people. I've got people running for Royal Diamond right now. I've got people running for Diamond, people running for Platinum. What I do is: I simply say, "Who do you have going to the event—that big event?" Those are the question marks. You fill those question marks with a body. I don't care how deep in that leg it is. I want somebody there who represents that leg, that perspective Silver, because within 45 days of that event they will be Silver and the statistics are astounding. 90% of the people who attend one of those big events, the lock-in events, the big ones and we **have a business plan for them, when they come home, they go Silver within the first 90 days.**

35:13

I was able to apply this process to helping people rapidly break Silver. When we apply this to a 90-day business plan in Australia, do you think we had lock-in events? We sure did. One event was their sponsor flew from Canada. Big fanfare. This is a little town, so for somebody to fly in from Canada is a big deal. That was a lock-in event. They organized an event around that one speaker. Then, the following month they get told their sponsor's sponsor (Carolyn) is flying in and she's a Platinum. They are impressed—a Platinum distributor flew all the way from Canada and came and did their lock-in event.

35:46

Then the third month, November, which was the final month of their 90 day launch, which was the month that we had to hammer that last

Silver, the "big Kahuna" flies in—Mike DiMuccio. And, we did a lock-in. By this time though, we had distributors in different locations. I think there were three or four cities, so we did 4 lock-in events and bang, bang, bang, bang—Silver, Silver, Silver, Silver.

36:11

I knew I was going to Australia, and I knew when I was going. I knew why I was going and so did they before we launched . . . because it was planned and they simply executed the plan and the results that they were experiencing was a consequence. It was a consequence. The cause was still a cause. They still believed in the cause. The cause is Nikken and the cause is Wellness. The cause is doing the right thing.

36:45

That cause has to be turned into something that they can apply themselves to and lead others to. It takes a little bit of planning and the process is very clearly defined. This is it, these are the events (see Page 243)—arrange them, organize them in sequence. Because these lock-in events are a little harder to come by, we tend to do them once a month. Which means I can do one, two, three weeks of the process (Page 243) and then get everybody from those three iterations to that lock-in event. So, in going from Silver to Gold, there might be one, two, three weeks, maybe even four weeks of those zigzags (the process) and then we do a lock-in event. Guess what happens? The 3 new Silvers show up after that and then we do it again. One, two, three, four, five, six maybe seven or eight, we might do eight iterations.

37:59

Then we do maybe one or two lock-in events and the next generation of people show up. Let me show you how the 90 days come into play and how the human condition factors into this. This is one month—but in real life when you take the human condition into account and you want your plan to work for sure, you'd take two weeks to do this. That's your pre launch—one month to do this (Silver), two months to do this (Gold). In other words, you are giving Silvers twice as long as it took you to find how many people? Let me ask you, what did you find to go Platinum? Six leaders, 18 candidates to generate 6 leaders.

38:40

What is their plan? What did you sell? Gold? Gold is what—12 to 4. So you are giving these people twice as long to do 80% as much or 75% as much. What are you doing with this group (3rd generation down)? The same thing. You're selling at least the Gold level because Gold is the minimum otherwise you are not understanding the numbers and rules. Ninety days to Gold is what you sell, but you're going to give them even twice as long, four times as much time it took you. Why, because **the further it gets away from you, the duplication starts to break down,** *so you've got to give people a little bit more time to do the same work.* But if you *build it into your plan, you can count on it.*

39:23

Two weeks, one month, two months, and there is your 90 days and your two weeks pre launch and you've got yourself at least a Platinum. But where is everybody focused? On the cause . . . not Silver (or the Board). What have you got everybody doing, where are they going? What is the **most important event—the next event?** Everybody has a calendar, everybody knows when the next event is—*that's their basic training.*

39:56

You know why you are doing these different events and activities. Together, you've generated your calendar. Now it's just a matter of keeping it going, keep fanning those flames. Your first lock-in event might be a small one because you had to organize it, and for it to work within your calendar, you might have had to create it. But the next lock-in event, you know there is going be to something going on somewhere in North America this month, so you make that next lock-in event. Hopefully it's local, and hopefully you've got a bunch **of Gold distributors who have figured this out and are putting on a monthly regional event** and you can tap in that monthly regional event.

40:45

The *next event* usually has to be even *more dramatic* because you not only want your frontline to excited, you want their front line to be excited. So to get these people who have already been to this smaller event even more excited—give them even a bigger event. Now everybody is even more excited. You are building a fire and you are pouring gasoline on the flame. So the *third event* in succession should be an *even bigger* event. Can you think of an even bigger event? Can you plug into one? Usually we have *Platinums putting on Expos* that bring in Diamonds from abroad. That's why we have a Platinum committee and they put on Expos every quarter, because without that you don't have a business.

41:25

The **leaders put on events,** followers don't. The people who are making all the money are the leaders; *the followers just do the business, have fun for a while until they get bored.* The leaders stay and grow and bring in new people and new leaders and new followers. But the beautiful part of this whole story is—*everybody wins.* Everybody wins. Maybe some people don't get what they came for, but everyone gets something. They get something more valuable than they probably expected. As the saying goes, if you don't have your health, you've got nothing.

42:15

Questions. When you are launching a big country, how much of your **time is devoted to individual meetings?**

42:49

What I try and do is I **try and leverage time.** I might be involved in more than one city and more than one town. There is no point in doing the same thing without good reason. In other words, there are some events that really need a personal touch and there are some events that you've gone far enough with your group of people that you can have them together. The **creating interest part—it's a one-on-one thing.** It may not be in person, it might be on the phone. But to create interest with the right people, you need to do that in a very personal and pointed way because there is going to be communication going on. There are going to be some interviews and there's going to be some dialogue, and you can't really generalize—it's particular.

43:47

You have got to create interest. Creating interest is getting interested in someone so that they get interested in you. There is a great series of books and tapes called **"Listening For Success" Get it.** Do not compromise your business by not getting that series.

44:01

The next thing is a **business briefing.** In a business briefing I can put two, three, four, five, *ten interested people* together because they are all interested in the same information. By now I don't have to worry about them being concerned about each other. What is even more interesting about that is; they see other people interested and what does that do to their level of interest? It brings their level of interest up. Now a **Wellness Preview?** Same thing!

44:25

A Wellness Preview is going to be a big event. It's a big event because it includes people who are not interested in the business. You might have a lady at the Wellness Preview because she heard that the magnets could help her wobbly walk! You are not going to see Aunt Sally building a Royal Diamond business, but she was invited because she heard that these products could help. **I want my business prospects** to come to that **Wellness Preview.** Understand **that the Wellness Preview is the store front**—that it is our store. It is where people come to buy the products and if I've got a lot of customers at that store and the right profile, then this is for everybody.

45:10

They are going to find out that Nikken has great products that apply to everybody. Just like at a McDonald's restaurant where you see all kinds of people, some in suits and some in running shoes, I want that at a Wellness Preview. I want my business prospects to come to a Wellness Preview to see and to look at all the customers. There are customers, all kinds of customers; every market profile in the world is represented here at the Preview. Not only that, but they stand up and talk about the products. They even cry, "Holy cow, is this ever cool." They even buy the products—not one or two dollars but one or two thousand dollars. I want to own one of these businesses. That is what I want prospects to feel at this Wellness Preview.

45:46

When I put on a Wellness Preview I need everybody, I want everybody. It is okay to have cross-line involved in Wellness Previews. Everybody's story is going to help everybody with their business prospects and your potential customers. So **a good Wellness Preview has 30 to 50 people** maybe more, but the **emphasis is on the products.** What is important at the Wellness Preview is the emphasis on the **testimonials**—particularly on the products. If I've learned that there is a good business here, what am I going to see? I am going to see testimonials. What does that tell me about the business? . . . that there is a market.

46:20

If I know there is a market for these products, I will be one of the first people to buy them. If I know there is a market for these products and you have **already explained the business and the compensation for that,** I will be one of the first people who wants to build this as a business.

46:33

There is a new presentation that's coming out and it's called the **Power of Wellness.** I'm pretty sure that it is going to be the next gem! You have all seen "It's About Time." That was one business presentation. Actually the very first one came with some 60 slides, but it was the only thing that there was back then. It was a Wellness Preview, but it was basically a business presentation and that evolved to "It's About Time," which evolved to "Trading Time for Money." How many are you familiar with that one? Now it is evolving into the Power of Wellness—by far the most superior product you will ever see in the business presentation. It was made by a group of us and it will be available through Team Tools.

47:25

Today I received a CD called "The Rollout Companion." Apparently, this is a very good CD to listen to and to have your prospect listen to while doing a roll out. It educates them and the person's voice and music are very soothing. It's a subliminal sell; it's really good. You get them where you want them and there is no resistance; it's really a good piece. You want to add this to your process. This is part of your process for creating an environment that's conducive to giving people a back roll. How many of you are serious about giving people a back roll?

48:04

Did you see a back roll in here; did you see it in this process? Did you see it? Absolutely! If you haven't given your people a back roll then how do they connect with this process chart? I will tell you one thing, when I had Marty Jeffery, and there is a great video called "Why Not You," get that video. Just the entertainment value alone is worth watching. But, when I gave him a back roll, it was at that moment he understood. He connected with the cause, he realized that Mike DiMuccio wasn't just a marketer but there was a real truth here, and it was the back roll that got this guy hooked—because it was something he would never have experienced in any other business situation.

48:46

There is a real power to this process that Nikken has developed. Many of you have seen this brochure "Investing in Your Business." If you haven't got it, then get it from Team Tools. What is it? How about this? What should my initial order be? Personal use products, business use products, tools! The importance of the initial order! Ensuring you have what you need, higher PV rebate and PGV override, ensuring success by setting an example. And it gives you examples, a $1,700 point example, a $3,000 point example and a $5,000 point example. It shows them the logistics to their investments, why it makes sense. That way you don't have to answer so many questions.

49:29

Let them educate themselves. You educate yourself. Not only that, but it even gives you sample orders of what would we recommend, good, better or best—here is what we recommend. You take the thinking process out. When you are launching the business at this speed, you want to eliminate as much of the thinking as possible. **You want people just doing, doing, doing** and when they get really big results and they get a really big fat paycheck and they are interested, now they are going to want to understand, what they were doing and why they were doing it, and why it worked.

50:10

You see, first you hit the rank and then you get the competence. Did you notice that? Many of us feel incompetent at times. It's OK, it's normal. First you hit the rank and then you get the competence. What tools do I need? A sample of the different tools. Listen to this, this is really cool. (Referring to a Team Tools brochure) Tools for your education, tools for their information. And it even breaks it down to, interest stage, building belief, presenting, and the validating stage at the end. It includes the activation stage, which is for their education.

50:48

It is working completely in tandem with the plan. So here is a tool that is made available to everybody to synchronize their business. A tool to get everybody on the same page at the same time, take the thinking out of it. All of the tools and all of the thinking has to happen before you start a business. That's what a business plan is, it's the thinking, and then the rest is just action.

Question: Where does the four $5,000 come from?

51:15

The four comes from our understanding of the dynamics. Let me give you an example of the four. It is explained in this brochure by the way. If I want somebody to go Silver, the minimum I would want them to do is four frontline people with $5,000 each. This is where it comes from, but then we found out something afterwards.

51:54

If this person is only told we need $5,000 here plus $5,000 here, what happens for this third person? If this person comes in the third week of the month, they will say, "Is this how you go Silver . . . me plus three others?" Well I can't get three others in the next week because I'm busy, but I can next month so I'll hold back my order till next month and then the whole system breaks down.

52:18

So we realized we had to eliminate this from the equation. This was a mistake we made when we were launching Marty's business. By the way we did $60,000 in volume the last day of the month. How? We achieved the volume because of the chart of four. Everybody kept coming to this conclusion and we said, "You know what, why don't you just do what Marty did?" because it didn't matter in the end. He not only went Silver, he went Gold—200,000 in volume, because he didn't get into the business to invest $5,000. He didn't get into the business to go Silver. Why don't you just do what he did—he bought his products on the last day of the month and, by the way, we did that on purpose.

53:00

When I was sponsoring Marty in August, his launch month was September. It was August 22nd when I met Marty for the first time. He bought $2,500 worth of products just because he wanted to evaluate the products before he made a decision to do the business. His wife had a phenomenal product experience and that was it, his wife's product experience was the lock-in for him.

53:17

Sometimes that's all it takes to have a lock-in is a phenomenal product experience by someone in the family. That was the case for Marty. But because Marty was presented a business, a business vision, the product experience was validation of the business. His wife's product experience assisted him to make a decision to do the business. We talked about the business and doing it in a big way, immediately. I had been around in this business for at least 2 years and I knew that this problem was imminent. I knew we were going to have the last day of the month in September, and I wanted to ensure that the last day of the month in September was going to be a good day and not a bad day.

53:47

Who has to set the example? It starts with us. So on the last day of the month Marty ordered the balance of his 2,500 points. On the last day of the month of August, we could tell everybody that on the last day of September he was going to have a big month. And that's what he did, by doing $60,000 points in volume that last day of the month—because of his wife's product experience. So **what you sow is what you reap.** Don't ever delay someone from placing an order because all you are going to do is to cause delays to happen exponentially. **If you do the right things, the right things happen exponentially.** If you do the wrong things, the wrong things happen exponentially.

54:37

So we went away from that (3) to the four. That was logical, but here is what else happened. We started looking at the dynamics and what we found was every single time when someone was breaking Silver, there were always four other people involved. It just seemed to be like clock work. So the magic number must be four, just like the rule of thirds; the minimum for Silver is four.

55:05

There is another way of looking at it. What if you do 1700 points? You have to drop down another generation for it to be duplicatable; once again it's 16. 16 times 1700 works out to 27,200. If you drop it down by 3 you drop too far below the 20,000 and once again it's that number four. Four keeps popping up as it relates to Silver. So there it is. It's simply by process of elimination; we know that four is the right number. Five is better, four is the minimum, and 3 is no good. That is why we have arrived at the number four.

56:56

We have a new magazine called "Leverage Magazine" available from Team Tools. Thank goodness Team Tools is our supplier. They have the best stuff out in the market as far as I am concerned. This article in the magazine is a great piece. I had seen something like this a long time ago in a company I used to work with, where they profiled some of their top-level people. Anyone of you can have this for your organization. I encourage all of you to get a copy of this great article.

56:35

Thank you for coming. I hope you got something out of this. You will probably want to watch this tape over and over again, because I don't know if I would have understood me, hearing this for the first time.
57:03

"Getting Started"—Building a Strong Foundation—Part 1

:40

Many of you are brand new to Nikken and are not yet Silver Wellness Consultants. Okay great! This training is primary targeted at **focusing on getting the business up and running.** These are in interesting times in Nikken even though a lot has changed since when I first got started and launched my business. As much as things have changed, some things just don't change. There are some things that are fundamental to the business and every once in a while we need a reminder what those fundamentals are, because during a lot of change—rapid change, we tend to sometimes get confused as to what are the things that are the grass roots and what are the things that are **fundamentals,** and how do we adapt to the new environment? So we are going to start from the very beginning and work our way through some fundamentals. I know some of you have been around the business for while and this could be a good refresher. As well, perhaps you will hear something you have not heard before.

1:58

I am going to be bouncing around here and there. You may have watched some of the video tapes that I've done in the last year. If you haven't, I would really strongly encourage you to because I think it will give you a great **background in the science of Nikken.** I think it is an exact business, and the more you understand your business, the more equipped you will be to deal with the circumstances that inevitably as the boss—you are the boss—the CEO of your company, you will be better equipped to handle the different situations that arise.

I assume that you are here or watching this because want to build the business—right? If you're here to learn about the products, wrong training! I'm going to focus on that and some people get those two confused because they think how can you have one without the other. And, you can't. But just as **every company has divisions . . .** they might have a personnel department, a product development department, a marketing department . . . our companies (**each of us have our own Nikken Wellness Consultant businesses**) need to develop our skills and to develop our departments because we do have **a personnel department.** What is it responsible for? **Recruiting!** Making certain that we have the right people in place so that our company can continue to grow. We also have **a marketing department.** What is it responsible for? **Products!** Educating the market about the products so that we can create a demand which ultimately results in sales. Therefore, Nikken steps in to fill that demand.

3:59

So I'm going to touch on all of these things especially now, since we have this thing called the Wellness Home Concept. In my humble opinion, I think it is the quantum leap that addresses the issue that I brought up in a video called "The Missing Link." In that video, I point out that a complete business is a complete business and Network marketing for a long, long time has been incomplete in the way of business. I think Nikken has completely closed the gap on this issue and has created the opportunity of the century and I'll explain that to you. Let me take a step back for a second and just cover one of the fundamentals.

Rick Tonitta, a good friend of mine, introduced me to this idea. He's a scientist. I think he is a brilliant man who has done so much in the way of research and has helped me to understand, from a completely outside point of view, what our business is. One of the things he introduced me to was this pyramid.

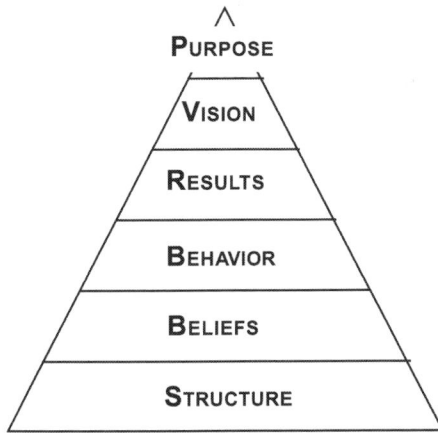

```
                    /\
                 PURPOSE
                 /      \
               / VISION   \
             /─────────────\
            /  RESULTS       \
          /───────────────────\
         /   BEHAVIOR           \
       /─────────────────────────\
      /    BELIEFS                 \
    /───────────────────────────────\
   /     STRUCTURE                    \
  /─────────────────────────────────────\
```

5:11

We live in a world of structure. Let's say you are a part of a company, or you are a part of a family, or part of a Nikken organization, or part of a church. These are all individual structures, even though I'm not thinking of a structure in terms of a hard, fixed building. I'm talking of structure in terms of an ideal. There is a structure to an ideal in that it is organized.

These structures that we were born into impart to us a perception of the world and, from that perception we develop some of our beliefs. It's easy to understand—if you look at religion for instance, because organized religion imparts beliefs. You grow into those beliefs and from those beliefs come behavior. We operate according to our beliefs and that's a fundamental truth. We operate according to those beliefs that are deep in our soul. Those beliefs have come as a result of our environment. We all started on neutral ground; in fact the only thing that we had a fear of when we first got started on this planet was the fear of falling. So everything else we've absorbed through the environment, if you will; it is our environment that has created our beliefs which has led to our behavior.

Behavior produces results and some people really like the results they are getting in certain areas, but don't like the results they are getting in other areas. However, all behavior leads to results and the reason why you like or dislike your results is that you have in mind what you like and what you don't like. You have a vision. You have a vision about what you would like your life to look like, or the kind of house you would like to live in, or the kind of car you would like to drive, or the time you would like to invest in having fun and how you entertain yourself. These are all visions of yourself and if the results you are producing are not consistent with that vision, how do you feel?

7:33

You feel disappointed, frustrated, stressed. How do you feel when you see other people get the results that you are seeking? Some people might say they're encouraged and others might be jealous, and some might be disillusioned. Inevitably, what usually happens at this point in time is we look at ourselves. When our results are not consistent with our vision, but we see other people are getting what we want, then we figure we must be stupid. We interpret it in a certain way that somehow we are lacking in some understanding or something, so we come back down Beliefs and we talk about us.

8:30

I must not have the right attitude, I must not have . . . I . . . I . . . I. It is an internal process. What we probably need to do is take one more step down (Structure) and evaluate where our beliefs came from.

How relevant is this when you are talking about money? Very relevant, because that is what most people don't have enough of, or feel they don't have enough of. It is where the vision is inconsistent with their results—it's in the area of money. So when we look at how people analyze that, what do you hear people say?

9:17

I don't have the money! But how do they justify the fact that they don't have the money? I need a better job, or maybe I'm not smart enough, or maybe they are smarter than me, or I don't need the money. Money does not make you happy; money is the root of all evil, etc., etc., etc. This is how we start to justify the inconsistency. What we have a tendency to do is, rather than raise our expectations or at least maintain our vision, we tend to lower our expectations. Let me give you an example. I didn't get Silver done in my first month so I guess it can't be done in a month. We lower the expectation and, in our business, that's an example of how it functions, how it works. Rather than maintain our vision, we have a tendency to become self-critical. We justify the fact that we did not succeed, especially if we see others who have succeeded, as somehow lacking on our part . . . because if somebody else could do it and I can't, that must mean I'm not capable or something is wrong with me.

That's typically the way we do things in life, that's how our mind functions. But there is something even more important and more powerful than a vision. A number of you have an idea of how you would like your life to be, if you really take the time to think about it . . . some of the things you'd like in your life. An older man from Alberta once said to me, "I'm so impressed with your youth and yet you had a pretty good idea what it was that you wanted to do in your life."

11:25

That struck me as "No! I didn't know what I wanted to do but, what I did know was how I wanted to live." That is a different thing altogether. I didn't know what house I wanted to live in, I didn't know what business I want to be in, etc, etc, but I did know how I wanted to live. Living is an expression, it's not an end result. That is a much higher degree of awareness. That's a much higher expression of yourself when you look at Purpose. Purpose is what drives the equation, but many people lack a sense of purpose or have lost their sense of purpose—which is their compass. They grow attached to vision, or they grow attached to results. You see this in society with programs like Reality TV. You see "Get Rich Quick" schemes on television, constantly bombarding people with the "Get Rich Quick" attitude and what that represents is a lack of purpose. They create, on the screen of your mind, a vision that

is completely inconsistent with your results. Lotteries—how many play and win the lotteries? In other words, we need to take a stronger look at why we are here?
12:55

I just came back from Tampa last month. Even Royal Diamonds need a reminder of what we are doing in the scheme of things. You might think you have it all at some point and then you realize there is no such thing. We had "Humans Being More" Silver training with over 300 people. There were a lot of Diamonds, Royal Diamonds and there were officers of the company there as well; it was an impressive experience. Just the star power alone was neat. But, to hear people share, again, as if it was their first time being there, or to be involved with a partner who had never been to a "Humans Being More" Silver training—was very interesting.

14:06

To relate and find that common ground is quite amazing. I proposed to the company that there be a mandatory "Humans Being More" Silver training for the Presidents Club annually. These are the people Nikken says represents the vision of this company, and I don't think they do. I don't think they all do. I think they represent a vision, but I don't think it's always the vision of this company. We need a refresher to start developing our sense of purpose. I think the "Humans Being More" Silver training is all about getting in touch with the higher purpose, the higher side of us, the compass—the thing that helps us to better see the reality of this equation, rather than attacking ourselves and justifying our behavior, justifying our results. By getting a strong sense of purpose, it drives you upward, rather than down. Let me see if I can better define it.

15:36

Earl Nightingale taught Bob Proctor, who taught me, the definition of success, which is the thing that we are all after. I've seen people in Nikken self-destruct, and they would do it anywhere and in any business if they had some success. The reason is they don't have a strong sense of purpose. They may have a strong vision, they may even produce some pretty strong results but without that purpose, without that guiding light, they go off on a tangent and self-destruct. So, this issue is a very relevant issue, a very strong and important issue to take hold of. Silver training for me reminds me of that definition of success.

16:40

It was Earl Nightingale who said:

**"Success is the
progressive realization
of a worthy ideal."**

Write that down, because if you start to use that as your definition of success, you will start to evaluate your Nikken experience in a different way. You won't look at the results, because they won't have nearly as much meaning—positive or negative. What will be important is your definition of success and how you relate that with what you are doing. I repeat—"Success is the progressive realization of a worthy ideal." It means you needs to be progressing. Some people say progress is moving in the direction of a vision. But, you know what . . . that all depends on the time frame you are looking at it. I'll give you an example. How many of you think the stock market is progressing?

17:43

It seems to be going this way and that way. Nobody can seem to guess which way it's going to go next. It's kind of an interesting experience. But if we look 50 years from now, we will see that this experience was part of a progression toward where it ended up 50 years from now. So it's the time frame you are looking at to determine whether you're progressing. In fact, we are always progressing if you are looking at it from that stand point. Sometimes you've got to take 5 steps backward to progress. Somebody came up to me and shared with me how I've changed as a person. And, it's true. I think I've had to take a few steps back and gotten in touch with things that are more relevant, so that I can take a quantum leap forward.

18:34

Progress is not measuring your results day to day and saying, "Did I get closer to where I wanted to go?" I'm telling you this because, for some of you, the Nikken experience is the first time you've been the captain of your own ship, and you are going to have a lot of people who to want to torpedo that ship. You can bet on it. Is success common?

Well, if success is the progressive realization of a worthy ideal, it is not very common at all. So let's continue with our definition. There needs to be progress. But, progress is not something that you measure in terms of a small window of time, it's a bigger picture. I look at Nikken's experience over the last 3 years and our sales are down. Does it surprise you? Does it concern you? It doesn't concern me at all, because I know this is part of the plan. It's progress in fact. I know, so well, this is part of the plan that in 1994, I co-authored a book—a training system called "You³." In that training system, I realized that people were going to experience something, every single one of them. So I published what they would experience, so when they experienced it and when they saw this, they would not be so concerned.

20:12

That curve (refers to diagram in You³) at first looks great at first, and then all of a sudden, it's like somebody has torpedoed the ship. It starts to sink. So you need to build a stronger hull. You need to do something, and that gets you back on track. What happens when you get to that next major quantum leap? You get to do it all over again, because that's the way life was designed. Can you imagine your life without any valleys? They say that the degree of your joy is in direct proportion to the degree of your sorrow. So, our life was not designed to go this way, our life is designed to go like this (making a wave motion) and over a large span of time what you will see is that it's actually doing this (going up motion). But, if you look at a short time, it's like this. Look at the stock market. Take a 10-year window of the stock market, take a 20 year window of the stock market and you will find that it is consistently going up. But if you take a two-month window, it's very confusing. I'm saying this because that's life. The stock market is a representation of human emotion, it's a snippet of who we are, the fabric of our being and it will affect you in a business environment and it will affect you in your Nikken environment.

21:53

Your Nikken business is not always going to go up. Mine didn't. It has had hills and valleys; the Nikken corporation is a macrocosm of the microcosm and therefore, it must experience that too, because it's a dynamic living thing. But progress, progress—is the important thing in success—as long as you are progressing toward something that is worthy. What does that mean, a worthy ideal? Well I like what Bob Proctor says a worthy ideal is. Bob says it's something you would trade your life for. It's something you would trade your life for. Well, let's just think about this in a practical sense—life. Would you agree that we know exactly the day we were born, but we don't know the exact day we are going to leave this planet? We are all given a certain amount of seconds, minutes, hours, days. So there is a finite span to this life; therefore, life and time are one and the same.

LIFE = TIME

23:10

What you are trading your time for is the same as saying what you are trading your life for, isn't it? So the big question remains: is what you are trading your time for worthy of your life? Is it worthy of you? How many people are thinking in those terms today? Think about that. There are some people who are preparing themselves right now for battle. These people are prepared to sacrifice their life for something they believe is worthy of their life—the pursuit of freedom. That is a huge contribution. Does everybody operate that way? In other words, how many people have their feet firmly planted on the ground (re. their purpose), because that's where the ground is. It's not at the bottom of the pyramid (Structure). Did you ever expect a company the size of ENRON would go upside down or WorldCom? We look at the structure and how big it is—Russia, the former Soviet Union—it's so big. We look at the structure; we are awed by its size and therefore, it must be credible because it's big.

24:40

The Health Care industry is so big. It's so relevant. It's so huge, therefore it must be so credible—whether it's producing results consistent with our vision or not. Our purpose or not is almost irrelevant isn't it? Once it gets to a point where it's so big, you must assume it is right. But size does not matter; size is irrelevant. What is relevant is whether you are progressing toward the realization of this worthy ideal (purpose), whatever that worthy ideal is. So what would you trade your life for? Would you trade your life for your family? I'm amazed how my life has changed concerning that. Some of you may have gotten my Christmas card; you've met the little guy. He's a cutie. The point is, I found my worthy ideal a number of years ago and I never expected it. I was not looking for it, or maybe I was deep down inside. I knew I needed to find something that would make my life meaningful because I came to this planet to make a difference in a very big way. I'm not modest; I came here to make a difference in a big way and I'm only getting started.

26:24

When Nikken landed on my doorstep, it was first introduced to me as an opportunity to make money. Of course somebody who is young and ambitious wants to make money. It was a nice vehicle for me to do that, but what I didn't expect was the human element. I didn't expect to fall in love with the idea and become impassioned by this idea. Then I met Mr. Masuda and it became really important to me, for some reason, to know if this guy was the real thing. Was he the real deal? Is he really what I think he is and what I perceive him to be? When I met Mr. Masuda and had an opportunity to interview him (we had a translator), I wanted to get to the heart of the man because if I was going to put my life into something, it had to be the right thing. It had to be the thing that best represented who I was, the core of my being. I was so enchanted by him and his simplicity, that I just knew in my heart that this guy was the real deal and the idea of the Five Pillars of Health was not just a marketing gimmick; it was something that struck a chord. I was also convinced that *he* knew it was a good idea, but he didn't have any idea how big this idea was really going to be. In fact, the question I asked him that left a mark with me was—did he ever think he would have such an enormously successful company?

27:53

Now if I was to ask a CEO who was completely out of touch with this (purpose), they would probably have said "Oh yes, of course, we knew we would be successful." They might even boast about how they've made the right decisions at the right time, that's why things are they way they are. But he wasn't like that. He thought about it and he said, "No, I was interested in my health and I thought others might be too." That was his response. "I was interested in my health and I thought others might be too." This is the response from a guy who founded this company, and you know the success of this company. It's a privately held corporation, so you know he is not exactly hurting financially. That's a remarkable statement because, for me, it was a transparent statement. It gave

> **Nikken is the most phenomenal opportunity.** I wear lots of shoes but I didn't get any attention until I started wearing Cardio Strides. **There is something magical about what we are doing that seems to affect people on a very subtle sub-conscious level.**

me a glimpse into this simple man who was not a businessman, but a visionary. He partnered with Mr. Tom Watanabe. Tom Watanabe studied business and he went to school in America. It was the visionary mind, the visionary experience and the heart of Mr. Masuda combined with the business savvy and steadfastness of Mr. Watanabe. I think the two together are responsible for making certain that this thing sets sail on the right course.

29:23

It is our responsibility to take it further. I consider the worthy ideal in Nikken to be the balance of the Five Pillars of Health. I think that's the deal. I don't think Mike DiMuccio could be doing anything worthier than the pursuit. The pursuit—because remember it's the progressive realization and therefore, it's the pursuit. It's the pursuit of this ideal that, by definition, is success. Is Mike DiMuccio trying to achieve balance in his life a worthy ideal (purpose)? Trying to expand who I am to express the divinity in me to higher and higher purposes? That's what it is all about. It's about expansion! Do you know that everything is for expansion? Spirit is for expansion. God is for expansion. Anything contrary to that is not true. The desire you have for more wealth is the very desire you have for more life. So for people who say "Oh well, you know, I don't need the money." or "Money doesn't grow on trees." or "Money isn't everything" and all that . . . they are saying something and demonstrating their ignorance by saying that. If you understand who you are and where you are from, and what your highest ideal is, there is no such thing as enough. Is there enough love? Is there enough health? Is there enough of a positive attitude? Is there enough of a contribution to society? Is there enough in the way of strengthening your relationships? Is there enough in the way of resources? What could you do if you had more? What would you do for others if you had an infinite amount of money coming in and all you needed to do is figure out how you want to direct it? When you get outside of yourself and you see the bigger picture, all of a sudden that ideal becomes rather worthy.

31:32

So I found in Nikken a vehicle that, if I continue this pursuit, I know that I'm doing the highest good. When I see hills and valleys, I just know that it's just part of a process. I've got a bigger picture here in my head. I see way beyond the hills and valleys. I know this company has got a map for my destiny because this is real, this is real (purpose), this is not (structure) This (structure) can change in a heart beat. WorldCom . . . kaboom! But this (purpose) won't change.

32:17

We might be selling magnets today, but wellness—we will always be selling wellness. A lot of people start here (structure). They've got to see it, touch it, and feel it to believe it. That's not how it works in reality. This (purpose) is how it works in reality. It begins here (purpose) and from here you work backwards (down to structure). For instance, if I now understand how I want to live . . . I want to live in the pursuit—that's my life. I want to be pursuing it because if I'm not pursuing it, by definition, I've stopped progression. And, if I've stopped progression, then what . . . I'm no longer a success. So when you talk to someone like a Bruce Black and think, "Oh my God, he is such a big success story!" How do you know that he may not be empty inside? I'm not saying that he is. He may have stopped the pursuit years ago. Here you are in the thick of the pursuit. You may not have the results to show for it yet, but what is the definition of success . . . it's a real time expression. It's how you are in the pursuit. Are you in the pursuit? Are they in the pursuit? A lot of people are not as passionate about what they are doing as I am about what I'm doing. Who do you think is going to win the conversation? Who do you think is going to set up an attractive force? Who are they going to want to be like? It's getting in touch with that passion and getting to that pursuit that is going to attract the people into your business.

33:42

That is what you want to do, isn't it? You want to attract people who have their own mind and their own desires. You don't want to have to tell them to go to work every day. They are just going to do it because they're excited, they're passionate. You want to attract those kinds of people. How does that work?

How do you attract? You've got to have a vision. You've got to be passionate about that vision and you need to pursue it. So this is the ideal (purpose) by which I live and that is why I can see past any of the little obstacles that happen. People get in a tiff because there might be a change in the compensation plan. Long term—think big. The compensation plan has been changed since I've been in the business—constant changes. That's what causes the business to progress—changes in the products, changes in the management, change. Change is inevitable. Change is the only thing that assures us of progress. Progression, that's the key word here. So, we've got to get in touch with this side of ourselves (our purpose).

34:52

"Humans Being More" Silver training is a critical component to the success of your business. Number 1—your commitment to it; Number 2—the people that you introduce to Nikken and their commitment to it. Your insistence on it. It has got to be part of the business start-up. In other words, when you sit down to tell somebody what they need to invest, it must be included in their initial investment. Do you know what I've experienced? If it's the last $300 that a person has, and you're thinking—if they buy product I earn a percentage, or should they go to "Humans Being More?" What should you sell this person? Think of the picture. How BIG are you willing to think? What is a Royal Diamond worth to you if this vision inspires them to those heights? You've got to think long term in business; you cannot be thinking short term. I know you're in Nikken because you're looking to change your life, and maybe for some of you, just to make a little bit of extra money.

36:21

I'm talking to the people who are building Royal Diamond businesses today, because I don't waste my time talking to people who aren't interested in that. Why think small. You've been given a mind to think—why think small? If you are going to take the time to do anything, do it big. We know what it is that makes our life meaningful (purpose). Nikken is the only company who has represented that. I've never seen it in any other experience. First of all, is money important? Yes, but It's relatively important. That's what I like about Nikken. They say money is absolutely important. It's at the foundation of a lot of what we are able to do, however, it's only 1/5 of the equation. There are other things that are just as important. It's getting it all together that matters, and from there we can set a vision.

37:21

What is it that we would like to achieve that would allow us to live in this manner and then what we can do is go down here and say—what is the structure that will provide us with this way of living? You may notice that this presentation is a little bit different than most presentations you've been to in the past. What did I start with in this presentation? I started with—what do you want? How do you want to live? What is the point of having a business if the business isn't providing you with the lifestyle? What's the lifestyle? What are you seeking? Let's get this clear, get the top end clear (purpose) and then we'll work backwards. Is there something out there that can provide us with that? Is there a structure out there that can provide us with this (purpose and 5 Pillars of Health)? That's why we work backwards. What was the last thing I talked about in that presentation? It was the company. Nikken was the last thing I talked about instead of the first thing. Nikken has no relevance until you figure out what the problem is and if Nikken is actually the solution to that problem. So, I started with the issue and worked backward to see if there was something that can bring us to where we want to go . . . and we arrived at Nikken.

39:01

There is some material out there that I suggest you get your hands on and become a student. Get a copy of "The World is Changing! 7 Questions That Demand An Answer," and the Recruiting Puzzle which has been put together by Bob Proctor. It teaches you how to think, how to think in terms of solving problems, human problems . . . instead of trying to sell your wares. What you have to sell is meaningless to people. What they have to buy is everything. It's just learning how to make that distinction. When you're brand new in the business, you are going to have a tendency to want to run out there and tell everybody about these wonderful new products, about this amazing new business. Good for you! But what's that got to do with anybody. So, as excited as you are, you want to take that excitement, that enthusiasm, that passion and direct it in a way that is inviting and attractive to another person. When they see you passionate, they want to be passionate. Everybody wants to be passionate about something

40:19

It's taking that energy of yours and directing it in a certain way that attracts people to want to know more about what it is that you're involved in. We get involved in a structure and it will build our beliefs. Do you know that the beliefs in network marketing are different than the corporate world . . . which means you have to change your mind about a lot of things. Are you prepared to change your mind? There are some things that are fundamental to the functioning of the corporate world that are irrelevant here. Did you know that we do not engage in competition, that we don't perceive you as a threat, that your brothers and sisters and cousins in Nikken are not your competition? There are enough people out there, that we don't have to compete with each other. We've got such a big task ahead of us competing with the real competition, that the last thing we need to do is worry about each other. We work in harmony—that's a different paradigm.

41:30

Are other network marketing companies a threat? Not at all. We are in the Wellness industry not the network marketing industry. Did you know that? Do you know network marketing is just a method of how we've modeled our business; it's the structure from which we operate. We are in a Wellness business not the network marketing business.

We used to talk about being the number one network marketing company.

42:32

I didn't care that Nikken wanted to be the number one network marketing company. I'm not "their" company, therefore I can't be a participant in that. But I can participate in being number one in Wellness. You see, your vision has to be big enough to include everybody. You and I are not Nikken Inc. and I don't care if Nikken Inc. is the number one network marketing company. But I really do want them to be the number one provider of Wellness products in the world. I want my marketing company, Good Vibrations International, to be one of the forerunners in the Wellness consulting business and therefore we will operate new behaviors. We'll start to actually do things a little bit differently than we have. These are all things that you have to be prepared to learn. I'm spending a lot of time on this subject because, too often, the big players, the ones who are going to get the prize are the ones who think long term, not short term. As important as it is to do the right things as quickly as possible, if you lose sight of the big picture, you're lost.

44:05

If an airplane is off course by one degree and it flies over the Pacific Ocean, where is that plane going to land? Even a slight error in your judgment can take you, over a long period of time, way off course. You have to always keep your eyes focused on where you're going, not where you are. But you need to know where you're at to make an adjustment if necessary. Most people just look at where they're at. If this month's check is lower than last month's . . . is that where you want to go? Keep thinking that way and that's exactly where you're going. I'm saying that because this is reality. This is a business that definitely goes where you think; it goes in the direction of your vision. The rest is history.

45:25

Let's move on! What has this Wellness home concept got to do with any of this? As long as we were in the network marketing business, we were off course . . . that had nothing to do with the Five Pillars of Health. So, we went as far as our structure could go, because it eventually got to the point where the results and vision were bouncing up against each other. There was an inconsistency, and that inconsistency was big enough that we had to change. Things were forced into change. Those of you who have been around for a while have seen some structural changes at Nikken. A structural change could be management, it might be compensation, it might be technology, it might be the NEAT system, it might be e-Nikken. Some of the things that were being introduced into the Nikken structure have changed. Now, you have to be a Silver distributor in order to sponsor internationally; that's a structural change.

46:43

These are all modifications in the structure. What happens if I don't modify the structure? Let me give you an example. You buy a race car and you're on a track and you've got a straight run. You hit that pedal and you go as fast as you can. That car is not going to go any faster than that car was built to go. What if you want to go faster? If you want to go faster, you can either buy a faster car or you can modify that car—maybe make it more aerodynamic, etc. Structural changes are important in order to keep things moving in a certain direction. So don't be afraid of things and afraid of change because it's totally relevant and necessary in order to keep things moving to newer heights.

47:44

So let's get to the Home Wellness concept. Nikken created the Five Pillars of Health and the idea of achieving balance in the Five Pillars of Health was the philosophy. They used to talk about the individual, an individual achieving balance in the Five Pillars of Health. By the way, when this was presented, we used to think of ourselves as being in the preventive healthcare business. Today we talk about being in the

BALANCE

---

wellness business. It's almost assumed now, that we understand that wellness means prevention, but it has taken 10 years in North America to come to that realization.

48:30

So Nikken was about creating balance in the lives of individuals and they created a business around that, so that you and I, as individuals, could participate in the promotion of this concept. However as things have evolved in the last decade and wellness has become a recognizable word, Nikken is modifying its definition of itself to be the number one wellness provider and it's modifying its definition of what that would look like. What would the top end look like if we were successful? Let's go to the structure. Where do we learn about wellness? Where's your first wellness encounter? I remember what mine was. Eat your spinach, it'll make you healthier . . . eat those peas, fish is good for your brain. My mom used to tell me all the time to eat lots of fish—it's got phosphorous, it's good for your brain. I don't know if that was true or not and you know what, I never saw my mother as a wellness provider. But what if she had a label that said PhD Wellness? I would probably have taken that information as a little more credible. There was never a world or structure in existence that gave her any credibility, even though she was an authority on the subject in one-way or another. There are some old wives tales that are actually true. Chicken soup makes you feel better. It has been discovered, as we've learned in science, that in fact there is something in the chicken soup that makes us feel better.

50:28

So, the first place where we are introduced to the subject of wellness—even though we don't call it that, even though we don't recognize it as that, even though we don't recognize it as a credible source, is the home. In fact, it's the place where we have the most influence. It is the place where you actually have the most influence. Let's go back to our vision. If you wanted to affect the world in a big way, where do you need to begin? Here is my example of this. If this is where we are right today in the area of wellness in the world, where, by the time we are 30 to 40 years of age, the incident rates of cancer and diseases and so forth is so much, and by the time you're 50 is this much, and by the time your 60 or 70 is this much, we know we are off course. We absolutely are guaranteed, we are certain we know that. But if I want to fix this problem, where do I start if I'm off course? At home. Somehow I lost track at the very beginning; I moved away from my home and the information I was getting there as credible, and then I became reliant on the exterior world to supply me with information. And then I looked at what's out there . . . thinking, the structure is so big, it must be credible.

52:03

Where do I go for my health information? Who do I have to check with to make sure that these products are safe to use? Think of the thoughts that people have concerning their well-being. Who is their source of creditability on the subject? Who? Doctors! Now, ask the doctors in the world how many hours they've invested in the subject of wellness, that they should be considered authorities on the subject. You can see where the problem is. The problem is we've given credibility to people and misread that. We call it a healthcare system and is it really? If you were a customer (and you are), to the tune of $1.4 trillion a year in North America, . . . if you are a customer of the current "healthcare" industry, what does that imply about your health? There is something wrong. There is something wrong with you.

53:17

So, are you actually a part of the "healthcare" system caring for your health or are you part of the "sick care" system caring for whatever is wrong? As long as we have that misnomer, we don't see what the reality of the situation is. The reality is "healthcare" is a subject and "sick care" is a subject. They're both relevant, but they're different. So, who are the healthcare professionals and who are the wellness professionals? Are they the same? Since there are not too many wellness professionals but there is a huge industry of healthcare professionals, we have a choice. We have a vision and we can create it. What do we want to create? We want to create a structure that is identifiable as a wellness structure, identifiable as a wellness structure that produces wellness beliefs . . . that creates wellness behaviors . . . that produces wellness as a result . . . which allows people to live the way they want to live, which is consistent with who they really are. What are we going to do? We are going to set up hospitals and call them wellness hospitals. Are we are going to give seminars and lectures in them? Exactly how is this structure to take shape and form? What does it look like?

54:38

It looks like your home . . . where you have the greatest degree of influence on the people you care about the most . . . the next generation. Because this generation . . . the one we are in right now—is tainted. We are already 30, 40, 50 years down the road of sickness. We've already ruined a lot of what is good about our health just by the habits we have and they are pretty hard to break. I'm not looking to resurrect the dead; I'm looking to save the world by saving the next generation. I'm building a model and giving credibility to that model so that 50 or 60 years from now, they won't know any better. For them, that's normal. For them, wellness is normal, and pursuing a balanced life is normal.

55:49

I have three young kids and the two older ones ask me the most amazing questions. We have conversations with the kids about what's good food and what's junk food. So, the other day my daughter asked me why they put commercials on television for junk food. They are starting to understand the difference between good food and bad food and at least they're asking the right questions. Take that child 10 years from now. If I am considered an authority or specialist on the subject of wellness, and there is a structure that gives me credibility on the subject, those kids are going to listen to what I have to say about the subject. They are not going to become reliant on misinformation.

56:56

The information they are going to be getting is information about wellness, about the latest discoveries on the subject of wellness, not "sick care," but wellness. All of a sudden, my house is a house of wellness. All of a sudden, everything I do and everything I talk about is related to wellness. Why not introduce some of those ideas into my home, make that home an environment that's conducive to wellness because an environment (structure) leads to beliefs, which leads to behavior, which produces results. Why not make the first structure a child encounters—a wellness structure—and give it credibility by identifying it as a structure. We need to call it a wellness home and it's different than the average home. A wellness home is a home committed to wellness.

57:53

A wellness home is a home that invests not only time and energy, but resources, in maintaining wellness. Many of you right now probably have a television, if not 2, 3 or 4 in your home. Many of you probably have more televisions in your home than bathrooms. That means you have more garbage going in than going out! You have already started to eye that flat screen TV. My guess is that you probably have a DVD player, a VCR, remote controls and you probably have a stereo. I'm sure you've spent quite a bit of money on making certain that your home is an entertainment home or a center of entertainment. In fact, they call it an "entertainment center" for your home. There is a whole industry out there that has been given credibility and authority that says you should have an entertainment home. Your home should be entertaining.

59:10

Because it has credibility, it has magnitude and real value . . . we have such a thing. We really like to be entertained as people. And, as they continue to upgrade the technology in that area, what do we do? We buy more. It's not like we need another TV, but the new ones look better. There's a predisposition, there a structure out there right now that has us consuming and creating in our home, an entertainment environment. Why wouldn't there be a structure that would do the same regarding wellness? Wellness is tangible. Wellness is practical. Wellness produces results that we all enjoy and like. The wellness home is something that some of us have already created—our homes have all the Nikken products. I hadn't understood the total impact of a wellness home until recently. But now, when we go to a restaurant and the server pours us water, my kids ask if it is Pi-Mag water. You don't think much about it, but do you think that the child at the next table will be asking that question? No!

1:00:44

So, what is it about our home that has my kids fascinated? They know how to turn on the Pi-Mag unit. They sleep on the magnetic sleep system and they know they are sleeping on the magnetic sleep system. They can say Nikken. One of the first things my daughter was able to read was Nikken. She would see the logo and say, "Papa, that's Nikken." She is in an environment that is promoting wellness, but the environment itself is "Nikkenizing" her. She has started to think in terms of Nikken. She starting to think in terms of wellness, even though she does not understand the subject. In other words, her environment is creating beliefs and is therefore creating behaviors on a subconscious level. Just because I made a conscious decision to improve the quality of my life and include the Nikken technology in my environment . . . she's touching it, feeling it and seeing it . . . so has she. I've observed people who are not necessarily building the Nikken business, but have the Nikken products . . . because the products are fascinating, they want to show their friends the technology, and that they've learned something new.

1:02:07

Don't you always talk to your friends about the news? Our products themselves are fascinating enough that you'll find people tell other people about them, just because it's an interesting subject. Does that have an effect? It most certainly does, because that person is affirming to themselves by virtue of saying something about it—that they made a good decision. They're becoming consciously and subconsciously involved in the subject and now they're developing a predisposition . . . which Paul Zane Pilzner says will cause them to become voracious consumers of more wellness products and services. It's stimulating them on a conscious level which creates a sub-conscious effect. By incorporating Nikken technology into our home and calling it a Wellness Home, and giving it a certification so that it's called a Certified Wellness Home . . . it gives it credibility. What makes it certified? Because we say so. What made a doctor a doctor? Somebody said so! Somebody said . . . this is what you have to do to get that label. So, all of a sudden the Wellness Home is an industry.

1:03:11

Sony is the entertainment giant that's turning your home into an entertainment center. Nikken is the Wellness giant that's turning your home into a Wellness center. You don't have to go and open up a Wellness center down the street because you've got the best Wellness center going for you. What a concept! We've got all of these technologies and all of these products and Nikken will continue to develop more unique technologies and products in the category of rest and relaxation, since it's such a fundamental part of creating a wellness environment. Fitness—they will continue to develop technologies and products that fit the category of fitness because it affects us on a physical level and creates an environment. Have you noticed that wearing the CardioStrides gets attention?

1:04:43

It's the most phenomenal thing. I wear lots of shoes but I didn't get any attention until I started wearing CardioStrides. It's really interesting. There is something magical about what we are doing that seems to affect people on a very subtle sub-conscious level. How about environmental development? Nikken is always developing more and interesting technologies to make certain that our home is environmentally friendly and is providing an environment that is healthy and safe. Nutrition—providing good nutrition is a whole subject that Nikken is getting further involved in, as we learn more and more of the long term impact and importance of nutrition. Nikken is becoming more and more involved in this subject. In fact, they've just asked the

Royal Diamonds to fly to Japan in March to spend three days touring some facilities with a doctor who is a world-renowned specialist on the subject and has developed some very interesting technology and products. That's Nikken's commitment to this concept.

Now, can you build a business? Let me remind you, you are not in Nikken. The second you say "I am in Nikken" you are categorizing yourself as somebody who is a subordinate or some sort.

1:06:27
You are not in Nikken, you are outside of Nikken. Nikken is a company that existed before you and will exist after you. It exists. It's a company. You are not in that company. You don't own that company. You don't have shares in that company. It's a company. It's a corporation that performs a function; it's a manufacturer, it's a developer. They've set up an infrastructure around the world to be able to support the distribution of their products to the community. That already exists without you, so you're not in Nikken. It's important to be clear on what the structure is, because the beliefs will determine the behavior. If you don't understand the structure, then the beliefs you have about the structure will cause you to behave in a certain way that may not be consistent. Many people wait for Nikken to decide what the next incentive will be. Think about that. Nikken is not a company you work for; Nikken is a company that works for you.

1:07:41
You've got to think in those terms because it changes your whole perspective on how to go forward and the success you'll have. I was in a meeting with all the Royal Diamonds and the subject of the Kenko-Creator came up. Did you know that the Kenko-Creator was created by a distributor, and do you know why? Nikken had made the mattress but nobody knew how to sell it. A distributor came up with the idea of creating a Kenko-Creator to demonstrate the product. The distributor, at the time (that is what they were called) was responsible for the solution. The distributor was responsible for the sale, not Nikken. Nikken is just

responsible for making good products; we were the ones who are supposed to figure out how to get those products into the market.

1:08:52

How many of us are waiting for Nikken to make that decision? You see, if your perception of the situation is skewed only a little bit, it skews your beliefs. It skews your behaviors and therefore it must skew the results. Then you wonder why the vision and the results don't line up. I realized later on in my business that my reason for being in Nikken is to guide Nikken into the future and not for Nikken to guide me. And I realized, that perhaps, my vision of Nikken is bigger than Mr. Watanabe's vision. In fact, I proved it to myself on several occasions. Thank goodness for that because I need him to mind the business; I need him to make sure Nikken stays in the business, so that I can make my vision a reality.

1:09:52

The Wellness Home is not an accident. It started as an idea almost three years ago, as part of a mission statement—even though it appears to have sprung up in the last year. Nikken—they need to exist, they need to do what they do. They make products, they develop technology, they support research and development. They build the infrastructure and support our ability to do what we do. I believe that the philosophy that gave birth to this company is why this company has been so dynamically successful. They've attracted people, people who want to promote this idea.

1:10:40

The Wellness Home concept has further refined and defined our position in the market and the value, the true ultimate value of what it is that we are doing. Can you see homes across the world being called Wellness Homes? I have a hard time seeing individuals, but I have an easy time seeing a home and the environment and what it means to that family in that home. I'm talking about creating an environment where they have a better life and a better future, a better hope for the future. If we did not have physical problems to deal with, we would be directing our energies toward better things, wouldn't we?

1:11:31

$1.4 trillion of our energy is devoted to something that nobody wants. This doesn't make sense to me. The future has got to be better than that. Nikken created an opportunity backed by a remarkable and ongoing commitment to the development of technology, to maintain their position in the market as the number one provider of Wellness Technology. That's their job. Our job is to make them the number one Wellness Company. Their job is to be the number one in Wellness Technology. It's very important that you make the distinction. It's our job to make sure they are the number one.

1:12:21

Let's suppose you were Celine Dion—rough around the edges, a brand new singer who had never sung in public and I was a producer who heard you sing. I'm thinking, "This kid has the potential to go all the way. This is a singer extraordinaire who could be number one in the music industry." As a producer, I would get behind you and bring the necessary people and money together to push you all the way to the top. It's my job to make Celine the star that's in her to be. So, my team and I make Celine Dion the number one female artist in the music industry. Why not think in those terms with Nikken. Let's make Nikken number one in the Wellness industry.

It's not up to Nikken, it's up to us to bring our resources and our talent and attract the people that we need to make that happen. It's not Nikken's job. Their job is very clear.

1:13:20

They write the checks, build the infrastructure to support the delivery of products to the market on time and make sure new products keep coming to us. It is not their job to create incentives; it's not their job to create marketing, that's our job.

Let's just review this—manufacture, technology, development—the company with an extraordinary vision provides an opportunity for people to go out and promote. That's how they create a sales force, that's how they create a marketing arm, by giving them an opportunity. Their job is to keep that product line, that pipeline filled so that the opportunity is viable, not twenty years ago, but in real time . . . today, tomorrow, and 5 years from now.

1:14:33

Do you know that 10 years from now Nikken is going to have technology that is going to blow our mind—10 years from now? You know you have a company that's committed to the future. Their research and development has spent more money than most of our competition combined. They've been doing this for almost 30 years and have millions of people who've experienced these products. They have hundreds of thousands of people who call themselves Wellness Consultants in some 30 countries already—quite a success story. Where does this leave you? Why should you join this now? Isn't it done? Isn't it finished? Isn't all the money to be made already being made? Aren't all the people at the top already at the top or is there room for somebody like you? What could you contribute to this situation that would be worthy of you and that would compensate you in a way that is worthy of you? What's the answer?

1:15:32

Do what Nikken wants you to do. We have been in Canada for 11 years and have less than 1% market penetration. Let me repeat: less than 1% market penetration. Richard Branson is a billionaire from England who has just pumped $200-$300 million dollars into cellular technology in North America. The market is 40% penetrated and he thinks it is underdeveloped because in Europe it's 60%, and he wants to take the company from 40 to 60% market penetration—billions of dollars. I like the way he thinks and I am probably inclined to agree with him. If we are at 1% market penetration, he probably wouldn't look at us until we were at 10-20%. We are faced with the ominous task of taking this company to 10 or 20% market penetration. If it has taken us 11 years to penetrate less than 1% of the market, do we have enough manpower? No, we don't. We're going to need more people because I'm not going to work 10 or 100 times harder.

1:16:42

That doesn't make any sense. What we need is more people.

We've got to grow the company. **Your job is to expand your organization. That is your first priority**—not to be confused with retail sales or exposing the products.

Your first priority and why the compensation plan is designed the way it is—to maximize your profits to you and make it worth your while—if you build an organization.

A lot of people think your business is your down-line but no, that's your organization. **Your business is taking Nikken products to the market. Don't get the two confused.** Your down-line needs to be empowered to take the Nikken products to the market.

I can honestly say we are in the business of building an organization that builds Wellness Homes. We are in the business of building an organization that builds Wellness Homes internationally and the compensation is more than you'll ever need, but you will struggle through and learn how to live with it. We're in the business of building an organization that builds Wellness Homes. That's how we make our mark in the Wellness industry.

1:18:24

Nikken is in the business of manufacturing products and developing a structure to support our efforts. We create the demand by creating an organization that exposes this concept, this technology to individuals and families all over the world. In doing so, we continue to expand our organization and we continue to expand our penetration of the market. The difference is that now there's an end in mind. Instead of an individual being a customer, they're the doorway to their home. Instead of it being a one-time sale, it's a process that will build a relationship forevermore. As this person develops a relationship with me and becomes a voracious consumer of wellness products and I, as a Wellness Consultant, bring them the most credible line of products in the world, they are going to see me with credibility and see me as their source of Wellness information in Wellness technology.

1:19:30

That is how they are going to perceive me. Even though I'm not a "doctor," I am a doctor of Wellness in today's society. What I do for that person gives them the credibility that they are at the leading edge of the Wellness movement. Their friends are going to know they're on the leading edge of something when their friends see them looking better, feeling better and by their sharing of the technology with them. We give them credibility—we are creating Wellness Homes, Wellness Centers around the world. This is just an example of a compensation that can be earned.
1:20:31

"Getting Started"—Building a Strong Foundation—Part 2

0:12

When people ask you what you do, what do you say? Most people refer to their old profession instead of talking about this business. Are you operating from your structure or are you operating from your purpose when people ask you what you do? When people ask me what I do, this is what I tell them.

1:09
"I'm a Wellness Consultant."

"What's that?"

"I develop a market with a company called Nikken. Have you ever heard of it?"

"No."

"They are the number one provider of wellness technology."

"What's that?"

"Let me show you."

"What exactly does it mean?"

"I help people set up their own consulting business creating a demand for these products."

You see how simple and easy it is to say, "I'm a Wellness Consultant," and that I help create a demand for wellness technologies and I work with a company called Nikken.

3:08

This is a business presentation that will be understood by business people. One thing that network marketing people rarely show is how they actually earn their money. The question that inevitably comes up is: "Who does the selling?" I think the reason why we continue to raise that question is that we continue to fail in showing them a business plan as opposed to a compensation plan. I've mentioned this to Kendall and told him that Nikken has one of the greatest compensation plans in the world, but it has no business plan whatsoever for the Wellness Consultant . . . and there is a difference. A business plan says you know how you are earning your income. You should know where it is coming from. A compensation plan outlines . . . here is how much you get paid if, and it's a big IF. You have got to answer that "if," because if people don't visualize it and see it, they won't build it. So here is a way of showing somebody a business vision, a business plan, starting with you.

4:42

Our function is to expand the organization and, in doing so, create Wellness Homes. We accomplish this by various sorts of presentations creating awareness about the Nikken technologies, their application and how that could change the quality of the someone's life, their environment and their children's life. In order to attract people to the business, you've got to show them the business—beginning, middle and end. They have to see that there is a business that can produce business results, that will produce a lifestyle that is desirable.

5:28

Every business has products and every business has products that move and that create volume, which creates income. This is how I show it. Notice in the diagram below, there are two organizations—two very distinct triangles. When have you ever shown that before? I bet you never have. Let's say the bottom triangle represents General Motors or ABC Company or perhaps the company you work for. Does that company exist just to employ people? No. Does that company provide

The Science of the Nikken Business

a product or service to people outside of the employees? Yes, it does. If it didn't, there would be no cash flow and cash flow is king.

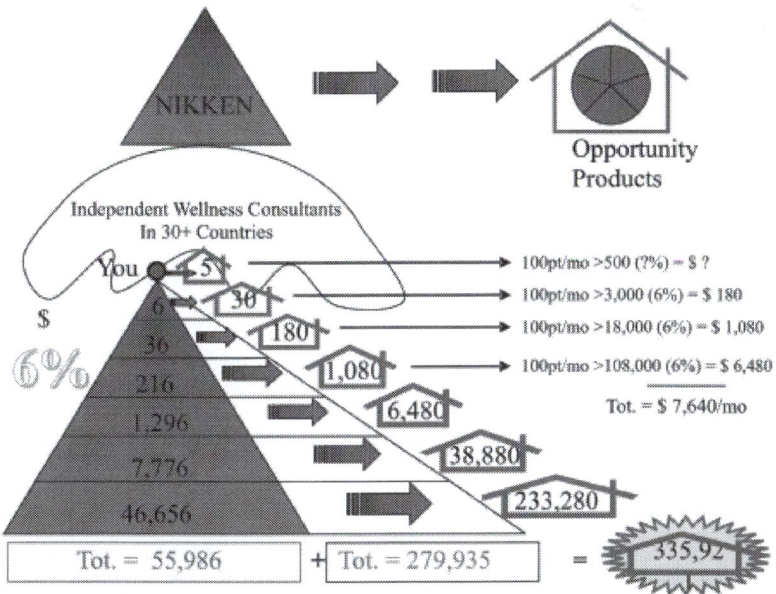

NIKKEN

Opportunity
Products

Independent Wellness Consultants
In 30+ Countries

You

100pt/mo >500 (?%) = $?
100pt/mo >3,000 (6%) = $ 180
100pt/mo >18,000 (6%) = $ 1,080
100pt/mo >108,000 (6%) = $ 6,480

Tot. = $ 7,640/mo

$
6%

5
30
180
1,080
6,480
38,880
233,280

6
36
216
1,296
7,776
46,656

Tot. = 55,986   +   Tot. = 279,935   =   335,92

There would be no way of staying organized and the company would disband. So, bringing people together is about accomplishing something outside of bringing people together. This seems fundamental, but it's everything. Business people need to know that you are building an organization that does something, not that you are building an organization from which you earn something.

6:53

For many years, network marketing has failed to present a legitimate argument as to why it's a viable business. They show the results . . . look at this! But a lot of people don't relate to the big numbers. They hear an income of a Royal Diamond and they think it's "pie in the sky." They can't see how it's possible. It's too big a quantum leap from where they are coming from. Their beliefs and the structure that they believe in produce what they see. Because there are so few multi-million dollar income earners in network marketing, they think . . . the results produced in the world they live in mean there's a 97% chance that what you're saying is a bunch of crap. "Prove it," is what they'll say. They relate to the world in which they live, and you are trying to get them to relate to your world. There is such a big difference in the belief systems of the structure we are a part of, versus the structure they are a part of.

8:04

How do you bridge the gap? How do you go to a business person and show them a business in network marketing? Why would Warren Buffet buy a network marketing company. Did he buy the network marketing company because it's a network marketing company? Absolutely not! That's not how he thinks. He thinks business and to him, network marketing is just one of the vehicles through which they distribute their products.

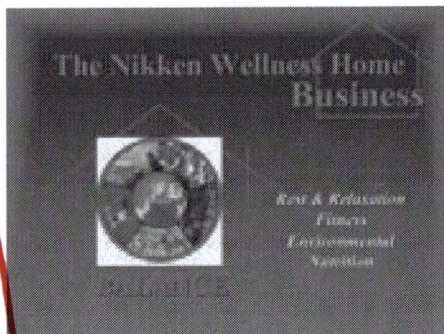

The Nikken Wellness Home Business

Rest & Relaxation
Fitness
Environmental
Nutrition

BALANCE

Diagram 22

8:47

He bought a business. So what is the business? Cash flow. Does this business have growth potential? Does this business have a legitimate product? Does this business have a market for that product? Does this business have the resources to grow? The method they use to distribute their product is secondary to the main issue—is it a business, is it viable? In fact, the ultimate litmus test for any network marketing company is whether or not its products are viable in the market besides the fact that it's a network marketing company. That is how you know whether

The Science of the Nikken Business

they are going to be around for a while or not because most network marketing companies are an excuse to network market.

9:31

Most are just looking to earn income from their down-lines and that's why it has that incestuous connotation associated to it. Nobody has ever shown them how it really works, how it's really viable and how it really does outperform the traditional business environment. If I'm going to build a pyramid whether you call it a franchise pyramid, a corporate pyramid, or a network marketing pyramid, this pyramid must perform a function, otherwise it has no reason for being. It's nothing more than a cult or a short-lived experience. Some people who get in at the beginning might make some money and be able to capitalize from its growth, but in the end there is nothing there to sell.

What we're doing is finding six people who want to build this business, not six people who want to own a Wellness Home. I want six people who want to build a business. Owning a Wellness Home of their own is a consequence of them embracing the idea of being in this business. How can you sell Toyotas and drive around in a Chevy Chevette? If you say you want to be in the wellness business, you have to embrace wellness and that means YOU have to be the first customer of your wellness company.

10:57

You have to be the first person to be a "product of the product." Why is there such a big emphasis on creating a Wellness Home—your own certified Nikken Wellness Home? How can you go out with any integrity and offer it to somebody if you aren't willing to be it, have it? So, six business builders is different than six consumers. You've got to "walk the walk" and "talk the talk."

Now, we're going to talk about the business building aspect. How do we create an ongoing growing organization? How do we attract more business partners, and duplicate that so it continues irrespective of us? We want an organization that goes down 5 and 6 generations. If you have weakness at the top of your organization, you will never have downline generations. You have to think long term, I'm talking about your 5th and 6th generation. Think in terms of family. Think in terms of the decisions you make right now and how you educate your children to ensure that you're going to have great, great, great, great, great grandchildren who are healthy, wealthy and wise.

12:22

That's what you want to be thinking. The Indians have a belief . . . that whatever they do today is based on how it will affect the 7th generation from now. That's long-term visioning. Anybody who thinks that far out is going to have a 7th generation. If somebody isn't thinking that far out, and is only thinking about themselves, that person is going to have a tough time having a first generation. This explains the people who have done really well at recruiting but aren't duplicating. You have a front-line with a bunch of zeros . . . what were they thinking. About themselves . . . look what I have! And not, look what I'm helping *them* build—look what *they* have. It's just a different perspective, a different vision. Your vision will cause you to behave a certain way. Remember it goes back to structure—you believe and you behave. Getting clarity on your vision and what it is you are doing is very important. I want everybody in Nikken to carry this vision forward, because we will see it if we believe it. That's how it works.

13:41

Building your organization is one thing but a business person wants to know that building the organization is not where they make their money. Will I make money building this organization? Has every one of these people become consumers of Nikken products, purchased their demo pak, purchased their Wellness Home, their dream kit, and so on? Will I be compensated? Will you be compensated? Absolutely. What happens when every one of them has one? The question you'll get is: where's the money going to come from? Instinctively business people feel something in the pit of their gut that says . . . if this is your business and you make 6% on all of these people . . . and the "languaging" and the communication is about "on these people," then you are making money on people and off people. It doesn't fit, does it? What has that got to do with the 5 Pillars of Health? They may think: am I taking advantage of people? Is that what you're telling me?

14:53

What if building your organization and the compensation you get for building your organization allows you to build the organization, and makes it profitable for you to build the organization, but that's not why you are building the organization? You are building the organization to make a difference. You want that organization to go forward and start promoting. I don't want to have six hundred people on my front line. I don't want to keep recruiting for the rest of my life. I want to build a solid organization that has a function, so they don't go away and I have to replace them. I want to give them a vision that sustains them for the rest of their lives. I want those six people, to be those six people today, tomorrow and for the next 50 years. Not that I have to find six more people because the people I found quit . . . because of my myopic vision or theirs. Let's build a business. What can I engage these six people in that will keep them coming back for more and keep them going out and promoting?

15:58

I want to teach them how they can make a difference by engaging in the public, by presiding over a small number of homes. What if it was just five? What if everyone agreed to make an effort to preside over five families, to become the Wellness Consultant to those families, to make certain you do everything in your power to ensure they have a full understanding of the value associated in owning their certified Nikken Wellness Home? As well, you will commit to demonstrate the products, or introduce them to a new product every month, so that over the next two, three, four, five years, they will have a certified Nikken Wellness Home. Of all the people you know and all the people you don't know, can you think of five homes right now that you would want to put that kind of energy into?

17:06

My guess is that probably there are a lot of people you care about. My guess is you really wouldn't care if you made a penny off of it, if those people embraced it and got involved in it and started to develop the benefits of having a certified Nikken Wellness Home. That would be reward enough, because it's your family and it's your friends.

17:30

What if we taught that model and duplicated it? Is there money to be made in teaching people to be crusaders of wellness for the people they care about, not just one time purchasers? I'm talking about people who are going to buy $5, $10, $15, $20 thousand dollars worth of Nikken products over the next 10 years. Can you make money at it? Yes, 6%. Let me just back up for a second and tell you something important (refer to diagram on Page 303). 100 points a month, around 500 points a month in volume that you create through those 5 Wellness Homes. I've put a question mark and a percent for a reason. How much money will you earn on that. That's your choice. Nikken allows you to choose how you want to sell the products and at what price. You can go from full retail down to wholesale. In fact we are looking at even pushing that envelope. What if you could check off on your e-Nikken site, check off that you want to extend your rebate to that person and what if they got the rebate cheque instead of you?

18:45

How many customers would come back for more if every month Nikken would send them a cheque as a customer? There are companies that are doing that now. Why are we not one? Stick around long enough and we'll see it. Think about that idea; it creates awareness. That Nikken logo coming in, even if it's a little money, $10, $15. If somebody is on $100 a month in consumables, it's like a reward for wellness. It's a reward for choosing wellness. It's like they just want to keep reminding us. Isn't that brilliant? Do I have to make a living on my 5 homes? Why? When I'm making

6% on all the Wellness Homes in the company that I'm building, it starts to multiply and add up. I use $100 as a simple demonstration, because it could be a consumable purchase on a monthly basis or it could be a one time durable purchase in a year. A consumer does not have a 6 month life-span or a 1 year life-span. How often do you buy a TV?

19:57

We have to look at a longer picture where a consumer is concerned. In 4 to 5 years they might consume $5,000 worth of Nikken products. One sleep system amortized over 12 months is about a $100 per month in business. So this is just an example of showing you how your business generates income beyond building an organization . . . so you can see where that money is coming from every single month. I don't want to have to recruit every single month to make money; I want my business to function like a business by having consumers every single month. Can you imagine a corporation relying on the personnel department for profit? Think about that. I'm talking in business terms because Warren Buffet doesn't buy a network marketing company because it's a network marketing company.

20:58

He buys it because it's a business; it's a viable business. That's what you are seeing; you are seeing a viable business. There is an organization of people who are committed to promoting a concept and, in doing so, they are creating a consumer. Not just a one time purchaser but somebody who is going to embrace and become a voracious consumer à la Paul Zane Pilzner. So this is ongoing residual income. Do I have to make a big deal of it? No, it's 5 friends or family and it could be one purchase.

21:30

If Nikken comes out with one new product a year, that would be enough because when they come out with CardioStrides, everybody wants CardioStrides. When they come out with a water system, everybody wants a water system. It's pretty simple. It is not difficult to maintain that and if you were making $100,000 a month maintaining that, would it be worth it? Is building this organization worth your time? Take it down one more generation. Now take it down one more generation. Take it down to the sixth generation and do the calculation. I'll tell you what it is. You certify—you build this company and certify those 335,000 homes and you will put over $90M in your pocket. Your company would have generated $1.5 billion in volume all over the world and whether it takes you 5, 10, 15 or 20 years to accomplish this, is it worth your while?

22:30

When do you want to get started? That's a business model? That's a business vision. That's something that gets me excited. Does it get you excited? This is the cash flow, it's not $90M in a day, it's a cash flow. It's an ongoing, growing thing and that's why I take it down through 5th and 6th generations, because I would rather be modest and show somebody that this is what we're building . . . the 5th and 6th generations. Rather than saying they're going to make $10,000 in their first month, which is highly unlikely. Not many people in network marketing make $10,000 in their first month. I want them to believe in me in this vision and not doubt me. There is nothing wrong in setting big expectations, but you are not building short term, you are building long term. I didn't get into Nikken to make $100,000 a year. I got into Nikken to have a life. If you want to make $100,000 a year, go and do what you were doing. But if you want to build something that's worth building . . . that will provide you and your family with a lifestyle. These are the things you must do.

23:46

If this is just about making money, you're already doing that. And, you're doing what you're doing better than you're doing this, so the chances are, you should just keep doing what you're doing. If your vision is that myopic, if it's just about making some money, you'll find a way to screw this up. But if your vision is about building a business that makes money instead of you having to make it, it's a different picture, a different idea, a different subject. Let's build a company, a business that creates income, cash flow and value, so that you can live in Barbados with your family whenever you feel like it.

24:31

So how do we do this? Actually, let's stick to this. Having just presented a business. Let's say I've just done a business briefing for you. This business briefing is part of a presentation that's called "The Power of Wellness." It's a brochure which starts with the end in mind and then works backwards . . . is there something out there that helps us create this (purpose). What happens after a business briefing? You say you want to build an organization. Building an organization is about showing people a business, it's not about showing people product. You've got to have product to have a business. You just have to understand the pecking order.

25:25

Now we move into a Wellness Preview. Nikken has just announced to the President's Club that you can purchase what they call a Mighty Moe, which is a little portable computer with a DVD player and a projector in it. Now we're looking smarter, a little bit more professional. Because, you know, if you want to attract smart, professional people, you've got to look smart and professional. This little gadget that everybody is going to learn how to use, empowers us to put on some pretty effective presentations.

26:11

That little computer also has a Visa card swiper and a wireless connection. That means you will be able to utilize it to go online and make immediate purchases. Picture this . . . a Wellness Preview and you've just taken someone through the business information, whether it was a one on one, whether it was in your home, whether it was over coffee or lunch or a business briefing, which is what we like to do . . . and you want to show them the retail environment, you want to bring them to the Wellness Store. Whether it's in your home or at a Wellness Preview, what they are going to get there is to experience the products, and get the experience of a customer. You're going to show them that this business of yours, this potential business has customers, real customers who don't just buy the products—they can't stop talking about them.

27:22

If I wanted to introduce you a restaurant or franchise of some sort, at some point you're going to ask to see it. You will want to go and "kick the tires" so to speak, see what it looks like and how it operates. Would you do that before or after a business presentation? After. You came to me to buy a business—now I'm going to show you a business and then I'm going to show you the business in its operation and what it looks like. I'm going to bring you to a Wellness Preview. Now, envision the back of the room after we've finished. At the far end of the room somebody sits down and processes orders because you're able to process anybody's order from any down-line. It's not limited to you to go online to e-Nikken and being able to only do your own. You've got your cash register and your retail environment. Isn't that powerful!

28:24

Do you see how things are starting to develop, things that are consistent with the vision? The vision has inspired a change in structure. We never use to have that, but we are going to because the vision has inspired that. We want to build a vision and so the Wellness Preview is going to be a place where people can not only experience and hear about the products, but they can purchase them right then and there. You'll actually be able to leave the Wellness Preview and go online and see the volume that was generated that night. It sounds more like a business doesn't it? It's a little bit of a break from network marketing. Does that bother you? We're getting to the point where you will be able to do this manually. Pretty soon it will be a hand held device (credit card swiper). It takes time, but that's the vision.

29:23

After a Wellness Preview with my business prospect, not my consumer, my business prospect is going to be pretty much committed to being my consumer. But that's not why I brought them there. I didn't bring them there to sell them the products, I brought them there to sell them the business. They bought the products because they liked what they saw. It's interesting how that happens and this is a process we can do with everybody. Once this business person has seen the business model and the presentation, I want to sit down with them and have a bit of a strategy session. I want to introduce them to "What it Takes to Build the Business." I want to introduce them to the infrastructure that has been put in place to support the activity of getting this business off the ground and how we are going to be involved in that. I want to introduce them to the business investment.

30:28

I want to introduce them to some of the considerations that they want to make, in terms of getting their business started, some of the resources that they want to take advantage of. It's just a familiarity process of how we get them up and running now that you know they like what they see. They like the business, they like how it operates and they like the products. Let's make a business decision about how they want to get started. Do they want to put their toe in, put their foot in or do they want to jump in with both feet? They decide, you're going to present the options . . . they choose. That's call a strategy session. I don't care how you do it . . . one-on-one, in your home, or at a formal presentation; where you do it and who is invited is the dynamic, but the content is the same. Does that make sense? I've mentioned previously that there is a private, a personal and a public presentation.

31:30

The content is the same; the venue changes the dynamic. Personal or private presentations are a little bit more intimate and provide more two-way communication, whereas a large, public gathering is more one sided. I use the smaller venues because they provide for a great exchange of information and that's how you know you are getting the information across. A Wellness Preview or a large gathering is more for validation, it's more to verify the facts and information. It's important for them to hear the stories, and the testimonies to reinforce what they've already heard.

32:24

These are the insights into the "how to's." What's in place for you to build your business? How important is the infrastructure that Nikken creates in order for us to be able to build our business internationally, nationally or locally? Critical. Nikken makes sure the product can go from their warehouse to the consumer, whether that consumer is a member of our organization or that consumer is a member of the consumer division. Remember, we have two divisions now . . . we have personnel who are building the organization and we have our consumers who are not interested in building the business, but who are interested in wellness.

33:28

So Nikken provides us with a structure to supply those people with products, but we need to build a structure that's conducive to bringing people into the business, into the organization.

Nikken provides the structure to fill the consumer demand We, however, must provide a structure to fulfil the organization demand. How do you build an organization? What is the environment that will attract? What are the beliefs that you will impart, so that you can create behavior out of these business builders to produce results that are consistent with your vision? First and foremost there is, in my opinion, an order to getting somebody started in the business. Some people feel that getting customers is the place to start . . . and when

People will join this business to build a business if they were presented a business opportunity. If they are presented the products that may not be the case. But, if they are presented the business opportunity, there is a way to build a business.

you get your feet wet, we'll turn our attention to building the business. I don't think that's wrong. I just don't think that's the best way to do it. I

think people would join this business to build a business if they were presented a business opportunity. If they are presented the products that may not be the case. But, if they are presented the business opportunity, there is a way to build a business. The organization is the first step in building the business. Let me make a distinction. When I say building the business, I mean building what was shown previously.

35:02

Those two very healthy organizations of organized business builders and consumers! That to me is a business. When I say building the organization, I am referring to the down-line, and these terminologies and definitions have not been in existence before, so I want to be sure you understand them. To build a down-line, I must create an environment to recruit and educate those people, empower them, support them and develop them . . . not just to get them in, but to keep them going all the way through the ranks. And, so, as all structures vibrate naturally; everything has a vibration. If it's a structure, all the structures have a vibration—we call those rhythms.

35:53

Imagine that you have a Royal Ambassador business. Think in terms of the big picture now. You are now a Royal Ambassador. Imagine where you are living? Imagine how you are living? This is important. Let's just get you there. Imagine where you're living and how you're living; do you see yourself with time on your hands? Do you see yourself keeping in touch with what's going on in your business by telephone with key people? You couldn't possibly talk to everybody in your organization . . . you wouldn't have a life. So, you can see that as a Royal Ambassador or as you elevate in the compensation plan, you're not exposing yourself to more work, you're just redefining what that work is.

36:50

If you are a Royal Ambassador, you obviously have people doing Wellness Previews since Wellness Previews are part of the process . . .

our retail store is part of the verification process for our business people. You obviously have people doing business presentations. You obviously have people doing a lot of things such as training like this throughout the world. You're a Royal Ambassador, it's happening. Is it happening because you're making it happen, or is it happening because it's happening? It's happening. So, all these things that are happening with or without your direct involvement are what we call rhythms of the business.

37:31

These rhythms are marked by successive events. We give you a calendar to show you the events that are being organized locally, and you will notice that there's a weekly repetition. When you look at next month's calendar and the months after that, you'll find that there are certain activities that happen only once or twice in the month but they happen every month. That means there is a monthly cycle. You'll also see there is something that repeats every three months, which is a quarterly cycle. We are hooking it up so that what we are doing in the field as an organization, Nikken is doing as a corporation. So it's going like this organization . . . consumer . . . organization . . . consumer . . . organization . . . consumer.

38:41

We start to develop that rhythm in sync with Nikken and we are working like a real company works . . . efficiently. That is what we're developing right now When you hear Nikken talk about Rhythm of the Business—that only took about 3 years! Everyone is talking about it, and the impact is going to be huge. These events that take place in rhythm give our business its ability to operate. At the same time, it gives us our freedom. If I don't have people doing what they need to be doing to build their business, I won't have freedom. So I've got to get to know these rhythms and start to develop and work with them. Start slowly. What's the daily rhythm? What should I be doing (a brand new person) on a daily basis to ensure that I'm building a business, and then what does that have to account for on a weekly and monthly rhythm?

39:44

As my business is growing and I have people in my organization, I'm going to start thinking a little further ahead because my vision is always long term. The big picture is always the big picture. But in terms of rolling out your business . . . phase 1, phase 2 . . . as a roll out . . . in terms of my thinking . . . I may be thinking immediate (now), and then I'll think a little further ahead and as things happen, I'll think even further ahead. We're not asking you to learn all of this now, but you need to know there's a road map. You have to go through the phases and follow the map to reach the end. If you went to university you knew that if you got started and kept doing what they told you to do, you'd get to the end. There was a curriculum. They weren't inventing it as they were going along, but sometimes they would modify it.

40:38

But, traditionally you would go and get a degree because you know that if you take these courses and pass your exams, you'll end up with your degree. You'll be a competent person with a label and you'll be able to go out into the work force and practice your profession. Well, there is no difference here but a lot of people have never seen network marketing as a structured business. They look at a Royal Diamond and they wonder what we do every day. I don't do what you do every day. I'm a Royal Diamond. What kind of life do you want as a Royal Diamond?

41:17

Do you want to be recruiting every day when you hit the rank of Royal Diamond or Royal Ambassador? Probably not. So there's a progression and there are things you need to become aware of when it's time to make the transition.

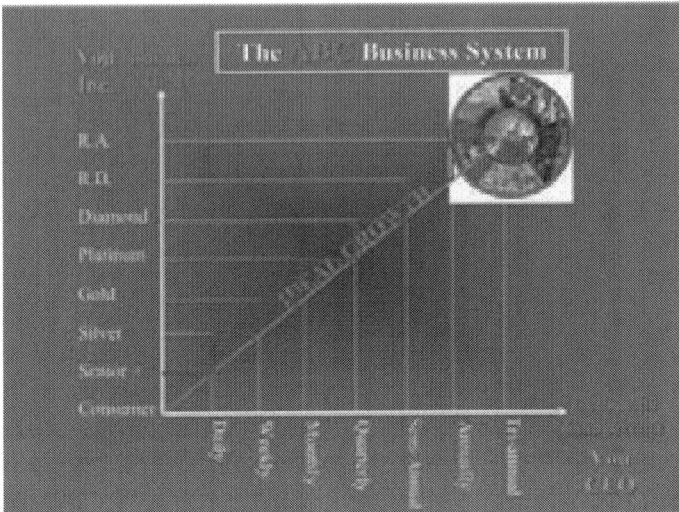

Diagram 24

In the diagram above, there's you and your business. Would you agree that a Royal Ambassador, if this business is worth its salt, would provide us with this life style (referring to 5 Pillars of Health and a balanced lifestyle)? If Nikken's business is really the gem of all businesses, then it's not just about making money—it's about having a life. A Royal Ambassador ought to have a life. If I start here, today, as a prospect, and I begin my journey, then at some point in time I should, if I succeed, reach a way of life that's accomplished and successful. Therefore, by our definition "success is the progressive realization." As long as I'm moving in that direction, I am succeeding.

42:42

But there's an ideal growth curve—making less mistakes is better. But, if I was making a whole bunch of mistakes, the ideal growth curve line would not be straight. There are hills and valleys right through the entire experience, just ask some of the Diamonds. These are the ranks we go through because our vision must be specific. Our way of life is intangible, it's nonspecific, it's ongoing; but our vision must be tangible, it must be specific. Setting a goal is critical for us to move in a certain direction. Without a specific goal to achieve something—long term, mid term or short term—we have no way creating a plan and if we have no plan, we will create nothing.

43:49

Our business requires a business plan and to have a plan you need a specific vision. We've got a long term vision—Royal Ambassador. We've got a mid term vision—Platinum or Diamond and then we've got a more immediate vision—maybe Silver or Gold for some of you. Let me give you the reason why Silver is the most important first rank when you join the business . . . nothing in between matters. Notice when I did my compensation plan, I said 6% in that big picture. Does anybody care to have a 5% override when you are building 6% residual income? A business person doesn't care about what a Silver makes on a Senior. That's comparable to what a baby-sitter makes. That's why the percentage is so high, because at that point you're baby-sitting. You're giving birth to new people. The real money in the business is the long term picture. It is the 6% down in the 5th and 6th generations. These are people who are doing the business and you don't even know who they are or where they are. They are just doing it for their own reasons. That's the big picture. That's the big picture paying off. So we don't talk in small terms, talk in terms of the big picture.

45:11

The first rule of business is what? To make a profit. You've got to get your business to the point where it's profitable. That's why we say Silver should be your first goal.

Would you rather be a Platinum making $2,000 a month or Silver making $8,000? *The advancement in rank should be driven by the economics, not the prestige.*

45:53

Assuming that you're here to build your resources, your first priority is business. Business. Now this is really important. This is why I'm here (balance in the 5 Pillars of Health). I'm never going to get there and be able to be there unless I take care of the small details when it's time. One of those small details is I've got to get that business to be profitable so that I can afford to be here full time. You've got to be able to afford to do this full time and you know what that means in terms of real dollars . . . so we've got to maximize our profit as quickly as possible. The maximum profit is at the Silver rank where you make a 20% rebate, which means overrides on all the new people in your business. You also make the most of the retail situation and so the most profitable place in the compensation plan in terms of activity is Silver. Therefore, I want people to get to Silver right away. If I sponsor somebody brand new, that's my first priority, because if I can't help them to become profitable they can't be here.

47:02

How many of you thought it was for a different reason entirely? How many of you didn't know why it was? It was just because your up-line telling you, you had to do it. I'm telling you as a business, because we're talking in terms of business today . . . that your business has to be profitable as quickly as possible and so do the people you sponsor. The first business plan, the first agenda is what? Help somebody break Silver. We seem to have lost sight of that. With all the new information coming in, we have a tendency to run all over the place. We are losing sight of the most fundamental thing; there are new ideas but there are some basics that just don't change. You will not have a business if you don't have an organization, so the first priority is in developing that organization. That organization will have

The Science of the Nikken Business

lots to do in the way of the Wellness Home, but we've got to keep things practical.

48:12

Silver is for profitability. There is one other reason why Silver because Gold is also for profitability. Why would somebody want go from Silver to Gold? For a business reason called profit. The difference between Silver and Gold is you earn on three generations instead of two. How many of you thought it was because you could walk around with a Gold pin on your lapel and people would think you were important? Your business doesn't care about that; your business is the only objective thing. It is complete objectivity. My message to you as a business person is . . . as wonderful as this business is in the way of recognition and as many opportunities as we create to recognize people . . . your business doesn't care about that. Your business isn't going to pay you that way. You will not be able to afford to stay here, if that is the way it pays you.

49:18

There are a lot of people who spend a lot of time just presenting because they like presenting. But then you look at their pay cheque and you wonder—what the heck they are presenting for? Get to work. They like the public appearances and stuff like that, but that's not what your business needs. Your business needs business. What does that mean? It means profitability. Advancing in rank is something you do to make certain there is profit for your business. I never advanced in rank until I needed to.

49:46

Until I was making $5,000 or $10,000 in that next generation that I wasn't getting compensated on, there was very little need for me to advance in rank. So, I would build and then it would get to a point where there was volume that was slipping out of the pay line. Then I would put that extra piece together and make it and grab that next generation. I talk to people in my up-line who are sitting on $40,000 a month in lost income for the last 5 years. What's the number come to? $40,000 a month x 12 is $480,000 x 5 is over $2,000,000—gone. Plus interest! What is that $2,000,000 worth 10 years from now at compound interest? So, would it have been prudent on their part to think business, to say . . . their business needs them to expand right now so that they can capture that next generation. Don't do it to be a hero . . . so that you can be paraded around. Wow, they are Platinum. How much do they make? I don't know. Ask them. How much do you make? Good! What does that mean—my best month or my average month? You start dancing around the issue. Would you rather be a Platinum making $2,000 a month or Silver making $8,000? The advancement in rank should be driven by the economics, not the prestige.

51:36

It's really important. I am sharing this with you because I've got eleven years of history in this business and I've seen it done the wrong way for the longest time. People blow their brains out because they don't get it! They get the rank, but they don't get the pay cheque, and they are wondering what's wrong with me? They are not building the business the way the business needs them to build it. They are building from the wrong perspective. It's the ego driving it and not objectivity.

52:08

Let me show your business in terms of real terms. When you are Royal Ambassador, you will have influenced people around the globe, wherever Nikken is doing business. If you look at Dave Johnson's business, I'm certain that as many countries as Nikken is in, there are people representing his company, so it's a global impact. If you think globally, then that's the kind of business you are building. You are building your Ambassador business. A Royal Diamond has an international impact, a Diamond has a national impact, a Platinum has a regional impact, a Gold has a municipal impact. Let me give you an example of a regional impact. If you are a Platinum, your business probably stretches from Toronto to Montreal, over to Ottawa and maybe some parts of western Ontario. It might even be inter-Provincial. But a Diamond, generally speaking, has built a business that has gotten people, who've got people, who've got people. It starts to spread out a little bit further and now it's global. I think of it as a drop . . . if you drop a pebble in a pond and it starts a ripple effect.

53:07

A Gold is somebody who is really involved municipally. You can see them. They're the ones who put the calendars together. A Silver is somebody who is doing business locally, they're just brand new. How far of a reach have they had so far? They may have some influence with their friends and family but it's a local thing. A Senior—what does it take to achieve the rank of Senior? Buy your products, buy your products, buy your products. It doesn't take much to be a Senior in this business; it's 1500 points of product. It doesn't take much to put 1500 points on the score board when you are just buying your own products.

53:51

So don't get overly excited if you're a Senior and don't get overly excited if somebody else is a Senior, that's not why we are here. That's why it's personal, because a Senior is only somebody who has said "yes" to wellness. It's a personal decision. So far, they have not influenced yet. Okay, so that's your business.

Now in terms of the rhythm of the business, there are events and activities that are necessary in order for us to support this. For instance, every day, if you are brand new to this business, you need to be in touch with new people. You can get help to do that in the way of an ABC. An ABC is when you are working with somebody who is already involved and interested in your success, someone who is capable. If you're out there everyday contacting new people, where is it that you need to bring these new people who have been contacted or perhaps presented to, so that they can see the picture? To a Wellness Preview.

55:04

So, every day you are contacting people so that those people can be directed into a Wellness Preview as the next step. There is the thing called business training which is what we are doing today, every week. Your new people who join the business need to get some basic training when they join, and if you've got people joining your company every week, how often do you need to have a training session in your company? Every week. Because we work a lot in groups, it's not necessary that every individual put on a basic training every week. That is why we have an organization that puts on public meetings, so we can leverage each other's time, leverage each other's expertise and share time. But that doesn't mean there should only be one in the city. Is there only one McDonald's in the city?

55:52

Would McDonald's sell more hamburgers having a restaurant ten times bigger than the one they have downtown and no other restaurant, or by having smaller restaurants spread out all over the city? More business, more volume by duplication, instead of having one huge event that everybody says, "Did you see how big that event was?" I suggest you don't get excited about big events for that reason. I'm more excited about having 10 small events going on than one big event. At one big event there is one presenter, one person doing the business; at 10 smaller events, there are 10 presenters. I'd rather have 10 leaders than one leader—any day of the week. That's an important point! Monthly, every month we put on a special event. What's the month's event for February? In February, it is a Super Saturday. What do you learn at a Super Saturday? You learn advanced stuff . . . stuff about events and about people, and it is great for those who have been around a little bit and who need the next piece of the puzzle, the next little bit of competence.

57:02

Then we've got the "Humans Being More" training or Gold training and Expos. We have not gotten to that level yet—where we're teaching specifically to the Golds and Silvers, but that's coming as the market in the Toronto area develops. We have something called the Rhythm of the Business working very, very successfully here. A lot of people were able to achieve the rank of Silver, Gold and Platinum because of it. Then their businesses have spread outside the area and that has created a vacuum. There's no longer that activity going on here, but that is just the same thing as having one big restaurant versus a bunch of restaurants.

57:43

You may look at the area and say the area is depressed. No. There is a great deal happening outside of the area because of what happened here—it's a dynamic. It develops like this—Wellness Previews grow—and they splinter off and they shrink. Then some people say . . . well things are really down over there. No they are not down over there! If you look at the impact, you now have a larger impact. We started one Expo in Toronto or in the neighboring area for New York, Ottawa, Montreal and Western Canada. I remember Marty's group from Manitoba came to the one in Niagara Falls.

We had one Expo once in six months that covered a huge geographic area. We had some 400 people at that Expo. Now we have one Expo every three months in Toronto, but they also have one every three months in Montreal, they have one in Ottawa, they have one in New York and they have one in Buffalo. So even though one event might have reduced the attendance at another event, we've increased the attendance overall by creating more events. That is what you have to keep in mind. You might be deceived if you see a Wellness Preview spike and then have attendance drop. It is not because overall attendance is down, it is because it's splintering into multiple events. This is another thing for you to put into those little footnotes because it does happen and you might confuse reality with what you think is reality.

59:11

Then there is the Team Diamond event that happens every six months and so on. So you could see there is a rhythm to this business.

There are events that propel us. What are these events? It's an ABC—if I want to make a "C" (a prospect) turn into a "B" (a Senior and above), I need the help of a Silver. And, I want that Senior to move up to the rank of Silver. So, the ABC is all about advancement, moving in a direction—always movement, movement, movement. Remember, we need to move, progressing toward. The "A" is the presenter, the "B" is the "Validator" and the "C" is the target audience. What's a validator? What do you say at Wellness Previews when you are given the opportunity—your testimony. Don't be shy about giving a testimonial at a Wellness Preview. We rely on your testimonies. Don't you be somebody who relies on other people's testimonies and then contributes none yourself. If you are at that meeting—participate. You can't be in the audience and not participate. Put your hand up and even if you are not picked every time. You can be a part of that meeting. There are prospects in that audience and they are going to decide on the future of their family in their business based on what they see. If you are sitting on your hands thinking, "Gee I hope they don't pick me. I don't have a good testimony." Think of this prospect in the audience who says to themselves, "Oh, there are only a few customers here." Even prospects are experienced. Instead, it should be every hand that goes up . . . pick me, pick me, pick me. That prospect now looks around and says, "Holy cow! Not only are they customers, but everybody wants to talk about their experience!"

1:01:12

This is a business that requires our attention if you want it to pay you the way you hope. Make every experience a positive experience for everybody. Contribute. When an "A" presents, you rely on the professionalism of that presentation. We are doing our best to improve on that. You are going to be exposed to a video that is a killer; it's the best video I've ever seen Nikken put together. You should use it every chance you get. Every event, whether it's a local Wellness Preview or Business briefing, is an opportunity to create an ABC. So an Expo is an ABC, it's just a different "A," a different "B," and a different "C".

The Science of the Nikken Business

1:01:58

Expos are usually hosted by Golds and Platinums for the benefit of Silvers to advance their knowledge and understanding of the business, and to create a bit more motivation, excitement and so forth. Expos happen every quarter. At a Wellness Preview or a Business briefing the "A" is the Silver, whereas at an Expo—"A" is a Platinum. It is still an ABC, just a different level of it, just a bigger picture. If you're a Silver Distributor, you will be able to relate to this. Remember the ideal curve, the ideal line. This assumes not only do you have a title (refer to Diagram 24 on Page 318), but you also know what you are doing. It's called being a conscious competent and it means you can help other people get to Silver. Many struggle with that . . . when you have new Silvers breaking Silvers, what you have is the experience of having become Silver, but you do not have the conscious awareness of how to create it. What you need is help moving up in rank.

1:03:04

That is what training is all about. That's what working with your up-line and capable people is about. It's because they've done it two or three times and they can say, "Let's just figure out what it is that you are doing. Is there anybody in your organization who's excited? Great, let's go and talk to them. Let's find out what they want. You want to build the business, fine, let us get together. Let us focus on a little strategy; let's create a Silver this month." It is just a little bit of confidence that you need. It's not that you aren't bright and don't know anything. You're in a certain place in this progression (ideal growth curve). When you are a perfectly competent Silver; that means you can help other people achieve the rank of Silver. That's what it means—you can duplicate your success. What happens if you don't? My guess is you

You are in the business of breaking Silvers as far as building an organization is concerned. Breaking Silvers and teaching your people how to break Silvers—it's that simple.

have not set a goal and decided the future. The second you make a decision about the future and you commit to it, all of a sudden you need things to happen. You can sit down and put a business plan together, and that means you can look through your organization and find out who wants to go Silver next. You are in the business of breaking Silvers as far as building an organization is concerned. Breaking Silvers and teaching your people how to break Silvers—it's that simple. Break Silvers and teach them how to break Silvers.

1:04:37
That is how it goes, how we progress. We are always incompetent in some way and always competent in others. But if we are not moving forward, we are not taking the initiative to learn what we need to learn, to set goals . . . to learn what we need to learn—set goals; learn—set goals, it's an ongoing development. It is always with the long-term picture in mind, because you won't do the baby steps if there isn't something worth going for. What I'm sharing with you, you need to share with everybody you come in contact with in this business who wants to build this business. It's easy for me to decide where somebody sits. If they're over here, all they lack is a little bit of competence and I can work with them on that. If they are over here, and they are there for a while, and they've gone through one month, a quarter, a half a year, an entire year . . . and they are still there, then they haven't set a goal. They have not set a goal because the second you do, somebody comes to mind. You need help right? You need to help.

1:05:54
Number one: you need to get help from the people in the business who can help you achieve that goal. And, number two: you need help from the people in your down-line, or the people you still don't have in your down-line to achieve that goal. When I got to Platinum, I had two people who were definitely going to build this business long-term and four who were undecided. When I made a decision to go Diamond, I had to replace two of those undecided people because they had decided that they were going to be undecided and had put themselves on the

undecided list. I had to go to my recruiting department, my personnel department and tell them we are short two strong individuals who want to build the business. We've got two "wanna be's," but that's all they've amounted to. They've helped us get this far, but they are not going to help us get any further. In my mind, I had to say: thank you for the experience, thank you for the time, I hope you continue to practice Wellness. And, now that I have a Wellness Home, I know exactly what to do with them. I'm going to make sure that they stay practicing Wellness, but they may not stay practicing the business or building it. That's OK. That should not affect me or affect my decision to move forward.

1:07:11

When I make a decision to move forward, that means I need new personnel. But this time I'm smarter. I was a Platinum, so I knew how to break Silvers, I'd already done it six times personally and helped down-line do it. I was a Platinum and I wanted to go Diamond and that meant I've got to break Golds, which is breaking second-level Silvers. I can't just think about breaking a first-level Silver, I've got to start thinking about breaking second-level Silvers. When I started talking to people, I was talking to them about the business we were about to build them. I saw their people already—before they saw them. I built the business plan around their three Silvers they were going to break in the next three months, instead of the Silver I was going to break in the next three months. I started breaking Golds as quickly as it used to take me to break Silvers, and I got pretty good at it. I thought, I wonder if I can break a Platinum in one month? You know what? It's a challenge, and it's not at all impossible, it has been done. All it takes is seeing it. I've just got to see it. I had somebody say, "I want to get going. I want to get going fast and I want to win this contest to Maui. How do I do it?" You've got to see it. What does it take? See it on paper? What is a Platinum, what is a Gold, and then bing, bing, bing.

1:08:36

I need to engage and bring to the table someone I can talk to about building a long-term business. But, I have to see their people as well . . . not just getting involved . . . but breaking Silver in the same period of time. That means I've got a plan with dates . . . I've got to get this person to the table by this day and I've got to get their people to the table by this day. Then I've got to launch those people to get their people to the table by this day so that they go Silver, so that *that* person goes Gold by then. So now I've got a plan and I've got a time frame and I think, "Wow, that's a lot of events! Let me see how I manage this time. Well, if I use this Wellness Preview for this group here, and this one here, for this group here, and this one here for this group here, I can round them all up. I need those trainings; we need that month end event, so that by this time, I should get this far with this. I need to know how many people I need to direct to what, by when That sounds like a plan. Even if it doesn't work according to your plan, it still works.

1:09:41

I tried to launch somebody to Platinum in the first month and it was a disaster. It was! But they still made $10,000 in the first month—nowhere near Platinum, but they are still in the business three years later. Even if you fail miserably in your attempt do it, do it again. One of these times you're actually going to surprise yourself and get it done.

You've got a handout that I am going to work through very rapidly.

Leaders Create the Structure

=

Rhythm of the Business

=

Creating Conscious Competence and Business
Goals at All Levels

1:11:04

Leaders create the structure that people take advantage of. That is what we call the rhythm of the business. The leaders are the ones who are the organizers of these structures, whether they are ABC's on a daily basis that you are doing, whether they are Wellness Previews that you are hosting in your home. It doesn't have to be on a public level, it can be private, personal or public. Leaders are those who create goals constantly and move people to the fulfillment of those goals. That is how you support and sustain growth and momentum.

Let's talk about investing in your business. You can read through this, but let me take you to the page which shows you the 1,700 point example, the 3,000 point example and the 5,000 point example. I'm not going to talk to you in terms of you. Notice that it doesn't matter what your level of investment is and it doesn't matter what your new Wellness Consultant's level of investment is . . . at least, it shouldn't matter from a business ethics and from an activity point of view. The activity is the activity in this business whether somebody starts at Senior, Senior plus or Executive—the activity is always the same. "What it takes" to build this business doesn't change because somebody puts more money in than somebody else. But, like a snowball, the size and the amount of effort necessary to make a snowman is going to be in direct proportion to the size of the first snowball that you start to roll. Do you understand that parallel? If I make a tiny snowball and I start rolling it, is going to require a lot of manual handling. To get that thing to be round and so forth and keep it growing, it takes a lot of personal effort. But if I make a large snowball to start with, then I could probably push it with one hand. It is a little bit easier and it will grow much faster, because it's already bigger.

1:12:55

The investment does not determine whether a person will be or not be successful. The investment usually determines the rate of growth. That's what it determines. Everybody's expectations are higher, depending on the level of investment of the person coming in. This is an example that shows you the effort is the same. Notice, they all sponsor 12 people and the goal was to sponsor those 12 people in one month. You can see the results of doing the same amount of work, only with a different level of expectation. The work is the work, that doesn't change. But depending on what you set up as the level of expectation, which is based on your ability to commit or their ability to commit—in terms of the initial investment, that will decide how quickly their business goes through those promotions. One of the first business decisions a person has to make when they join the business is . . . what level of commitment, financially, are they prepared to make? But you need to be able to explain this to them (book called Investing In Your Business) which is why this is a tool that you can use. They could read through this or you can read through this and explain it to them. How they decide to do this is their decision.

1:14:21

However, there has to be something that we duplicate—there must be something, as in a way of a level of expectation that we need them to duplicate. You will not expect others to do something that you, yourself, have not done. You just won't. It's a violation of your own integrity and you will never let it happen. But, can you expect others to buy products you haven't bought? Can you expect others to create a Wellness Home if you haven't? People ask me what products they should buy. What do you think my answer is? Everything! Wrong question! Where should I start—that's the right question. Then I explain this and then they can make a business decision, because I will work with them no matter which of these three choices they make. But, there is a point where I won't. There's a point where I say it's a violation of my personal integrity if I allow you to distort a process that I know has succeeded for so many. If you think by buying a pair of MagSteps and a MagBoy you are going to go out and build a multinational, multi-billion dollar business on my watch, then I have to say "Sorry." That's not to say that it's not possible, that's not to say it's not been done, but it is not the norm and why should I set you and I up for failure?

1:15:45

This next page has the initial business start up order. This is something Guido and I worked on as an advancement and evolution to the one that's in print. You'll see that what we have here are the categories: personal product, business product and tools. We've included some of the new items that are available. The form shows you the point value both in Canadian and US dollars. You'll see three columns: good, better and best. Here is a good way to start, here is a better way to start and here is the best way to start . . . in real terms—in today's dollars, it is the best way if you have a choice. And you have a choice. You choose. Some will say, "I don't have the money." Well, I guess their problem is not the money. If somebody says they don't have the money, what is their problem? If they're saying to me . . . and this is important for you to be able say to them . . . is that, what stands between you and the life you choose and the life you want is that amount of money. Then, you don't deserve this (balance in the 5 Pillars of Health), if you are going to let that hold you back. Think about it.

1:17:08

The next page talks about tools, how to utilize those tools, and what is available to you. Let's move beyond that to the brochure called "The Career Plan and Launch Strategy." There's also a video tape called "The Career Plan and Launch Strategy." There's very little point in me covering information that's covered on that video. I walked through this entire presentation in that video "The Career Plan and Launch Strategy." What this presentation basically does, is focus your effort on one thing. Turn to this page called "Breaking Silvers".

1. Blueprint

Strategy for Silver . . .
Position for Gold

Requirement A
Find 4 leaders.
Recruit 12 to find
4 serious leaders.
the Rule of 1/3.

Requirement B
38,666 points
Volume in one
business month.

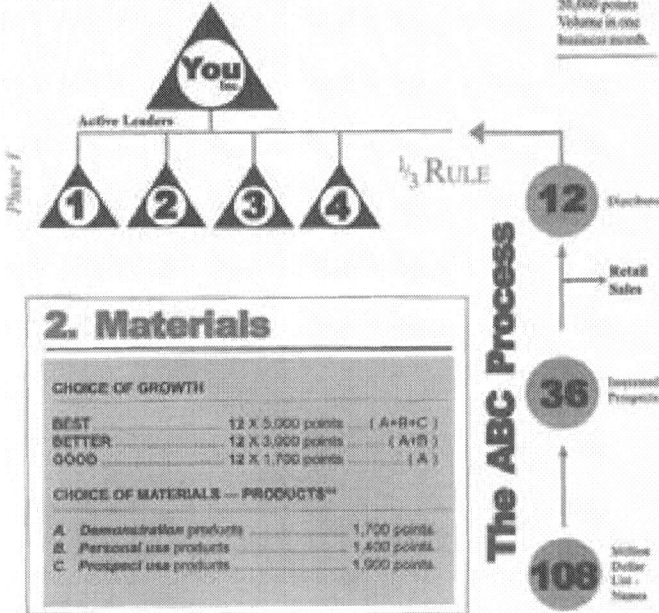

You
Inc.

Active Leaders

Phase I

(1) (2) (3) (4)

1/3 RULE

12 Distributors

Retail Sales

The ABC Process

36 Increased Prospects

108 Million Dollar List . Names

2. Materials

CHOICE OF GROWTH

BEST .... 12 X 5,000 points ... (A+B+C)
BETTER .... 12 X 3,000 points ..... (A+B)
GOOD .... 12 X 1,700 points .... (A)

CHOICE OF MATERIALS — PRODUCTS

A Demonstration products .... 1,700 points
B Personal use products .... 1,400 points
C Prospect use products .... 1,000 points

** Nikken® has no minimum purchasing requirements.

Diagram

Breaking Silvers is our primary function as a sponsor. When we are bringing somebody into the business so that they can become profitable as quickly as possible, then we need a plan of action. Even if we don't get it right the first time, we can keep using the same plan of action, working with people who have gotten it right . . . to develop our understanding, our conscious competence as to how to break Silvers.

You should be able to break Silvers in your sleep. You should be able to get so good at that you could say, "I'm a master in breaking Silvers."

1:18:47

If you can't say that a year from now, or two years from now, then all the other stuff that you are doing—just stop it, because it's not helping you go where you want to go. You want to learn how to teach people to launch the business because breaking Silver, in my opinion, is a consequence of activity. It's a consequence of activity. If you set up the conditions and you plan your calendar around this individual, such that their activity is "X" amount, even if we fail and achieve only "Y" amount of activity, that "Y" amount is still enough to accomplish our initial objective which was to break Silver. When I'm launching somebody, I always do three times as much in the way of activity and expectation necessary to achieve the end objective. I'll tell you why. I learned something a long time ago . . . this idea of breaking Silver . . . if you want to break a board and you keep your eye on the board, no matter how strong you are and how fast you are, there is something about eye-hand coordination that causes your hand to stop short and hit that board. And it hurts.

1:20:18

To break the board with even less effort, you just have to do one thing—keep your eyes focused beyond the board. See something in your mind that is beyond the board. Then that board, regardless of where it is, it doesn't matter—snap—your hand goes right through it. It is true in life and it is true in principle. There are things that happen in our every day life which do not go according to plan. If you are thinking beyond the board, what generally happens is you do far more to compensate for those shortfalls. You still snap through that board. Thinking beyond the board in terms of a strategy is on the next page. Sponsoring 12 people who purchase the equivalent of what I purchased or more, creating the activity necessary with my sponsor/my up-line, my capable up-line . . . of planning and doing the activity necessary. This is going to take some time. It's going to be a priority—the month you go Silver is a priority month. You may have to make some plans with your family;

you might have to get some concessions on their part concerning what it is going to take. Because it's a focused effort, there is no question about it. It is absolutely a focused effort. The month that you are going Silver or the month that you are helping somebody go Silver, make sure they understand that there are going to be some concessions as far as their activities outside of their business are concerned. Their business requires complete focus for that month.

1:22:00

The activities you organize are: the Business briefing, Wellness Previews, and Trainings so that you can create the volume necessary and the outcome necessary for that person to go Silver. Here is how it generally works. By sponsoring 12 people who purchased as you did, or as they did in that one month, you will create the volume necessary to break that Silver. But because our vision is long term, what we are presenting to people has to be the business and the business vision. Because, what we hope to gain out of presenting the business vision . . . are business people . . . people who want to build the business. And, of the 12 people who say they want to build the business, probably 4 of them actually will. That is why you see the 12 breaking down into 4. This has been our experience over the years. But, when you've got 4 people on your team who are as excited about this as you are, then things start to happen very, very quickly. Then, your focus turns to developing and working in a team environment.

1:23:10

The team now becomes the number one issue, not the individual. It becomes a team effort. This process is a Million Dollar List. We call it that because, quite literally, it is worth at least that. I don't want you to think in terms of people as dollar signs; people are not dollar signs, they are people. But that Million Dollar List is all the people you know and who know you, who can either a) become involved with you or lead to somebody who will become involved with you, and b) who could at the very least, appreciate the value that your company has to offer in the way of wellness and wellness technologies. We'll give them all the options they need. From that list will come the people we feel are most relevant as far as building the business. From that list will come the people who actually decide to join us. And, from that list will come the people who actually decide to build.

1:24:11

This is a strategy (referring to the book Investing in Your Business), this is the way to approach this business in a calculated way, to create an outcome consistently. If you keep working this so that you perfect your strategy, what you will find is that it produces consistent results. Here's an example. Somebody is going to go Silver. They are three weeks into the business and have sponsored 8 people already. Keep this in mind, this is important . . . pay close attention to this. You are the "B". You are operating with your beliefs, not hers. This new person has higher expectations, and so she's working from her perspective and you are working from yours. My guess is she will make any course corrections necessary to keep you on track so that, in the end, the goal is accomplished. So, a person who is in the process of becoming Silver does not have the awareness of a person who is in the process of orchestrating that person's run to Silver. And, you will probably hear her say, "It ain't over till its over."

1:26:02

I've seen people with 8,000 points volume with less than 24 hours to go—break Silver. One time in Montreal I had 5 people out of 5 people do that. I went there and the lowest volume was 8,000 and the highest was 12,000. I said, "Bring me those people and I'll have lunch with them." One at a time we had lunch, we drew it out. I said "Okay, I know what you see or what you think you see, but you don't know what I know or what I see." So I started asking questions, only questions that I would know to ask. When they started to give me answers to those questions, I was able to see past what they saw. I said, "Here is the strategy for the next 24 hours." Every single one of them broke Silver in those 24 hours. How important is it to work with somebody who has been through it? Who can see more than you can see? Going through the experience of getting Silver done is not enough, you also need to learn how to take others through the experience. This means you need to learn the perspective of the person who helped you, and that's what it means to become a master at breaking Silver. To break Silvers you need a strategy and you just keep working at it . . . you keep working it . . . you keep working it . . . keep working it and fine tuning it.

1:27:19

Some people will build Wellness Homes during this. I don't see a Wellness Home as a one-time thing. I see people starting the business who are real business builders . . . putting their Wellness Home together. All it takes is 4 of these people. If these 4 people did nothing more than put their Wellness Homes together this month, they're Silver. But you haven't built the business yet, you've just gone Silver and so now your company can be profitable. Now, let's duplicate. I recommend you learn how to be teachable, very important . . . to follow directions. In order to be a good teacher, you have to be a good student.

1:28:04

Let's talk about "The Process." Please turn to this page (Career launch brochure—arrow facing down). Bringing people into the business is not an event, it's a process. If you want "X" number of people to be in the business by a certain date, how do you guarantee it? Keep putting people into this "The Process" by a certain time of the month or on a regular basis. If I want to cook spaghetti, there is a process. You've got to boil the water, put salt in the water, let it come to a boil, and then toss your pasta in. If you like it al dente, you've got to check it once in a while, stir it up a little bit and take it out just when it's just right. You strain it, you put it through a strainer and you dump it out and then you put your sauce on it.

1:29:21

Would you agree that it's a lot easier to cook a plate of spaghetti than it is to cook one strand at a time to make a full plate? Even though the process is the same . . . you still have to boil the water, you still have to put salt in the water, you still have to put the noodles in, you still have to strain it. But, wouldn't you agree putting a whole bunch in at same time is a lot easier than putting one in at a time? In fact, if you did it one strand at a time, by the time you had enough noodles, most of them would be cold—it wouldn't be worth eating! The process is the process. What it takes to take somebody from not knowing anything to knowing enough to say yes to Wellness . . . is the same, for the most part is the same. But, whether I do it one person at a time or 5 or 10 or 15 at a time . . . what's going to be different? The difference is whether I'm going to starve to death or I'm going to fill my tummy and that analogy is exactly true in this business.

1:30:18

Putting a number of people through the process at the same time will produce results that doing it on an individual basis will not produce, even though it's the same people. Let me repeat this—putting a number of people through the process at the same time will produce results that cannot be produced by putting the same people through the same process individually . . . even if it's the same people. There is something that happens beyond my level of understanding that is called a dynamic! There's just something that happens between who you are as a person and who they are as a person . . . when there's a bunch of us all at the same time getting excited—it creates a dynamic, rather than just one person at a time. If it is just one person at a time over a period of time, then the energy tends to dissipate. I liken this to nuclear physics. A controlled nuclear reaction is allowing the uranium to have a reaction with itself by putting the rods in it, so it

> Putting a number of people through the process at the same time will produce results that doing it on an individual basis will not produce, even though it's the same number of people.

does not get out of hand but it just keeps producing a nice, steady and stable result.

1:31:27

That's not going to build you this business. You want excitement, passion, enthusiasm. You need to take that same uranium, pull all the rods out (in other words, pull out all the stops) and let it react. And that same uranium creates a nuclear explosion, if left to react all at once. There's a dynamic that takes place that is simply inexplicable.

When I start somebody with a list, we are not going to take the next year to go through this list because I'm not going to give you a year of my time. When I sponsored my cousin Flavio in Italy, he only had two days of my time because I could only be there for two days. He was on his agenda and I was on mine, and the only way those two fit was in two days. I went to Italy and I prefaced it and made sure that he knew that he needed certain products to be there for display. He needed to invite certain people with certain characteristics, and he did this. We had two presentations in his home, back-to-back one evening, and on another evening, eight people the first evening, 7 the second evening. By the end of those first two days, he had recruited 5 or 6 people and had 8,000 points in volume.

1:32:42

What he learned was how to do a presentation in a very simple way. Given that I knew I only had two days to work with him, I had to make the presentation so simple that even he could follow it. Because I wasn't going to be there to do the third presentation—he had to. So, given my notes and what he had learned, he was able to carry on for the balance of the week. I said before I left, "I think you could be Silver by the end of the month." He said, "What's that?" He didn't need to know, but I needed to know that. He needed 20,000 points volume and the month ended in 5 days! He doesn't need to know it's not possible. He is operating according to my expectations and my beliefs. He doesn't know any better.

1:33:26

When I sponsored Marty Jeffery, it was Platinum and $200,000 his first month. He said OK. He didn't know any better. He didn't have contact with anybody else, so he didn't know. I was able to keep him from intermixing with people who have been in the business for 5 years and were still Silver. Thank goodness for that. He went to the first presentation in Niagara Falls. He was a brand new guy, two weeks old in the business walking around just being himself. Somebody says to him, "So how long have you been in the business?"

He says, "A couple of weeks."

"Do any volume?"

"Umm, about $90,000 something like that."

"Yeah right!"

Was that a lot? He didn't know. You see, he was working according to my beliefs, my expectations, not his.

1:34:23

I built a structure to support that. So, don't limit the people you sponsor by your limiting beliefs. They're a chance for you to experiment on them. What if you had to do it all over again, knowing what you know now? Could you do better? Every time I sponsor somebody, it's an opportunity for me to try it—knowing what I know now and they don't know anything . . . it's a chance for me to give them my brain, my mind. And, so I set up a situation to see if I can get them moving a certain way to produce certain results. That is how you break a Platinum in a month. You just keep trying and eventually you are going to find the right person who has the right spirit of intent. You finally get that little detail fixed and bang! Then you realize that it is achievable, it is doable.

1:35:18

So don't limit. This is for all of your endeavors. When you're a Platinum, you're going to be able to break Gold faster than if you were breaking Silver as a Silver. What that means is you can grow faster, it doesn't have to take you as long to go through those ranks as it took you to get you where you're at. Another paradigm. Some of you may think "Oh my God" if it takes me this long to go Silver, how long is it going to take to go Gold? It's a paradigm. Shift your paradigm.

We have a video that we'd like to close this part of the session with. I think it encapsulates what it is that we're doing. You should be very proud to use this video tape and I highly recommend you use this in your business briefing, before you begin a Nikken business presentation either in your home or in public. This video sets the tone; it shows people the big picture and then you can come back and say, all right, you're here to build a business. What do you want out of your business? Then, begin the process of the power of a wellness presentation.

The Video . . . . THE NIKKEN FACTS
About Nikken Certified Wellness Home

1:37:53

In a world of marketing glitz and hype, sometimes it is hard to see the facts. For the next few minutes we invite you to see the facts about the company called Nikken.

FACT
one

1:38:14

Nikken is the undisputed leader in Advanced Wellness Technology. With over 25 years of leading-edge research, design and development, Nikken has developed an extensive range of unique products that has changed millions of lives. Patented Magnetic Technology, Advanced Sleep Technology, Far-Infrared Technology, Bio-Directed

Nutri-Technology, Pi-Mag Technology and revolutionary new Biaxial Magnetic Technology. Cutting edge products that are unique, patented and unduplicated in the industry, and cutting edge distribution through the new Wellness Home concept. (Via Testimonials) I think the Wellness Home strategy is rather genius. Most people have people come over to their house; it makes it really easy. What we are going to see is a change in the way the world looks at health care and everything else. And I honestly believe it starts in the home.

FACT
two

1:39:28

Nikken is the most dynamic, most stable company in the network marketing and direct sales industry. With over 25 years of continuous success and stable growth, Nikken has the financial strength and corporate expertise to remain the dominant company in the wellness industry. With a 5A1 rating by Dunn and Bradstreet, the world's leading provider of financial information, with over $1.5 billion annual sales and with more than 30 million satisfied customers, Nikken is solid, rock solid. (Via Testimonials). This company has everything going for it. Take a look at Nikken's track record. We are celebrating our 30 year anniversary; millions and millions of people in several countries around the world. This company's products have substance; these products work for people.

FACT
three

1:40:30

Nikken has established itself as the world leader in wellness. With operations in more than 30 countries, Nikken continues its global expansion strategy and 100 year strategic plan to become the largest wellness company in the world. Undeniably, Nikken is poised to dominate the multi-trillion dollar wellness industry. (Via Testimonials) "The sun never sets on the Nikken market place." "Now in Australia, in New Zealand and in Jamaica." "We're being paid on 17 countries" . . . people in Ireland, Scotland." "I never wanted to point to a building and say that's where I work; I wanted to point to a map and say—that's where I work."

FACT
four

1:41:20

Nikken is the number one business opportunity in the world. You need life-changing patented products . . . a multi trillion dollar global market place, stability, marketability, integrity. Our incredible new Nikken Wellness Home distribution concept, and our advance training, systems and services that are designed to help you succeed. For hundreds and thousands of Wellness Consultants across the globe, these facts add up to a phenomenal business and an incredible lifestyle.

(Via Testimonials) "Financially, we've done very well." "In my sixth month in the Nikken business we made just under $17,000." "My first check was $22,500.00" "In our 5th year, we created half a million a year." "We currently own 9 homes." "Our cheque was $42,000 per month." "By the 8th year, it grew to $1M in earnings." "We are pretty much able to go and do whatever we want to do." "We made a good 6-figure income in our first year." "I was actually working less and earning more." I play more golf in a month than I did in a year because of Nikken." "After about 8 weeks in the business, I decided that my heart was not in the car business anymore and I actually quit and went full time in Nikken last year. In fact, we took our two young daughters in a motor home, we headed south in January and didn't come home for 3 months." "I have found so much satisfaction out of the Nikken opportunity, and so many rewards that I now realize, that's what's being created here is the greatest stage anyone could ever want."

In a world of economic decline, we are expanding, expanding, expanding. In a world of lay offs, down-sizing and right-sizing, we are looking for people—people who are ready for a change. (Via Testimonials) "The timing couldn't be better." "Most people's 401Ks are now 201Ks. The stock market drops 206 points and I don't get nervous." "Wellness is a huge business." "They don't care if you're 18 or 88. They don't care what color your skin is. They don't care if you're a man or woman. You produce and you get paid. I love that about this business." "We have what the market is looking for now . . . which means being at the right place, at the right time."

Many companies have a mission statement. At Nikken we have a philosophy and it is called the 5 Pillars of Health. Beyond the facts, the numbers, the trends, it is this philosophy which drives us . . . healthy body, mind, family, society and finances.

(Via Testimonial) "Our family lifestyle has been changed so dramatically because I've got time now to be with my family."

"Every day I become more aware of the impact that Nikken can have in people's lives and in all of the 5 Pillars of Health. That is what it's all about. That is what life is all about!"

"Find people who are like-minded with positive attitudes and you'll have a chance to succeed. So, it means more than just a business to me."

"I never apologize for the money that I make in this business . . . for every dime that I have earned has been because the product has helped another individual and maybe even saved their lives."

"I would say the experience of being able to be at home is probably the greatest gift that Nikken has given."

"What more can anybody ask for in their lives? I just feel so grateful and so blessed that we stumbled on Nikken and through it our whole lives have been transformed in every way imaginable."

"What a way to make a living!!"

1:45:46
Nikken . . . a business that you can work from home, part time or full time, locally or internationally. No employees, no inventory and little or no overhead.

Whether you are looking for an additional income stream, a rewarding part time opportunity, or an entirely new career, take a look at the facts and call the person who gave you this program.

Nikken, the undisputed leader in advanced wellness technology, the most dynamic the most rock-solid company in the network marketing and direct sales industry. Nikken is the world leader in wellness, the number one business opportunity in the world.

(Via Testimonial). Nikken has the products, they've got the company, they've got the marketing plan. They've got it all." End of DVD.
1:46:44

1:46:51
Can you see yourself using that? I just love what Ed Wiens says . . . I never want to point to a building and say that's where I work. I want to point to a map. The DVD is called the Nikken Facts. Let me just tell you how many things are on that DVD, the Wellness Home overview; Rest and Relaxation—Sleep System, Environment; Nutrition; Biaxial Magnetic Technology; Skin Care; Fitness; the Nikken opportunity section has Nikken facts that you just saw; another one called Plan B; another one called Six Minutes to Success; and then Lifestyle Success Stories which I think are the Distributors of the Year and then the Nikken Story. This is all on one DVD.

1:47:37
So, you can literally pick and choose the one that you feel best suits the situation and the audience that you have in your particular

The Science of the Nikken Business

meeting . . . whether it is in your home or a live presentation. This is a phenomenal tool and another demonstration of where we are going . . . the direction we are going with the development tools to make our job as Wellness Consultants—really Wellness Consultants. A consultant—what does that mean in your life? There are consultants for many different things. For instance, you have an insurance person . . . don't actually make the insurance product, they just recommend and they usually have two or three insurance products. So, you consider them your insurance consultant and what they have are suppliers and they bring you what they think are good products for you . . . then you pick the one you want.

1:48:28

They provide you with information; they facilitate your buying experience and help you select what is best for you. Nikken is our supplier. We, as consultants, do just that—we bring the technology to people's attention, and we help them choose what is in their best interest. That is true about the business as well, because we are business consultants. What I'm doing is consulting; I'm giving you my experience, my knowledge and some insights as to how you can go forward in building a business of your own. We are consultants. Even for our organization, we are business consultants. The more you treat this like a business, the more questions you ask of it as a business, the more you will start to have the answers. Asking the right question leads to the right answers. So, get asking questions and ask the right questions. Don't be shy about approaching the people you feel might know the answer, because we grow if we grow together, and it is vital that we stick together.

1:49:42

Keep learning. Thank you.

Printed in Great Britain
by Amazon.co.uk, Ltd.,
Marston Gate.